HOW TO

LIE ABOUT

YOUR AGE

D0284989

5

HOW TO LIE ABOUT YOUR AGE

by Sona Holman

and Lillian Friedman

Collier Books

A Division of Macmillan Publishing Co., Inc.

NEW YORK

Collier Macmillan Publishers

LONDON

Macmillan Publishing Co., Inc.
866 Third Avenue, New York, N.Y. 10022
Collier Macmillan Canada, Ltd.

LIBRARY OF CONGRESS CATALOGING IN PUBLICATION DATA
Holman, Sona.
   How to lie about your age.

   1.   Civilization, Modern—20th century—Miscellanea.
I.   Friedman, Lillian, joint author.   II.   Title.
CB427.H64   1979   909.82   78–32038
ISBN 0–02–000550–4

Second Printing 1979

Designed by Jack Meserole

Printed in the United States of America

For Karl, Celia, and Jac;
Rachel, Joe, and Soren

Contents

Foreword

This book tells you everything you need to know to lie about your age and be believed. It assumes that you will want to subtract, not add, years. In a world where 12-year-olds make it in the entertainment big time, where the step after graduate school is a $25,000-a-year job, and you're never too young for sex, who needs to lie upward?

Nevertheless, the system set forth here for the subtraction of years can be applied as easily to their addition, if that's your folly. But we have devised our book for those whom society has superannuated prematurely and it is to them that we dedicate it.

S.H. and L.F.

Introduction

A well-known Washington hostess who never divulges her age explains that "you're always too old or too young for something."

Right she is. But secrecy is a naive and imperfect solution. Keeping your age to yourself may keep them guessing but chances are the guesses won't be in your favor as you see it.

In a youth-oriented society which often interprets over-35 as over-the-hill, even the scrupulously truthful meet with situations—social or professional—that make frankness madness. To get a job or save one, to gain entrée to a club or a romance, we lie by a year, or a few, or more—if we can get away with it.

There's no need to list the circumstances that might lead you to lie about your age. If you hadn't figured out a few, you wouldn't be reading this book. Instead, we will provide the tools that will enable you to dissemble with style and credibility: guidelines for selecting an Assumed Age, basic rules and techniques for lying, and, most important, the historical facts you will need to live your newly Assumed Age with poise and conviction.

It is impossible to overemphasize the significance of allusions to recent history in creating an environment that supports your lie. If you are to contribute with your customary assurance and wit to discussions about sports or schooldays, pop music or hobbies, politics or books, you'll have to fix a newly assumed chronology firmly in mind, rewrite your personal history—and have the appropriate recollections to back it up. *The secret of successful lying is in knowing what to recall and what to forget in all the areas of interest and trivia that ordinarily pepper your conversation.*

The historical facts of your Assumed Lifetime will be the foundation of your lie for, except for business purposes, you will never openly acknowledge the age you have adopted. If you do, you will be suspect. Most adults don't talk about how old they are, unless they are remarkably old. Your game is to *suggest* your Assumed Age through memories, association of events, and casual references to notable dates—to drop hints that will enable others to deduce how young you are.

Starting on page 25, you will find a year-by-year summary of significant events for the years 1910 to 1969—major and minor happenings, fashions, fads, and scandals. These invaluable aids cover politics and the arts, hit songs and popular dances, disasters and exposés, affairs of state and affairs of the heart, catchphrases and slogans, architectural landmarks and automobile models, personalities and causes célèbres, the clothes that were worn, and the heroes and heroines who were worshipped. The chronological summaries are followed by Checklists of special interest areas: Bestsellers, Landmark and Children's Books, Periodicals, Comic Strips, Movies, Theater, Radio, Television, Catastrophes, and Great Ocean Liners.

Depending on how many years you decide to deduct (a decision you will make after careful study of the chapter "Choosing Your Age"), you will use the summaries and checklists to guide you in selecting memories to be eliminated from your conversation and consciousness because you have become too young to recall them. And you will use them to provide the necessary memory update, to fill yourself in on the recollections of your new lifetime—the hit tunes of your rewritten high school years, the radical causes you supported in college, and the dances you danced while falling in love.

In the next few pages, we ask you to consider whether lying about your age suits your needs and your personality. We establish criteria and rules of behavior. And we ask the critical question: "Can you get away with it?" If your answer is affirmative, we tell you how to go about it with panache.

GUIDELINES

Should You Lie?

Philosophical and moral arguments clearly are beyond the modest intellectual scope of a simple how-to book. We do not presume to offer counsel on matters of conscience. Pausing only to note that lying does not qualify as a Deadly Sin, we turn from questions of principle to the pragmatic aspects of deception.

Before committing yourself to a life of pretense, it is vital to estimate your chances for success—to determine whether you are really suited to such a course. To help you, we have devised a brief feasibility study. We urge you to be honest in your replies to the questions that follow. Should you find that impossible, you are fortunate, indeed, in your gift for guile.

1. DO YOU HAVE THE TALENT?

Some people are natural liars; others are born without flair, going red or ashen before the first false word is uttered, spluttering in confusion through the smallest fib, breeding disbelief with every shifty movement of the eyes, blurting forth the truth when cornered.

If you are one of these, don't be discouraged. A recent study reveals that of a hundred inept liars, ninety-six were able, through practice, to overcome blushing, shortness of breath, confession, and other symptoms of hyperactive conscience within three months, *without professional help.*

A single case history suggests the type of longer-term self-discipline that can prepare an aspirant for carrying off the Big Lie, even though he or she lacks innate talent:

A successful and scrupulously honest businesswoman in her early 40s, spotting 50 coming up fast, wisely decided to prepare herself by undertaking a low-risk deception before embarking on an age change. She fabricated a brief but mildly glamorous earlier career in the theater, claiming to have played secondary roles in road companies and admitting modestly that she abandoned the stage after facing the fact that she wasn't quite good enough to make it to the top. For three years, she practiced her lie at every opportunity, adding convincing but unverifiable details one by one. By her 47th birthday, she was a pro, ready to turn 41.

Natural or self-made liar, if you have a track record of effective deception under varied pressures, you have a strong base on which to build.

2. DO YOU HAVE THE MEMORY?

A key to success is consistency—the ability to recall your lies so that when you repeat them to people to whom you have already told them, your recollection of details is at least as accurate as theirs. A simple test of your memory skills is to jot down three lies about yourself—that you were high school valedictorian, are related to the Roosevelts, and once climbed the Statue of Liberty, for example. Tuck the paper away in a drawer; in a week or two, try to recall the lies, then check for accuracy against the record.

If you can reconstruct all three lies, your memory is dependable. If you believe the written record, you have rare talent. If you find you can't recall where you put the piece of paper, you still may be qualified to lie about your age. But such a lapse should be a warning to keep your lies simple and direct, free of elaborate detail, colorful descriptions, and other sophisticated embellishment.

3. DO YOU HAVE THE TEMPERAMENT?

A celebrated psycho-historian has hypothesized that George Washington suffered from severe anxiety neurosis, a disability early manifested in a childhood compulsion to tell the truth.

Victims of Cherry-Tree Syndrome usually are poorly equipped by temperament to sustain lies about their age. Fear of discovery negates any benefits they might derive from restructuring the truth. The nagging discomfort of cold sweats and palpitations frequently drives them to impetuous confession. The cosmetic ravages of sleepless nights challenge their claims to youthfulness.

Only you can evaluate your psychological aptitude. To do so, draw on experience, reconstructing your emotional state under the stresses of past deceptions:

Were you filled with remorse? Troubled by insomnia? Apprehensive that you would be found out? Were you ever discovered and, if so, did discovery lessen your self-esteem? Two yesses and we recommend that you read this book for nostalgia value only. Playing fast and loose with fact is not for you.

If, on the contrary, you had no qualms (or few), perceived white lying as palpably different from outright falsehood, considered the possibility of discovery remote and the consequences insignificant, you are emotionally equipped to face the future and your doctored past guilt-free and light of heart.

4. WILL YOUR LIFESTYLE SUPPORT THE LIE?

Where and how you live and work and the social circles in which you travel are crucial in determining whether or not you can get away with lying. For example, if you still live in the small to medium-sized town where you grew up, anyone worth lying to probably already knows the truth.

Even in a huge city, lying can be risky if you maintain friendships with a number of former classmates or have a closely knit group of friends who will greet your newly assumed age with sniggering, if not helpless laughter. Of course, if you're determined to lie, you have the option of tossing friendships aside and building your social life from scratch in virgin territory.

Without question, the ideal time to begin establishing your Assumed Age is when you move to a new community or take a new job. But these are far from the *only* times to start. Provided you haven't advertised your age in the past, any time can be the right time.

5

The Risks of Lying

Any reason that makes sense to you is reason enough for assuming a new age. Whatever your motives, it is advisable to establish in advance whether you plan to follow a course of soft or hard lying.

As a rule, soft liars aspire primarily to social gain. They establish their Assumed Ages through suggestion alone, avoid outright falsehood, and never misrepresent their ages in writing.

Hard liars tend to assume new ages out of perceived necessity, such as landing a job or attracting a partner whose ardor might be dampened by the truth. Circumstances often force them to establish a written record of their lies—to fill in Assumed Year of Birth on pension, insurance, or marriage license applications, and Assumed Graduation Dates on job applications.

In deciding whether you will limit yourself to social situations or go whole hog, recognize that the risks increase in direct ratio to the size and complexity of the lie. About the worst that can come of a soft lie, with its moderate tampering with truth, is a little egg on the face. Hard lying, with its written record, is a more serious undertaking. Uncovered by a disenchanted marriage partner or a disagreeable employer, it could lose you a spouse or a job on the grounds of fraud. And if you're cursed with lack of foresight and rich relatives, it might even do you out of a legacy under the terms of an only mildly eccentric will.

Fortunately, many of the penalties one might expect to be inherent in anything as reprehensible as lying can be minimized by exercising reasonable judgment and taking a few precautions:

1. *Never lie about your age under oath.* The law takes a dim view of perjury. If asked your age in court you can coyly claim "21 plus." But if pressed for a precise answer, give your true age, whatever it costs you to spit the numbers out.
2. When applying for a job, watch your step with large corporations. Many routinely verify educational data. While employers no longer are permitted to ask an applicant's age,

even a would-be boss with no curiosity about your age might question your reliability on discovering that your recalculated graduation dates don't jibe with school records.

3. Before committing yourself to your Assumed Age, be certain to have in your possession convincing documents with which you can verify your Actual Age, should you need to withdraw your lie in the future.

Why would you want to withdraw it after all the trouble you've gone to? To establish eligibility for a pension or Social Security, perhaps. Or let's say your bachelor uncle dies, leaving the whole of his substantial estate to his eldest surviving niece or nephew—*you*. But since you've been advertising for years that you were born in 1939 rather than 1935, you've established that you're two years younger than a greedy cousin who was born in 1937. Unless you can document that you're actually older, there goes your million.

Don't wait until the moment of truth arrives. The older you grow, the harder it becomes to track down the necessary verification. (A lawyer who has handled many such cases says that, judging by explanations he's received from town clerks unable to provide needed documents, the buildings housing birth records have an unseemly penchant for burning down.)

The most reliable documents to keep on hand are a birth certificate, certificate of baptism, or a family Bible. If those were lost in moving or in the Town Hall fire, various other documents—ranging from an old report card to a lapsed passport—can be acceptable substitutes, although you may have to submit two or more of them to prove your case.

Provided you observe the foregoing precautions, there's ro markably little trouble you can get into by tampering with the truth about your year of birth. The practice is so common, in fact, that it's an acceptable deception to many normally prissy officials, who tend to take a relaxed attitude toward it. Let's see what's likely to happen when, at Actual Age 65 or 67, you want to collect the financial goodies due you as a senior citizen while your records all show your age as 60:

Your company pension will be the same as it would have

been had you told the truth in the first place. While any extra years you've worked beyond the cut-off age for "credited service" won't increase the pension payout, you'll have been earning full salary for those years, so who gives a damn?

Your Social Security checks will start coming, regardless of what age you've claimed in the past, when you produce your birth certificate or alternate documents acceptable to the government.

Your insurance won't be jeopardized. You'd never guess how sweetly reasonable an insurance company can be. If you try to collect on your annuity five years before they figured you would, they'll simply adjust the face value of your policy, calculating what the premiums you have paid have legitimately bought you in the way of coverage.

And what happens if The Company finds out you've been lying, before you're ready to retire? If you're between 40 and 65, relax; your boss can't fire you for hiding the truth without violating the Federal Age Discrimination in Employment Act. If you're under 40 and the truth comes out, things *could* get sticky; an unfriendly boss might seize on your duplicity as a handle for dismissal. But anyone who wanted you out that badly would find another excuse if lying about your age didn't turn up.

Fact is, you're always taking *some* risk when you depart from the truth, so if you can't live with anything but a sure bet, don't lie about your age. But if you do lie, the odds and the law are in your favor.

Choosing Your Age

If you're prepared to chance dropping a few years, it's time to determine how old you should be. *Should* be; not *want* to be. Capricious choices are certain disaster in the Age Assumption process.

Be realistic. This entails a long, objective look at yourself in a harshly lit mirror. Don't rush the decision and don't try to fool yourself. If your first self-assessment is made after a relaxing weekend in the country, make another after a night on the town or an exhausting week at the office. Examine yourself at your worst, then summoning all the cold detachment you can, ask yourself how old you really look.

If you're 45 and admit you look it, abandon plans to lie. A frank and open 45 will get you further professionally and socially than a prematurely aging 40.

But if honest evaluation tells you that you look perceptibly younger than your contemporaries, you are ready to make one of the important moves of your life—lying about your age. Deciding what age you will assume must, of necessity, be a lonely process. Asking your spouse, sibling, or other close relative will mislead you; their judgment will be biased by the momentary position of the love-hate pendulum. Consulting your best friend will be counterproductive; each one tells one and you'll have given away the game before it's started. In your soul-searching you will, however, have three rules to guide you:

Rule 1

Don't be greedy. If you're 54 and can pass for 47, don't go for 42. Remember, Jack Benny's claim to being 39 produced laughs for years precisely because it was improbable. You're after credibility, not yoks.

Rule 2

Choose one of your great years as a starter; it will give you an immediate psychological lift. Let's say you're a believable 37. Then *be* 37, provided you recall your actual 37th year as a vintage one—exciting, productive, and fun. If it was a year of a leg broken while skiing, a failed romance, and a job lost, *don't choose it;* chances are you'll live it that way all over again. Instead, move *forward* to the nearest good year and settle for being 38 or 39. Do *not* move backward to 36 or 35 (see *Rule 1*).

Rule 3

Maintain a sense of proportion. The older your Actual Age, the larger the number of years you can convincingly subtract. A

9

youthful-looking 70-year-old might easily drop eight to ten years and pass for early 60s. A 50-year-old will have trouble getting away with more than a five- or six-year deduction, and a 40-year-old should probably be content with four years. If you believe that you are an exception, try to be certain that you look as young to others as you do to yourself.

Once you have settled on your Assumed Age, you are almost ready to start scattering the crumbs of harmless pretense that will lead those you would convince back up the trail from your Actual Age to the age you have decided to be. But, first, a few rules to help you dissemble without blowing your cover:

1. Stick as close as possible to the truth. The less you stray from solid recollections, the greater your chance of being convincing.
2. Edit dated slang from your speech. It's a dead giveaway. Listen to yourself and eliminate "goshes," "swells," and "gee whizzes," unless you're a 1920s person trying to pass for a 1930s person (e.g., George Brent to Ruby Keeler in *42nd Street:* "Remind me to tell you I think you're swell.")

   Once you've dropped the passé speech, you can relax; there's no need to acquire the comparable jargon of your new age group. In fact, there's a risk of getting it wrong if you try. While you're struggling to be a swinger, the expression may go out of style. With slang missing from your conversation, you'll appear timeless and your speech will gain in color and precision.
3. Adjust the ages of family members to your own—and stop bragging about them. If you are flying to another city to help celebrate your parents' fiftieth wedding anniversay, think up another reason for the trip. You're not old enough for those parents. If your daughter has a birthday, be vague about which one.
4. Move your high school and college yearbooks from the living room shelves to a back closet. No sense in furnishing the curious with reference sources.
5. Stop using your driver's license to establish your identity

when cashing checks, charging purchases, or opening bank accounts. It carries your birthdate, which anyone you happen to be with can clearly see. Show your license only when ordered to do so by the police, and make an extra effort to avoid traffic violations when you have passengers who might spot the date.

6. Revise your résumé, bringing your work history into line with your personal history. Do not tamper with dates of past employment; a computer check could trip you easily. Simply drop your earliest jobs from the list. Occasionally this tactic threatens to eliminate important experience; in that case, rewrite your résumé in nonchronological form, emphasizing range of experience and being noncommittal about which function went with which job.

7. If you haven't been back to your hometown in years, brush up on events, make necessary corrections in dates, or stop talking about it altogether. Say you left Cincinnati in 1955 at the age of 23 and you're dropping five years; you have two options: Stick to 23 as the age at which you left home but update yourself on major doings in Cincinnati between 1955 and 1960, when you are implying you were still there. Or stick to 1955 as the *year* you left home (in which case your memories of the old town will be accurate) but make certain to remember that you were only 18 when you left.

8. When old school friends show up in town, look them over carefully for signs of wear and tear. If they have aged less gracefully than you, fight the urge to introduce them around.

And, finally, resist the temptation to dress more youthfully, color your hair or, if you're a woman, to put more snap in your makeup at this time. The coincidence of your trying to look younger at a time when you are starting to suggest that you *are* younger will arouse suspicion. Instead, stay as you are and start lying.

The surest way to look older is to struggle to look young. Later, when you're at ease in your Assumed Age, you'll be able to make changes with assurance and taste. Besides, as soon as you're in the swing of it, you'll feel younger and in no time will appear younger in ways no superficial changes of dress or hairdo can possibly achieve.

What to Forget

Sixty-year-old Gordon J., who has Assumed 54 with grace and conviction, attributes his success to a single resolve taken at the time of his age change.

"I decided to sacrifice my pride in having total recall of the political events of my adults years," he explains. "Fact is, ninety-nine out of a hundred people can't tell you who was governor of their state twenty years ago, even if they voted for him. I figured I'd have trouble remembering what I should forget. So I joined the majority, stopped being an expert on the past, and switched to current events."

Instinctively, Gordon had grasped a fundamental principle of age change: The more you decide to forget, the less you have to learn. To avoid the need to learn facts to replace recollections you're too young to have, give up your expertise in the troublesome area.

Nevertheless, the system has its drawbacks. There's a limit, after all, to how many topics one can drop from one's conversational repertoire and still pass for an intelligent member of society. Fortunately, there are better devices than total amnesia available to help you avoid recalling, in public, an event you should not be remembering.

By far the most reliable of these is the EPR (Earliest Possible Recollection), a dependable watchdog for any age change. The EPR is established by reaching back in memory to your first awareness of an event outside the intensely egocentric world of the young child—a major air disaster, for instance, a parade for a hero, a baseball pennant race—and then determining your Actual Age when it took place. Now substitute a comparably newsworthy event that occurred during the year you are Assuming to have been that age. The event is your EPR. Here's how it works:

Say your Earliest Actual Recollection is Pearl Harbor Day, December 7, 1941, when you were 5 years old. You're dropping four years. Your EPR could become April 12, 1945, the day Franklin D. Roosevelt died, or August 6, 1945, the day the atom bomb was dropped on Hiroshima.

Using your EPR as a benchmark and this book's summaries of annual events and its checklists as reference sources, you can quickly determine which events you are free to have lived through and which you merely know about from hearsay.

With your EPR firmly in mind, you can talk about the Triangle Shirtwaist Factory Fire or Paul Whiteman at Aeolian Hall or Christian Dior's New Look—or the San Francisco earthquake, for all it matters—as long as you also remember that you weren't around at the time.

The EPR, however, is an aid, not a complete system, for avoiding error. Growing younger is not a process for the lazy. It requires dreary rote-unlearning of certain things you absolutely *must* forget.

1. Forget obscure events and personalities prior to your EPR, even if they were widely known at the time. Take radio comedy. You can claim to have heard parts of the Jack Benny–Fred Allen feud on recordings. But if you insist on quoting Joe Penner's catchline "Wanna buy a duck?" you might just as well pass your birth certificate around the room.
2. Forget how obsolete objects felt in use. There's no harm in describing a rumble seat, we've all seen them in the movies. But talk about what it felt like to ride in one, and you're either an antique car buff or older than you say.
3. Forget dated nouns. It's a refrigerator or fridge, not an icebox; a helicopter, not an autogiro; a stereo or hi-fi, not a Victrola; social studies, not history or civics.
4. Forget about having read defunct newspapers, unless you are certain of the years of their deaths. The *Los Angeles Mirror* or *New York Sun* may be meaningful parts of your

life but mention of the fact will sound a death knell to your youthful image.

5. Forget that you saw any movie more than five years old anyplace but on TV. It's the safe way of avoiding error. Get into the habit of introducing comments about films with a covering statement, such as "When I first saw *Casablanca* on TV . . ."

6. Forget that you read any book when it first came out. The only exception should be current bestsellers; it's difficult to be completely safe about publication dates for most others. However, if reading is an important part of your life, you may want to ignore this advice; in that case, consult the checklists of bestsellers and landmark publications at the back of this book.

7. Forget the book series you read as a child unless they seem, like Nancy Drew, to be immortal. Heartbreaking though it may be to you, Honey Bunch, Poppy Ott, and Elsie Dinsmore haven't grabbed flashlight-under-the-blanket readers for quite a while. Talk about children's classics, instead— Robert Louis Stevenson, A. A. Milne, or E. B. White.

8. Forget the outcome of long-past minor political events that can't possibly have been documented more recently on TV.

9. Forget the names of advertised products that no longer exist —Cocomalt or Castoria or Herpicide or Sen-Sen.

10. Forget what things used to cost. Get penny candy, 35¢-pounds of coffee, and $28 three-piece suits out of your conversation.

11. Forget old novelty pop tunes. While there are some freak survivors like "A Tisket, A Tasket," you'll have some fast explaining to do if anyone catches you whistling "Open the Door, Richard."

A final warning: Be wary of the nostalgic personal anecdote. It's the arch foe of the age-dropper, slyly promising to deliver to its victim a reputation as witty conversationalist or sensitive raconteur. As you fill in the lovingly remembered details that will add shape and elegance to your anecdote, you take an unnecessary chance of revealing that you have, in reality, lived through moments in history you have carefully suggested only to have heard about.

Fallback Positions

Nobody's perfect.

Regardless of how careful you are about recollections of your revised past, you're bound to goof now and again. When you do, don't panic. Provided you have taken the precaution of establishing a few reliable fallback positions, you'll have little trouble covering your tracks.

Never in the history of civilization have circumstances conspired so felicitously to abet those who would lose part of their past lives. In every previous generation, men and women have been confronted with the need to forget thousands of details associated with years they were claiming not to have lived through.

Today, in response to public hunger for earlier, simpler days, TV and films bombard us with nostalgia-filled dramas and documentaries; newspapers and magazines deluge us with excursions into the past; tapes and recordings re-create the speeches that stirred, and voices that thrilled, other generations. The world is filled with young people who are familiar with the mood, look, and sounds of earlier decades and who speak knowingly of them.

This universal fondness for the past forms the solid base for most fallback positions. Knowing that the conversation of others is filled with trivia from the past, you can explain away any inadvertent reference to an era you supposedly are unfamiliar with by putting one of the following assertions into play:

1. You saw it on a TV documentary.
2. You read it in the *Wall Street Journal*.

3. You almost bought one at a flea market last week.
4. You learned it from the definition in a crossword puzzle.
5. You're a nostalgia buff.

Or claim special competence:

6. You read incessantly.
7. You study *Collier's Encyclopedia* the way other people study the Bible.
8. You were a weirdly precocious and observant child.

Or invent a sibling, precisely your Actual Age. All of your favorite stories and recollections can be attributed to your brother or sister, if the going gets tough.

It is advisable to have several of these fallback positions clearly in mind, not only to avoid repetition that might call attention to itself, but to provide sufficient flexibility to cover varied situations. But however well you have prepared yourself, there may be occasions when you are forced to improvise, when a major inconsistency might require as strong a measure as the instant creation of a new hobby.

Let's say you realize you've described the abdication of Edward VIII in suspiciously accurate detail. No sweat. You merely add, "It's really the only interesting thing in his autobiography."

But suppose you say something that's wildly anachronistic in relation to your Assumed Lifetime: you recall a flight from Chicago to Cleveland in a DC-1—not just a propeller-driven plane but a two-engine plane that hasn't been in service since 1942. If you have your wits about you, you assume a faraway look and add, "In September, the Midwest Chapter of the Orville Wrighters will be chartering a mint-condition Ford Tri-Motor; I don't know if I'm going to be able to resist." With rotten luck, there could be a genuine old plane freak in the room, eager to exchange notes. Plead migraine, leave, and bone up on old planes.

The substance of your cover-up statement is not nearly as important as your manner of delivery. The more casually you can slip it into the conversation, the better. When repartee is too speedy for you to be casual, let your lapse pass and trust to luck that no one will have noticed. Most people don't listen, anyway.

Preparing to Lie

You've determined the age you're going to be and made the necessary preparations. Now believe it. If you don't, no one else will.

Selling yourself on the truth of your Assumed Age starts with *thinking* the age you want to be, not much of a trick, considering that you've been there before. Three simple exercises will help reestablish you in the familiar territory. Once you feel secure, it's a simple matter, working with this book, to flesh out your conviction with the facts you will need to back it up.

EXERCISE I   Positioning Yourself in your Assumed Era

1. Calculate your Assumed Birth Year.
2. Turn to that year in the Year-by-Year Summaries in this book.
3. Check the events of the year but don't trouble to memorize them.

Now think about the condition of the world when you claim to have been born. Consider how the events may have shaped your personality differently. For example, if you have decided to have been born in 1943 instead of 1938, you have become a war baby whose father probably was not present during the early formative years. If you're moving your birthdate from the 1920s to the 1930s, you are switching from boom years to bust. A shift from 1917 to 1926 takes you from trenches and lisle stockings to ukeleles and flappers.

EXERCISE II   Recasting Your Lifetime

Turn to the first Checklist, "Books: BESTSELLERS."
1. Find the year corresponding to the first bestseller you recall reading.
2. Add to the year of publication the number of years you have subtracted from your age (if you are adding years to your

life, subtract from the year of publication the number of years you are adding to your age).

3. Select the bestseller of the Assumed Year. It is the first you read.

Example

1. Your first bestseller was Margaret Mitchell's *Gone With the Wind*, which you read in 1936, when you were 12.
2. Your Assumed Age is five years younger. Add five years to 1936, bringing you to 1941.
3. Your new first bestsellers are A. J. Cronin's *The Keys of the Kingdom*, Alice Duer Miller's *The White Cliffs*, Eric Knight's *This Above All*, or if you're claiming special precocity, William L. Shirer's *Berlin Diary*.

EXERCISE III   Learning to Pass for Your Assumed Age

Arrange to lunch with an acquaintance of your Actual Age—one outside your usual circle of friends. This difficult exercise requires practice and if you fail on the first try, it had best be with someone who won't blab about it to everyone you know.

After pleasantries, direct the conversation to an important event that occurred when both of you were actually 14—the 1933 bank holiday, Frank Sinatra at the Paramount Theater, Sid Caesar and Imogene Coca on *Your Show of Shows*. Permit your companion to proudly pull forth detailed recollections.

Wait for the last memory to die on the air, then say with some regret, "I envy you the experience. I was only nine [or seven or two] when it happened."

When you can perform Exercise III without pausing to do arithmetic, you are psychologically prepared to come out of the closet and live your Assumed Age.

How to Use This Book

Persuasive lying must be backed by convincing fact. The pages that follow provide the facts you'll need. There are two sections:

1. YEAR-BY-YEAR SUMMARIES FROM 1910 to 1969—what people were saying, products and institutions that were introduced or that ended, song hits, fads, pastimes, and fashions, what was happening in the world and in the United States. The summaries set the scene for each year you must either recall or forget, including major events, social trends, crimes, newsworthy romances, foolishness, and trivia.

   The chronology starts with the year 1910 to accommodate would-be liars now in their seventies; it ends with 1969 on the theory that anyone young or old enough to want to lie has a fairly solid recollection of the past decade and that any reader of this book is sufficiently alert to have been paying attention to what was going on. If you're not familiar with the pop songs, entertainers, or fads of the 1970s, you probably don't care about the pop songs, entertainers, or fads of the 1970s and won't need to talk about them; should you be unable to remember what happened at Watergate, there's no point in our trying to tell you.

2. CHECKLISTS of specific categories of information. For Bestsellers, Landmark and Children's Books, Movies, Theater, Radio, Television, and Catastrophes, these are presented chronologically. For Comic Strips, Great Ocean Liners, and Periodicals, most of which survived for many years, the time spans of their existences are recorded.

A word about the goings-on that appear in the pages that follow: *How to Lie About Your Age* is not an encyclopedia; we have selected the events, the people, the trivia, that seem to us to reflect the tempo of the years chronicled. The criterion for inclusion in the listings was simply whether most people knew that whatever-it-is was happening. In such areas as scientific discovery, sports, and the arts, you'll find the heroes and heroines known even to people with no special interest in those areas in which the notables excelled. People who've never been near a boxing ring know about Muhammad Ali; those who don't know physics from Ex-Lax know about Einstein.

It is assumed that if you have a special area of interest—baseball or chess or railroading or tennis—you can draw on your own memory to make necessary adjustments in your conversation.

As to fads, games, dance steps, and other such non-events, if dates given here don't agree with your recollections, feel free to interpolate. Fashions and crazes have a way of starting somewhere at one time, spreading gradually (or, sometimes, like wildfire) to other places, subsiding and, in some cases, resurfacing elsewhere at a later date. Hula hoops first appeared in 1959 but they've been wiggling ever since; Inky Pinkies were a fad in the late thirties and again, under various names, in the late fifties; they may even now be on their way back. The tango never died, but we record it when everyone was doing it.

Your first step in putting these facts to work for you is to turn to your Assumed Birth Year. To the left of the heading, you'll find a small outlined rectangle. Insert the letter "B" to indicate that you were born. Now turn to the following year and insert the numeral 1 in the rectangle to indicate your first Assumed Birthday; proceed year-by-year through to 1969, inserting your Assumed Age for each year. You will no longer have to calculate your Assumed Age for a specific year; it will all be there in front of you.

Now start reading the facts of your Assumed Lifetime and fixing them in the appropriate compartments of your memory. Keep to your own interests—and learn them completely. Don't clutter your mind with a Kentucky Derby winner if you automatically turn off the radio or TV when a horserace comes on.

At first, this book will be your constant and secret companion, to be consulted in the bathroom at cocktail parties, under the desk in your office, or behind a column at theatrical events.

You will study it in the privacy of your home, committing

the rich lore of your new lifetime to memory. If you apply yourself diligently, you will awaken one morning to find that you have outgrown the book. You will no longer have to learn to be your Assumed Age, for you will, in your heart, *be* it.

YEAR-BY-YEAR SUMMARIES 1910-1969

1910 "I'm for it, I'll vote for it, now don't bother me."
—N. Y. STATE REP. FIORELLO H. LA GUARDIA
to committee of women's suffrage
supporters seeking his support

FOUNDED The Boy Scouts of America; The Camp Fire Girls; The Carnegie Endowment for International Peace; The MacDowell Colony, Peterboro, New Hampshire

INTRODUCED The "one-man top" for cars, replacing folding canopies requiring two to operate; the Oval Room in the White House; suction cups for shoe soles, forerunners of sneakers, by Spalding Rubber Co.; the word "moron," to designate an IQ below 75 but above idiot level; a cure for syphilis, by Dr. Paul Ehrlich

SONGS "Ah, Sweet Mystery of Life" "Chinatown, My Chinatown" "Put Your Arms Around Me, Honey" "Let Me Call You Sweetheart" "Some of These Days" "I'm Falling in Love with Someone" "Mother Machree"

DANCE STEPS The tango was the rage.

FASHION Women wore full-length, tight skirts; enormous hats; high-button shoes. The typical bathing costume: sailor dress worn over knee-length bloomers, black stockings, high bathing shoes. ☐ For men: narrow trousers, Chesterfield coats, stand-up shirt collars and, in summer, loose-fitting, double-breasted suits, straw boaters.

THE WORLD An era ended with the death of King Edward VII of England. ☐ Halley's comet reappeared for the first time since 1835, is due again in 1985. ☐ Japan annexed Korea. ☐ China abolished slavery. ☐ Marie Curie isolated radium. ☐ The British liner *Mauretania*, queen of the Atlantic, crossed from Queenstown to New York in four days, eleven hours, forty-two minutes.

THE UNITED STATES The U.S. population was nearing 100 million. For half the work force, a workday lasted twelve

25

hours. The weekend as an institution gained popularity. 7,500,000 women were employed. ☐ The national divorce rate was .9 per 1000. ☐ Women's suffrage was on the move. Among marchers in a New York Right-to-Vote parade were Lillian Russell, Mrs. Otis Skinner, Mrs. O. H. P. Belmont. "Anarchist" Emma Goldman toured the country, lecturing on free love. ☐ Former President Theodore Roosevelt returned from his East African hunting trip. ☐ There were 114,000 automobiles manufactured, including the Model T Ford, priced at $825, less than any other four-cylinder car on the market. ☐ Congress passed the Mann Act (the "White Slave Act"), prohibiting transportation of women across state lines for immoral purposes. ☐ The first flight from shipboard took place when Lt. Eugene Ely, USN, flew a Curtiss plane from the deck of the cruiser *Birmingham*, at Hampton Roads, Virginia, to Norfolk. In radio, pioneer Lee de Forest broadcast the voice of Enrico Caruso singing at New York's Metropolitan Opera House. ☐ The ladies garment workers struck to protest sweatshops. ☐ The magazines people were reading were the *Saturday Evening Post*, the old *Life*, *Outlook*, *Delineator*, *Collier's*, *Vogue*, *Harper's Bazaar*, *Good Housekeeping*, and *American Weekly*. ☐ Aviator Glenn Curtiss won the $10,000 prize offered by the *New York World* for the first continuous flight from Albany to New York—137 miles in 152 minutes. ☐ There were 2,202 daily newspapers in the country.

SPORTS Baseball achieved new status when Pres. William Howard Taft started the presidential custom of throwing out the first ball of the season. ☐ Jack Johnson knocked out Jim Jeffries to become America's first black heavyweight champion.

ARTS AND ENTERTAINMENT John Philip Sousa made a world tour with his band of one hundred players. Igor Stravinsky's *Firebird* ballet premiered in Paris. Puccini's *Girl of the Golden West*, written for the New York Metropolitan Opera Company, opened, starring Caruso. Also at the Metropolitan Opera, Anna Pavlova of the Imperial Russian Ballet made her wildly acclaimed American debut; she went on in *Coppelia* shortly before midnight, following the regular opera program. Twenty-six-year-old Wilhelm Bachaus made the first recording of a piano concerto, actually part of the Grieg, abbreviated to

26

fit the record's running time. ☐ American architect Frank Lloyd Wright was acclaimed in Europe for his revolutionary home designs. ☐ An Englishman, Charles Chaplin, toured the United States with a pantomime troup and appeared in a vaudeville act titled "Karno's Wow Wows." ☐ American realistic painter Robert Henri and several colleagues formed a group, "The Eight," which became better known as the "Ashcan School." ☐ The Morton Salt umbrella-girl trademark debuted, with the slogan, "When it rains, it pours." ☐ Thomas Edison, in an interview, predicted three-dimensional television.

On December 12, Dorothy Arnold, heiress to one of Manhattan's important fortunes, lunched with friends, walked to Brentano's, bought a book, was seen leaving the store by a friend, and disappeared, never to be found.

☐   **1911**   Germany has "a place in the sun."
—KAISER WILHELM II, *promising that his navy would secure it*

FOUNDED   *The Masses,* Socialist magazine, with writers John Reed and Carl Sandburg among contributors; the postal bank system; the Indianapolis 500-mile auto race; the collegiate carnival at Dartmouth College

INTRODUCED   The automobile self-starter (Charles Kettering); the hydro-airplane (Glenn Hammond Curtiss); the Studebaker and Chevrolet cars; Kleig lamps; the gyrocompass (Sperry); two movie fan magazines, *Photoplay* and *Motion Picture*

SONGS   "Alexander's Ragtime Band" "Everybody's Doin' It" "Oh, You Beautiful Doll" "I Want a Girl (Just Like the Girl)"

DANCE STEPS   The turkey trot, most popular for ragtime music

THE WORLD   The coronation of King George V and Queen Mary of England was the event of the year. ☐ Follow-

27

ing a revolution in central China, pigtails were abolished, the calendar was reformed, Sun Yat-sen was elected president, Chiang Kai-shek was appointed his military adviser. The country had the world's largest population: 345 million. □ The *Mona Lisa* was stolen from the Louvre museum. □ In Mexico, Porfirio Díaz, president since 1877, was deposed. □ Roald Amundsen reached the South Pole via dogsled three months after starting out. □ Marie Curie became the first woman to win the Nobel Prize.

THE UNITED STATES The U.S. Cavalry was dispatched to protect the neutrality of the Rio Grande during civil war in Mexico. □ The House of Representatives voted for direct election of U.S. senators, formerly selected by state legislatures. □ An investigation in Ohio revealed that a fourth of the electorate had sold their votes. □ The first transcontinental air flight was made by C. P. Rogers from New York to Pasadena; it took eighty-four hours. Airmail delivery was initiated when the first airmail pilot was sworn in to deliver mail from Garden City to Mineola, New York, a distance of approximately two miles. The first American woman pilot, Harriet Quimby, a magazine writer, was issued a license. □ The Stanley Steamer was a popular car; its usual speed was 30 mph. □ In a classic sweatshop disaster, a fire in the Triangle Shirtwaist Factory in New York killed 154 workers, most of them women. □ The Standard Oil and American Tobacco companies were dissolved by the U.S. Supreme Court as monopolies.

SPORTS Ty Cobb batted .420, again leading the American League, as he had since 1907. □ Nine-year-old Bobby Jones won his first golf title, the Junior Championship of Atlanta. □ Jim Thorpe was named to the All-American football team. □ Winner of the first Indianapolis 500 was auto racer Ray Harroun, who averaged 74.59 mph in a Marmon.

ARTS AND ENTERTAINMENT Stravinsky's ballet *Petrouchka* and Ravel's *Daphnis et Chloé* both debuted in Paris. The focus in ballet was on Nijinsky, who joined the Diaghilev company, danced in Paris, and became the rage. He seemed to leap effortlessly and hang in the air. Said Sarah Bernhardt, "I am afraid, I am afraid, for I am watching the greatest dancer in the world." ☐ Richard Strauss' opera *Der Rosenkavalier* and Gustav Mahler's *Song of the Earth* had their first performances. ☐ Georges Braque painted *Man with a Guitar;* Matisse, *The Red Studio;* Renoir, *Gabrielle with a Rose;* Paul Klee, a self-portrait. Millionaire Peter Widener bought Rembrandt's *The Mill* from the Marquis of Landsdowne for $514,000. ☐ Architect Walter Gropius designed the Fagus Factory in Germany. ☐ Artist Max-field Parrish was doing covers for *Collier's* magazine. ☐ As part of its parlor furniture line of phonographs, Columbia issued a $200 "Regent" design with Chippendale legs; it was mahogany, doubled as a table. Victor pooh-poohed the idea: "The Victrola is not a piece of furniture," ads said.

☐ **1912**   "My hat's in the ring."
—THEODORE ROOSEVELT, *announcing his decision to run as the Progressive (Bull Moose) Party candidate against Republican incumbent William Howard Taft and Democrat Woodrow Wilson*

FOUNDED   The British Royal Air Force; the Girl Scouts of America; the United States Chamber of Commerce; the U.S. departments of Labor and Commerce; Hadassah, the Women's Zionist Organization of America; *Poetry* magazine, in Chicago, giving voice to the free verse movement

INTRODUCED   The newsreel, by Pathé; stainless steel; cellophane, in Switzerland (1923 in the U.S.); Sani-Flush; the Packard and Rambler automobiles; phenobarbital, introduced under the trade name Luminal

SONGS   "Waiting for the Robert E. Lee" "It's a Long Way to Tipperary" "Moonlight Bay" "My Melancholy Baby" "Sweetheart of Sigma Chi" "When Irish Eyes Are Smiling"

DANCE STEPS   The tango, still the rage, joined by the fox-trot, camel walk, kangaroo dip, bunny hug

FASHION   Tunic tops of dresses dipped in the back; skirts were narrow, with slits at the side; small hats were elaborately decorated with feathers; walking sticks were chic; the show *The Pink Lady* made that color popular.

THE WORLD   There was war in the Balkans—Montenegro against Turkey—as Bulgaria and Serbia mobilized. ☐ Nikolai Lenin called a conference of adherents in Prague, where the Central Committee of the Bolshevik group was formed. Lenin also decided to launch a newspaper in St. Petersburg; the first number of *Pravda* appeared May 5, 1912. ☐ In Germany, the Socialists emerged as the largest party. The Reichstag was adjourned after Socialist attacks on Kaiser Wilhelm. ☐ Captain Scott and companions reached the South Pole. All died on the return trip. ☐ The White Star liner *Titanic*, on her maiden voyage, struck an iceberg and sank, with the loss of 1,503 of her total complement of 2,207 passengers and crew. Young Marconi radio operator David Sarnoff won world fame when he picked up faint wireless signals, alerted ships and the press, stayed at his wireless key for seventy-two hours sending news of survivors.

THE UNITED STATES   Woodrow Wilson was elected president, defeating incumbent William Howard Taft, Theodore Roosevelt, and Socialist Eugene V. Debs, who received 897,000 out of the 13 million votes cast. Shot at by a would-be assassin while he was campaigning in Wisconsin, Theodore Roosevelt was saved by the bulk of the manuscript he was holding. ☐ Arizona and New Mexico became states. ☐ Textile workers in Lawrence, Massachusetts, struck, the first indication of the power of the Industrial Workers of the World (IWW), also known as the Wobblies. ☐ Eastman Kodak's Brownie box cameras cost from $1 to $4; folding Brownies were $5 to $12. A two-passenger Packard runabout with rumble seat was $4,750. Arrow shirts cost from $1.50 up, without the separate collar, of course. The complete works of Mark Twain from Harper & Brothers cost $25 for the twenty-five cloth-bound volumes. Riverview Academy, a home for the development of "the better kind of boys," charged $360 a year. Hamburg-American Line's 110-day round-the-world cruise on the S.S. *Cleveland* was $650 and up, including railway, hotel, shore excursions, carriages, and guides. ☐ Cherry trees, a gift of the Japanese government, were planted in Washington, D.C. ☐ The slang of the moment was "It's a cinch," "Beat it!" "What do you know about that?" "classy," and "peachy." ☐ There were 400 Great Atlantic and Pacific Tea (A&P) stores. ☐ Among popular products were Fairy Soap, made without lye, which advertised, "Have You a Little 'Fairy' in Your Home?"; Sapolio, a cleanser that "makes the cleaning arm strong"; and Sen-Sen Chiclet Company's Chiclets, "the Dainty Mint Covered Candy Coated Chewing Gum." ☐ In the United States, approximately 5 million people visited the movie houses each day. In England, there were 400 cinemas in London alone.

SPORTS American Indian athlete Jim Thorpe won the Olympic Games pentathlon and decathlon events, then was stripped of his medals when it was discovered he had played semiprofessional baseball the year before. Many still consider Thorpe the greatest athlete of the century.

ARTS AND ENTERTAINMENT Leopold Stokowski was appointed musical director of the Philadelphia Symphony Orchestra. ☐ Georges Braque did the first collage, gluing a piece of imitation-woodgrain paper to the surface of a drawing. French artist Paul Emile Chabas' painting of a nude woman bathing, *September Morn,* was a scandal; it later became one of the most popular pieces of calendar art of all time. ☐ The Victor Co. published a 375-page *Victor Book of Operas.* The company's catalog contained recordings by Caruso, Scotti, Louise Homer, Tetrazzini, and included six versions of the mad scene from *Lucia.* ☐ Maria Montessori, whose book, *The Montessori Method,* was a bestseller, wrote articles for *Collier's* magazine.

Otto Titzling almost invented the brassiere, when he designed a chest halter to provide uplift and shapeliness for the bosom of an opera singer who had complained of the heavy boned corsets she had to wear. He never patented it. ☐ *Century* magazine spoke for many when it said, "The fight against the cigarette is a fight for civilization. There is no energy more destructive of soul and mind and body or more subversive of good morals than the cigarette." ☐ Casimir Funck introduced the word "vitamine" into the language.

FOUNDED The Rockefeller Foundation, with some $165 million; Be Kind to Animals Week; The National Safety Council; The American Cancer Society; Actor's Equity; The Anti-Defamation League of the B'Nai Brith; The Federal Reserve Bank System

INTRODUCED Crossword puzzles (the first appeared on the Fun Page of the *New York World*); Camel cigarettes; the Indian-head-buffalo nickel; a radiation-detection counter, invented by Hans Geiger; Life Savers, patented as "nothing enclosed by a circle"; the Pierce Arrow automobile; parcel post service; the X-ray tube; Schick test for diphtheria

RETIRED The cylinder system of phonograph recording, abandoned in favor of discs

SONGS "If I Had My Way" "Peg o' My Heart" "Trail of the Lonesome Pine" "You Made Me Love You" "Sweethearts" "Too-ra-loo-ra-loo-ral"

NEW GAME Ping-Pong

FADS The country was dance crazy, doing one-steps, hesitation waltzes, tangos, and turkey trots to phonograph music.

FASHION England's Queen Mary started a vogue for turbans.

THE WORLD Germany increased the size of its army. ☐ King George of Greece was assassinated. ☐ Balkan wars continued. ☐ Mahatma Gandhi, leader of India's passive resistance movement, was arrested. ☐ Emmeline Pankhurst, British suffragette leader, was convicted of disturbing the peace and jailed after huge suffragette demonstrations in London. ☐ The *Mona Lisa*, stolen from the Louvre in 1911, was recovered in Italy. ☐ Albert Schweitzer opened his hospital in Lambarene, French Congo.

THE UNITED STATES Woodrow Wilson was inaugurated. ☐ The Sixteenth Amendment, authorizing an income tax, was ratified. ☐ Ten thousand women marched for the vote on

Fifth Avenue, New York. ☐ There were 2,250,000 cars on the road, including electric cars that could go 125 miles without a recharge. ☐ The first passenger flight took place, from New York City to Albany. ☐ The first loop-the-loop by a plane was performed at San Diego. ☐ Henry Ford pioneered the assembly-line technique with the use of conveyor belts. ☐ Grand Central Terminal, which opened in New York, was designed to accommodate eight hundred trains daily. ☐ There were fifty thousand men and women in U.S. prisons. Sarah Bernhardt entertained inmates at San Quentin. ☐ Secret Service protection was granted to presidents-elect. ☐ Leo Frank, Jewish manager of a Georgia factory who had been convicted of murdering a young girl, was lynched by a mob, which took him from the jail and hanged him. ☐ On Easter Sunday, tornadoes and floods struck Nebraska, Iowa, Illinois, Indiana, and Ohio, leaving three thousand dead or missing. Flood damage was worst in Dayton, Ohio, where the downtown business area was inundated to a depth of twelve feet. ☐ The sixty-floor Woolworth Building, the world's tallest at 792 feet, was dedicated by President Wilson. ☐ It was announced that persons addicted to the drinking habit would not be considered for fourth-class postmastership positions. ☐ Popular advertised products included Eagle Brand condensed milk, Budweiser beer, Postum, Pond's Vanishing Cream. ☐ Circulation of the *Saturday Evening Post* reached 2 million. Cartoons by T. A. Dorgen, known as TAD, began appearing in Hearst's *Boston American;* he coined the word "yes-man" during the year. ☐ Among notions around but not accepted were feminism, psychoanalysis, Socialism, and trade unionism.

SPORTS   The first Army–Notre Dame football game was played; Notre Dame won, introducing heavy use of the forward pass.

ARTS AND ENTERTAINMENT   Robert Bridges was appointed poet laureate of England. ☐ In New York, 100,000 people jammed the Sixty-Ninth Regiment Armory Art Show, organized by Walt Kuhn and Arthur B. Davies, and bought 238 pictures. The show introduced cubism, expressionism, fauvism, and futurism to the nation. Monet and Picasso were among the artists shown, but the sensation was Marcel Duchamp's *Nude*

Descending the Staircase, which critics variously termed hideous, pathological, stupid, and ugly. ☐ Igor Stravinsky's *Rite of Spring* premiered. Arturo Toscanini made his first American appearance as a symphonic conductor with Beethoven's Ninth Symphony. Moussorgsky's *Boris Godunov*, sung for the first time at the New York Metropolitan, was thought by the *New York Times* critic to have no lasting appeal, as it had no love interest. ☐ Isadora Duncan's schools of modern dance were flourishing in Europe. ☐ Exotic dancer Roshanara toured the United States with her troupe, doing Eastern dances. ☐ The HMV phonograph catalog, just published, listed violin records by Mischa Elman, Fritz Kreisler, Pablo de Sarasate, and Joseph Szigeti. ☐ In science, Albert Einstein began publishing his theory of relativity. ☐ In New Orleans, 13-year-old Louis Armstrong picked up a pistol, shot it off, was arrested and sent to reform school, where he received his first training in music from a Captain Jones.

☐ **1914** "It is not part of our curriculum nor is there any present plan for making it one." —PRESIDENT LOWELL *of Harvard University on aviation and the study of aeronautics*

FOUNDED The U.S. Federal Trade Commission; ASCAP, the American Society of Composers, Authors and Publishers; King Features Syndicate, organized by William Randolph Hearst; Mother's Day, by presidential proclamation; The National Birth Control League, by Margaret Sanger; Greyhound Busline, with a seven-passenger car with seats added, in Minnesota; *The New Republic*, as a weekly magazine

INTRODUCED Plastic surgery; the conditioned reflex, discovered by Pavlov; the racy, open, large-engined Stutz Bearcat

GAINING POPULARITY Electric vacuum sweepers

SONGS "They Didn't Believe Me" "Aba Daba Honey-

moon" "By the Beautiful Sea" "St. Louis Blues" "Keep the
Home-Fires Burning" "Twelfth Street Rag" "When You Wore
a Tulip"

DANCE STEPS   The Castle Walk

FASHION   Women's dresses were ankle-length, slightly
shorter in front, and multilayered—brief jacket, over tunic, over
skirt.

THE WORLD   World War I began. Following the June
28th assassination of Austria-Hungary's Archduke Franz Ferdinand and his wife at Sarajevo by a Bosnian revolutionary, Germany, as Austria-Hungary's ally, declared war on Serbia's ally,
Russia, on August 1. Great Britain declared war on Germany
on August 4, following Germany's invasion of Belgium and
declaration of war on France. Soon the Central Powers (Germany, Austria-Hungary, Turkey, and Bulgaria) were pitted
against the Allies (England, France, Russia, Belgium, Serbia).
□ St. Petersburg in Russia was renamed Petrograd. □ Benedict
XV became pope. □ The first aerial combat in history occurred
in August, when Allied and German pilots and observers started
shooting at one another with pistols and rifles, with negligible
results. □ Dr. Alexis Carrel performed heart surgery on an
animal. □ The Panama Canal opened to commercial traffic.

THE UNITED STATES   Following the arrest of American
sailors by the Mexican government, the United States landed
marines and sailors at Vera Cruz and sent troops to Tampico;
it was one of a series of incidents that brought the two countries
to the brink of war. A change in Mexican political power resolved that threat but brought a new one, with the appearance
on the scene of rebel Gen. Pancho Villa. □ The new income tax
took effect. Tax on $7,500 income was $35; on $20,000 it was
$160. John D. Rockefeller paid $2 million in taxes; J. P. Morgan
and Marshall Field, $250,000 each. □ In Colorado, nine thousand
coal miners were on strike and violence broke out. In a bloody
fight with federal troops sent by President Wilson, twenty-one
lives were lost in the "Battle of Ludlow." □ Work began on
the Lincoln Memorial in Washington, D.C. □ Cotillions were
fading from the social dance picture. Vernon and Irene Castle
were the pacesetters and innovators in dance. John D. Rocke-

35

feller, Jr. took tango lessons from them at $100 an hour. Nevertheless, the U.S. Federation of Women's Clubs banned both the tango and the hesitation waltz as immoral. □ Ford's assembly line worked so well that the company turned out 240,700 cars during the year and its profits doubled. Pay for Ford's workers increased from $2.40 a day for nine hours to $5 for eight. □ Wages for women at Marshall Field and Sears, Roebuck in Chicago averaged $9 a week; the heads of both companies told a vice commission that they saw no relationship between the salaries they paid and prostitution in the Chicago area. □ The popular cars were the Jackson, Hupmobile, Hudson, Mitchell, Maxwell, Overland, and Franklin; but the Ford Model T, always black, outsold them all. Ford jokes swept the land, with the car fondly called the Tin Lizzie or the Flivver. You could buy a Ford joke book for 10¢. □ Motor traffic was so heavy in Cleveland, Ohio, that the first traffic signal was installed; there were red and green lights, plus a loud buzzer. □ Evangelist Billy Sunday conducted ninety-five meetings during the year, touring the country and convincing eighteen thousand people to hit the sawdust trail. □ An around-the-world cruise via Hamburg-American Lines cost $800, all-inclusive; a quart of milk cost 9¢, sirloin steak 27¢ a pound, eggs 34¢ a dozen. To replace a fender on the ubiquitous Ford was $2.50. A dustless mop cost $1.25.

SPORTS   Walter Hagen won his first National Open golf tournament. □ Yale Bowl, an eighty-thousand-seat stadium, was completed. □ Jack Dempsey started his pugilistic career under the name of Kid Blakey.

ARTS AND ENTERTAINMENT   Italian tenor Beniamino Gigli made his debut. □ Movie houses were proliferating. The first of the deluxe versions was opened in New York, when Samuel (Roxy) Rothafel took over the Strand Theatre. □ Charlie Chaplin made it big during the year. *Tillie's Punctured Romance* and *Making a Living* brought him fame; from earning $150 a week he soared to $1,250, when Essanay made him an offer. □ Maude Adams, "the idol of playgoers everywhere," toured in *Camille*. □ Edgar Rice Burroughs introduced "Tarzan of the Apes," who ultimately starred in twenty-five books, movies, and comic strips and was translated into fifty-six languages. □ In New Orleans, 14-year-old Louis Armstrong formed his own band and started working around town.

□ **1915**

"What this country needs is a good five-cent cigar."
—VICE PRES. THOMAS R. MARSHALL

"Don't mourn for me, organize."
—JOE HILL, *poet and labor leader convicted of murder, before being executed by a firing squad in Utah*

FOUNDED The first Kiwanis Club, in Detroit; the U.S. Coast Guard; the Women's International League for Peace and Freedom, with Jane Addams as president

INTRODUCED The neon lamp; a tough, sturdy new car —the Dodge Four—at $785; an all-metal plane for warfare, by Hugo Junkers of Germany; serum injections to control tetanus in the trenches; poison gas

SONGS "Pack Up Your Troubles in Your Old Kit Bag" "I Didn't Raise My Boy to Be a Soldier" "Hello, Frisco" "Jelly Roll Blues" "Memories"

THE WORLD The sinking of the Cunard passenger ship *Lusitania* by German U-boats off the Irish coast, with the loss of 1,198 lives, including 124 Americans, brought the United States close to war. Italy, previously neutral, declared war on Germany. U.S. loans to Britain and France for war purchases reached $500 million. The British blockaded Germany. □ Germany launched its first zeppelin attack on London. The czar took personal command of the Russian Army. British nurse Edith Cavell was executed by the Germans in Brussels as a British spy. □ The names of the emperors of Germany and Austria were struck off the rolls of the British Knights of the Garter. □ The sale of absinthe was prohibited in France. □ The remains of Marco Polo's city of Etzina was discovered in southern Mongolia.

THE UNITED STATES German ads in U.S. newspapers warned that ships flying the British flag would be sunk. American sentiment turned against Germany when that country introduced poison gas, and atrocities in Belgium were reported. ☐ Haiti became a U.S. protectorate, following a revolution. ☐ A telephone line was opened between New York and San Francisco, inspiring the song "Hello, Frisco." Speech was transmitted experimentally from Arlington, Virginia, to Honolulu and across the Atlantic. ☐ A proposal to give women the vote was defeated in the House of Representatives. Margaret Sanger went to jail as author of the first book on birth control. ☐ An easy divorce law, requiring only six months' residence, went into effect in Nevada, assuring the future of the city of Reno. ☐ Pres. Woodrow Wilson, widowed for over a year, married a widow, Mrs. Edith Galt. ☐ In Chicago, forty thousand men paraded to protest the closing of saloons on Sundays. ☐ The Pierce Arrow car was offered in a choice of fifteen body styles, from a runabout at $4,900 to a landaulet at $6,200. ☐ Henry Ford, with the slogan Out of the Trenches and Home by Christmas, determined to send a "peace ship" to Europe to stop the war. On December 4, Ford, 163 pacifists, and a group described as ribald journalists set sail on the Danish vessel *Oscar II*. Everything went wrong; the ship made it to Norway, but Ford fell ill and abandoned the venture. ☐ Ernest Muenter, a German instructor at Cornell, planted a bomb in the U.S. Senate cloakroom, then went to the Glen Cove, Long Island, home of J. P. Morgan, to attempt to shoot him. Failing in both efforts, he shot himself.

SPORTS Jess Willard defeated Jack Johnson in twenty-six rounds to become the heavyweight champion. ☐ Ty Cobb set a baseball record by stealing ninety-six bases during the season. ☐ Paul Robeson started a sports career at Rutgers that was to make him an All-American football player.

ARTS AND ENTERTAINMENT Classic New Orleans jazz was in full bloom. Paul Whiteman left the classical music field to organize an orchestra to play "syncopation." ☐ *Musical Quarterly*, the first American musicological journal, was founded. ☐ Two theaters, which were to become centers for experiment and innovation—the Neighborhood Playhouse and the Provincetown Players—opened. ☐ Dancers Ruth St. Denis and Ted Shawn, who had married the previous year, formed the Denishawn school and dance company in Los Angeles. ☐ Pablo Picasso painted his first harlequin, and Marcel Duchamp his first Dada picture. ☐ David Sarnoff, assistant traffic manager of the Marconi Company, suggested the idea of a radio music box but his superiors found no merit in the scheme.

☐ **1916** "He kept us out of war."
—*Slogan for the reelection campaign of Pres. Woodrow Wilson*

FOUNDED The National Research Council, to coordinate scientific study for defense; the Professional Golf Association; General Motors, Incorporated

INTRODUCED The Mercury dime and the Liberty half-dollar; refrigeration of blood for transfusion; plastic surgery for treatment of war casualties

SONGS "I Ain't Got Nobody" "If You Were the Only Girl in the World" "Li'l Liza Jane" "Nola" "Pretty Baby" "Yaaka Hula Hickey Dula"

FASHION Little boys were wearing baggy knickers, pleated Norfolk jackets, high shoes and, at the neck, pussycat bows.

THE WORLD Germany introduced steel helmets into its army. The British introduced tanks on the Western Front. Zeppelins raided Paris. ☐ The Easter Rebellion took place in Ireland. ☐ Austria's Emperor Franz Joseph died after a sixty-year reign. ☐ In Russia, the mysterious and powerful monk Rasputin was killed by aristocratic relatives of the czar. ☐ T. E. Lawrence, to become known as Lawrence of Arabia, was appointed political officer by Prince Feisal of Mecca, leader of the Arab Army of Liberation.

THE UNITED STATES Woodrow Wilson was reelected president by a close margin, defeating Associate Justice of the

Supreme Court Charles Evans Hughes. ☐ War fever ran high. A munitions arsenal at Tom Island, New Jersey, was blown up, allegedly by German saboteurs. In San Francisco, a bomb exploded during a Preparedness Day Parade, killing ten, wounding forty. Labor organizer Tom Mooney was accused of the crime, convicted, sentenced to death; the sentence was commuted to life imprisonment in 1918. Mooney was pardoned in 1939. ☐ Louis J. Brandeis became the first Jew appointed to the U.S. Supreme Court, despite objections that "his Oriental mind could not function effectively in a legal system based on Occidental principles." ☐ Jeannette Rankin of Montana became the first woman to win a congressional seat. ☐ Margaret Sanger opened the first birth control clinic, in the Brownsville section of Brooklyn, New York, and ended up spending thirty days in jail. ☐ The United States arranged to purchase the three Danish Virgin Islands, via a treaty. Also in the Caribbean, U.S. troops landed in Santo Domingo to help settle internal strife; they stayed eight years. ☐ Pancho Villa, protesting American recognition of Mexico's Carranza government, shot eighteen Americans in Santa Isabel, Mexico, and attacked Columbus, New Mexico, killing seventeen. Gen. John Pershing, with a force of twelve thousand, pursued Villa, on horseback and in Dodge Fours, but was unable to capture him; Pershing became a hero, nevertheless. ☐ An eight-hour day for railroad workers became law. ☐ Auto production soared. There were 3,500,000 cars on the road, 98 percent of them open models. A Ford cost $600.

SPORTS The Rosebowl Game, played once before, in 1902, was resumed; Washington State won over Brown, 14–0.

ARTS AND ENTERTAINMENT Architect Frank Lloyd Wright designed the Imperial Hotel in Tokyo. ☐ Sergei Diaghilev brought his Ballet Russe to New York's Metropolitan Opera House. The great Russian dancer Vaslav Nijinsky debuted there three months later. ☐ The Provincetown Playhouse produced Eugene O'Neill's first one-act plays, notably *Bound East for Cardiff* and *The Moon of the Caribbees.* ☐ Movies, familiarly known as "flickers," were now America's fifth most important industry, with 25 million people a day spending from 5¢ to 25¢ to see them. ☐ *The Ziegfeld Follies* of 1916 glorified the

American girl, whose dimensions had to be bust, 36; waist, 26; hips, 38. Her salary was $75 a week. Marion Davies, later made famous by William Randolph Hearst, was one of a number of Ziegfeld girls who went on to better things. □ Norman Rockwell began illustrating for the *Saturday Evening Post*. □ Albert Einstein formulated the General Theory of Relativity.

□ **1917** "Lafayette, we are here."
—GENERAL PERSHING *in Paris, after landing in France with the American Expeditionary Force*

ESTABLISHED The Pulitzer prizes in Journalism and Letters; Boys Town in Nebraska, by Father Flanagan; Mt. McKinley National Park, Alaska; the U.S. Tank Corps; the International Association of Lions Clubs

INTRODUCED Erector sets; Keds sneakers; the zipper; Nash automobiles; the Flexible Flyer sled; the Liberty 25¢ piece

SONGS "Over There" "Beale Street Blues" "Darktown Strutter's Ball" "For Me and My Gal" "Thine Alone" "Oh Johnny, Oh Johnny, Oh!"

FASHION Irene Castle bobbed her hair and a nation of newly liberated women did the same.

THE WORLD The February revolution in Russia forced the czar to abdicate. Alexander Kerensky became prime minister. After ten years in exile, Lenin returned to Russia. The July uprising of his Bolshevik Party failed; a second try in November succeeded. Lenin formed a government and became the first chairman of the Soviet of People's Commissars. The imperial family was sent to Siberia. □ The United States declared war on Germany in April. The American Expeditionary Force made its first landing in France in June; the first American died in November. □ Mata Hari was executed as a spy by the French. □ With Germany the enemy, the British Royal Family changed its name from Coburg to Windsor.

41

THE UNITED STATES War hysteria and anti-German sentiment ran high. German measles became liberty measles; hamburgers, liberty steak; sauerkraut, liberty cabbage. Pretzels were banned in Cincinnati and the teaching of German outlawed in New York, Iowa, and Montana. New York's Metropolitan Opera House banned German opera. ☐ Ten suffragettes picketed the White House; four were arrested and given six-month sentences. ☐ Liberty Loans to finance the war were hawked by such stars as Mary Pickford, Douglas Fairbanks, George M. Cohan, and Charlie Chaplin, who drew great crowds to bond rallies. Liberty savings stamps, at 25¢, carried the legend, "Lick a stamp to lick the Kaiser." ☐ Evangeline Booth, head of the U.S. Salvation Army, sent hundreds of her "lassies" to the Western Front, where they served coffee and doughnuts in the trenches, cared for the wounded, helped boys write letters home. ☐ Food rationing was instituted, as were meatless Mondays, coal-less Tuesdays, and gasless Sundays. Prohibitionists exulted when federal decree prohibited the manufacture of whiskey. ☐ A draft call by lottery for men 21 to 30 was started; other men enlisted in answer to James Montgomery Flagg's poster of Uncle Sam pointing an imperative finger and saying, "I WANT YOU." ☐ As a sort of sideline to the war, the U.S. Marines landed in Cuba at the request of the Cuban government. ☐ With men at war, women went into the factories, became elevator operators, streetcar conductors, auto mechanics.

SPORTS New York's Polo Grounds opened. Team managers for both baseball teams were arrested on opening day, since it was an illegal Sunday game.

ARTS AND ENTERTAINMENT Storyville, the New Orleans red-light district where most jazzmen made their living, was closed down by the U.S. Navy, and the nerve center of jazz was forced North. Chicago became one of the new jazz centers. Jelly Roll Morton was playing with a group in San Diego and Los Angeles. ☐ Hotels and restaurants introduced the *thé dansant*, featuring the fox-trot. ☐ The original Dixie Land Jazz Band, playing at Weisenbeber's Cafe in New York, cut its first jazz record, "Indiana," with "Darktown Strutter's Ball" on the flip side. ☐ Sixteen-year-old violinist Jascha Heifetz made a triumphant New York debut at Carnegie Hall. The Ballet Russe made an extended U.S. tour. Ballet lost its greatest figure when Vaslav Nijinsky, whose mental state had been deteriorating for several years, was forced to retire. ☐ Sarah Bernhardt made her last American appearance, at 72, in *The Merchant of Venice*. ☐ Picasso did surrealist sets and costumes for Eric Satie's ballet, *Parade*. George Grosz, in Germany, produced his lithographs, *The Face of the Ruling Class*. John Singer Sargent painted a portrait of John D. Rockefeller. Auguste Rodin died, leaving his personal sculpture collection to the French nation. ☐ In the movies, Charlie Chaplin's salary reached a million dollars a year. Between 1911 and 1917, Tom Mix had made close to a hundred films.

"Even God Almighty has only ten."
—FRENCH PRIME MINISTER GEORGES CLEMENCEAU, *commenting on Pres. Woodrow Wilson's Fourteen Points*

FOUNDED   The Berkshire Festival of Music, in Massachusetts; in England, the RAF became the first fully independent air arm, equal to the army and navy; the Theatre Guild

INTRODUCED   Airmail stamps; Daylight Savings Time in the United States; motor scooters; automatic toasters; the Buick Six, which lasted, with minor changes, until 1923

SONGS   "Oh! How I Hate to Get Up in the Morning" "After You've Gone" "Beautiful Ohio" "K-K-K-Katy" "Smilin' Through" "Till We Meet Again" "Ja-Da" "I'm Always Chasing Rainbows"

FASHION   Women's skirts crept up to slightly above the ankle but high shoes kept things modest. The bellboy hat, tall and turned down over one eye, was in vogue.

THE WORLD   The first U.S. air squadron made independent raids over enemy lines. ☐ World War I was winding down. The year began with a great German offensive and ended with peace. In January, President Wilson issued his Fourteen Points as a basis for lasting peace. Russia and Germany signed a separate peace treaty. The German fleet mutinied and Germany began to withdraw to its own lines. In Berlin, the imperial government was overthrown, the kaiser was forced to abdicate; the German Republic was proclaimed. □ The Armistice came November 11. 8,200,000 had been killed in the war and 21 million wounded. An influenza epidemic swept the world, killing 20 million before it was over. □ Czar Nicholas of Russia, the czarina, and their children were executed.

THE UNITED STATES Eugene V. Debs was convicted of violating the Espionage Act and sentenced to ten years' imprisonment. □ Prior to war's end, many consumer products were in short supply. In homes with infants, most of the two-pounds-per-month sugar ration went into homemade baby formulas. □ The fight for women's suffrage grew stronger; parades for the vote were common in many cities, including New York, where eighteen thousand women marched in one parade. □ The first airmail flights were flown between New York and Washington, D.C., and New York and Chicago; the New York–Chicago time was ten hours, five minutes. □ The Anti-Saloon League called the liquor traffic "un-American, pro-German, crime-producing, food-wasting, youth-corrupting, home-wrecking and treasonable." □ One of New York's great parades for a returning hero was staged for Sgt. Alvin York, who had single-handedly killed 23 Germans and persuaded the remainder of the company, 132 in all, to surrender. □ The Mt. Wilson telescope was completed near Pasadena.

SPORTS Knute Rockne became head football coach for Notre Dame. Before his death in 1931, his team was to win 105 games, lose 12, tie 5.

ARTS AND ENTERTAINMENT The U.S. Post Office seized and burned early installments of James Joyce's *Ulysses,* which had been sent for publication in the *Little Review* magazine in Chicago. □ Dixieland music was everywhere; a band even toured Europe. The Victor Company, in Camden, New Jersey, issued phonograph recordings of the Boston Symphony. Igor Stravinsky's *Histoire du Soldat* premiered in Switzerland.

The St. Louis Municipal Outdoor Theatre, to become known as the Muny, opened. Rosa Ponselle, American soprano, debuted at the New York Metropolitan in *La Forza del Destino*, with Caruso. ☐ Joan Miro's paintings were exhibited for the first time, in Paris. ☐ Paul Whiteman's band gained national recognition. ☐ Enrico Caruso, a meticulous man, married Dorothy Benjamin and entered in his notebook the cost of the ceremony—$50.

☐ **1919** "Tell it to Sweeney; the Stuyvesants will take care of themselves."
—JOSEPH MEDILL PATTERSON'S *motto on forming the first tabloid newspaper, the* New York Daily News

FOUNDED The Communist Party of America; The American Legion; Radio Corporation of America; Father Divine's first Heaven, at Sayville, New York

INTRODUCED London-to-Paris passenger air service; the mechanical rabbit, which marked the origin of modern greyhound racing; Little Blue Books, published by E. Haldemann–Julius, ranging from classics to junk at 5¢ each

SONGS "Dardanella" "Alice Blue Gown" "Baby, Won't You Please Come Home" "A Pretty Girl Is Like a Melody" "How Ya Gonna Keep 'em Down on the Farm" "There's a Long, Long Trail A-winding"

POPULAR GAMES Auction bridge

FASHION A revolution for men: returning soldiers, accustomed to the soft, comfortable, attached collars of army uniform shirts, rejected conventional stiffly starched or celluloid separate collars; manufacturers were forced into attaching collars. ☐ Women's fashion: skirt lengths were on their way up—six inches off the ground; some hems had handkerchief points; hosiery was still mainly lisle or rayon, in dark colors.

THE WORLD The Peace Conference opened in Paris in January, with President Wilson attending. The treaty was signed

45

in June at Versailles. ☐ American-born Lady Nancy Astor became the first woman member of Britain's Parliament.

THE UNITED STATES Gen. John J. Pershing and his Yanks marched up Fifth Avenue in a great victory parade but returning veterans began to find that being conquering heroes did not guarantee them jobs. Herbert Hoover was named director general for food relief for Europe. ☐ Women won the right to vote, and Americans lost the right to drink, with ratification of the Nineteenth and Eighteenth amendments. Prohibition was to become effective January 1, 1920. While the liquor still flowed, the Bronx cocktail—vermouth, orange juice, and gin— was popular. Few women smoked in public or sat at bars. ☐ A bad year for labor and management: more than 4 million workers were on strike or locked out during the year. 350,000 steelworkers struck, followed a month later by 400,000 miners. Union demands were for shorter hours, increases in pay. With the aid of the military, steel management broke the strike. ☐ In Boston, there was looting, and stores closed when 1,117 out of 1,544 policemen struck. Gov. Calvin Coolidge took charge, wiring union leader Samuel Gompers that there was "no right to strike against the public safety by anybody, anywhere, anytime." ☐ Capt. E. F. White made the first New York-to-Chicago nonstop flight, and two Englishmen, Alcock and Brown, made the first transatlantic flight. ☐ An average Wall Street trading day ran between one million and one and a half million shares; the price of a seat on the New York Stock Exchange varied from $60,000 to $110,000. ☐ In September, President Wilson suffered a paralyzing stroke. Vice Pres. Thomas Marshall, who had said he loved his job because it had no responsibilities, sidestepped Cabinet meetings and other official duties. Sen. Albert Fall summed up the situation: "We have a petticoat government. Mrs. Wilson is president." ☐ The high cost of living brought milk to 15¢ a quart, sirloin steak to 42¢ a pound, butter to 61¢ a pound, three pounds of coffee to $1.05. ☐ The standard speed limit for cars was 20 mph. The Model T Ford (three thousand were being built each day) still had to be cranked, but many other cars sported self-starters. Other popular cars, only 10 percent of them closed models, were the Maxwell, Lexington, Dodge, Briscoe, and Templar.

SPORTS Close to 200,000 watched Jack Dempsey, "the Manassa Mauler," become heavyweight champ, when Jess Willard failed to answer the bell for the fourth round. ☐ Babe Ruth, who had started the season as an obscure pitcher for the Boston Red Sox, ended it with twenty-nine home runs and was bought by the New York Yankees for $125,000. Ty Cobb was still the big star.

ARTS AND ENTERTAINMENT The Los Angeles Symphony gave its first concert. ☐ Charles Griffes' *The Pleasure Dome of Kubla Khan* premiered in Boston under Pierre Monteux. ☐ Manuel de Falla's *The Three-Cornered Hat* ballet opened in London.

☐ **1920** "Harding is not a bad man; he's just a slob."
—ALICE ROOSEVELT LONGWORTH

FOUNDED The first commercial radio broadcasting station, KDKA, in Pittsburgh; the Farmer-Labor Party; the American Civil Liberties Union

INTRODUCED The permanent wave; Kotex, the first feminine napkins; the radio compass for aircraft navigation; four-wheel hydraulic brakes, in the fast, expensive Duesenberg car (and the expression "that's a doozy," derived from it); the Rolls-Royce "Silver Ghost"; the first American submachine gun, nicknamed Tommy gun for its inventor, Gen. J. T. Thompson; the Bloody Mary cocktail, at Harry's New York Bar, Paris

SONGS "Whispering" "Margie" "Avalon" "The Japanese Sandman" "Down by the O-hi-o" "It's All Over Now" "Look for the Silver Lining"

PASTIMES Mah-Jongg; ouija boards.

FASHION Skirts rose to calf length; hair was shingled or

47

curled with the new permanent wave; silk stockings in flesh tones replaced conservative dark shades. Elastic foundation garments began to replace boned corsets. A new suedelike fabric, duvetyn, was popular. ☐ For men, white tennis shoes, introduced by the visiting Prince of Wales, became the rage.

THE WORLD The League of Nations held its first meeting, in London. ☐ In Germany, Adolf Hitler announced a twenty-five-point program to his party of seven members at the Hofbrauhaus, Munich. ☐ Mahatma Gandhi emerged as the leader in India's struggle for independence, and converted his follower, Jawaharlal Nehru, to vegetarianism. ☐ In China, an earthquake in Kansu Province claimed 200,000 victims.

THE UNITED STATES The postwar economy slumped. ☐ On January 1, Prohibition, "the noble experiment," went into effect and no liquor could be had legally except on doctors' prescriptions; only near beer was legal. The coastlines of the United States offered 18,700 miles for smugglers to breach; there were only 1,520 enforcement agents. ☐ The gangster era began when Johnny Torrio found there was money in the outlawed liquor business and decided to take control of Chicago. The business card of his lieutenant, Al Capone, read "Alphonse Capone, 2nd hand furniture dealer." ☐ The previous year's strikes led to a Red scare. Two Italian anarchists, shoeworker Nicola Sacco and fish peddler Bartolomeo Vanzetti, were arrested for murdering a paymaster in South Braintree, Massachusetts. In what became known as the Palmer Raids, foreigners and suspected radicals were arrested, often without warrants. What was thought to be a radical act, a bomb explosion on Wall Street, killed 35 and wounded 150. In Centralia, Washington, a lynching followed a raid on IWW headquarters. ☐ The Ku Klux Klan had risen again, in both the North and South. In Jacksonville, Florida, Klansmen paraded openly. ☐ As the presidential conventions approached, Ohio politician Harry M. Daugherty predicted a Republican convention deadlock, saying that his man, Warren G. Harding, would be chosen as the candidate "by tired men in a smoke-filled room." He was right. Campaigning on a platform of "a return to normalcy," Harding defeated James M. Cox. ☐ Every second car on the road was a

Ford. The 1920 Model T now was offered in a closed-sedan model, with window shades and side-mounted spare tire. The luxury Cadillac added a searchlight. Also on the road were the Appersen and Essex and the remarkable Briggs and Stratton Flyer, a five-wheeled contraption with little more than two bucket seats and a steering shaft. □ Henry Ford's newspaper, the Dearborn *Independent,* embarked on a series of anti-Semitic articles with a front-page story headed, "The International Jew: The World's Problem." □ There were 8,500,000 women in the U.S. work force and 117,823,165 people in the country. □ Airmail flights started between New York and San Francisco.

SPORTS Man o' War won the Belmont and Preakness. □ Bill Tilden won at Wimbledon and again took the National Singles tennis title. □ A man died of excitement when Babe Ruth swatted one into the bleachers. □ The "Black Sox" bribery scandal nearly wrecked baseball when a Chicago grand jury indicted eight members of the 1919 White Sox club on charges of conspiring with gamblers to throw the World Series to the Cincinnati Reds. The players eventually were acquitted. □ Rogers Hornsby of the St. Louis Cardinals began a six-year reign as batting champion. □ Paavo Nurmi of Finland won the 10,000-meter gold medal and set a record for the 10,000-meter cross-country run at the Olympics.

ARTS AND ENTERTAINMENT Visitors to the exhibition of Dada art in Cologne were permitted to smash paintings. □ English conductor Albert Coates conducted the American premiere of Ralph Vaughan Williams' *A London Symphony* at Aeolian Hall, New York. Also premiered in the U.S. were Sibelius' *Finlandia* and Elgar's *Enigma Variations.* □ Agatha Christie published the first of her mysteries, *The Mysterious Affair at Styles. Main Street* by Sinclair Lewis drew praise and attacks, including censure from a California organization which accused the book of creating "a distaste for the conventional good life of the American." □ Jazz was now a worldwide rage; Paul Whiteman's band made a triumphant European tour. □ The romance of the year was the marriage of two film favorites, Mary Pickford and Douglas Fairbanks. Also in Hollywood, film star Harold Lloyd lost his right thumb when a prop bomb turned out to be real.

Among expressions new to the English language: "All wet," "applesauce," "baloney," "banana oil," "belly laugh," "bump off," "carry a torch," "fall guy," "gate-crasher," "sex appeal." □ Polly Adler embarked upon a profitable career as a madam, opening her first house in New York's West 50s. □ While England's visiting Prince of Wales was being entertained on Long Island, robbers entered the host's home and relieved guests of about $150,000 in jewelry.

 **1921**

"I am not a healer. Jesus is the healer. I am only a little office girl who opens the door and says 'come in.' "
—AIMEE SEMPLE MC PHERSON, *faith healer, whose miraculous cures drew a great following*

FOUNDED The Miss America Contest, at Atlantic City; the American Birth Control League, by Margaret Sanger

INTRODUCED Self-service marketing, with the first Piggly Wiggly store; the Eskimo Pie, first chocolate-covered ice-cream-on-a-stick; the first state sales tax, in Virginia; the first popular-priced home radio receiver, by Westinghouse ($60, not including headset or loudspeaker); Hermann Rorschach's ink-blot method for probing the subconscious

SONGS "The Sheik of Araby" "Say It with Music" "Three O'Clock in the Morning" "April Showers" "I'm Just Wild about Harry" "Ain't We Got Fun" "Wabash Blues"

FASHION Demure bathing beauties in Atlantic City wore tunic bathing suits, long stockings, hats over their long curls. One maverick Miss America contestant wore a one-piece swimsuit, rolled her stockings, showing bare knees. The form-fitting suit quickly caught on.

THE WORLD Economic crisis hit Germany. The mark began its plunge and the country reneged on payment of war reparations, due this year. Fascism was making inroads in Germany and in Italy, where twenty-nine Fascists won in the elections. ☐ The United States announced its refusal to trade with the USSR.

THE UNITED STATES   Warren G. Harding became president; commenting on his inaugural address, a British reporter termed it "the most illiterate statement ever made by the head of a civilized government." ☐ The Ku Klux Klan gained strength, instigating violence, destroying property, carrying out beatings and burnings. In Oklahoma, where the Klan was extremely active, marshal law was declared. ☐ The U.S. Communist Party and Communist Labor Party merged to form the Workers Party. ☐ Rioting followed showings of D. W. Griffith's film about the Civil War, *Birth of a Nation,* which featured scenes picturing blacks raping white women; the film was banned in Boston as inflammatory. ☐ On July 14, Sacco and Vanzetti were found guilty of murder. The case, which went through many appeals, grew into a major national and international controversy which continued up to—and following—their execution in 1927. ☐ Cigarettes were illegal in 14 states and anticigarette bills were pending in 28 states. Young women were expelled from some colleges for smoking. In Iowa, sale of cigarettes to adults became legal. ☐ President Harding commuted the ten-year sentence of Eugene V. Debs, who had served two years, eight months, for wartime sedition. ☐ A New York doctor was arrested for selling Dr. Marie Stopes' book, *Married Love,* which detailed contraceptive methods.

SPORTS   The first million-dollar fight gate was recorded when seventy-five thousand watched Jack Dempsey defeat French champion Georges Carpentier in Jersey City. It was the first major prizefight to be broadcast, and the first broadcast by RCA. ☐ Judge Kenesaw Mountain Landis was appointed czar of baseball, a result of the "Black Sox" scandal of the previous year. ☐ Golfer Bobby Jones caused shock and furor when he lost his temper at the British Open, picked up his ball, walked off the course, and quit the match. ☐ Big Bill Tilden again won the U.S. singles and Wimbledon tennis matches.

ARTS AND ENTERTAINMENT   American interpretive

dancer Isadora Duncan, now 42, was invited to the Soviet Union to establish a school of modern dance for children. While there, she married the poet Essenin. ☐ The highest price yet recorded for a painting, $640,000, was paid by Collis Huntington for Gainsborough's *Blue Boy,* sold by the Duke of Westminster through art superdealer Sir Joseph Duveen. ☐ New on the musical scene were "race" phonograph records, which record companies thought would sell only to the black market; they were mistaken. ☐ Enrico Caruso died in Naples. ☐ In Paris, *Die Walküre* became the first Wagnerian work to be performed at L'Opéra since 1914.

"My God, this is a hell of a place for a man like me to be."
—WARREN G. HARDING, *on the office of President of the United States*

FOUNDED *The Reader's Digest,* introducing condensed articles, a new concept, to publishing; the vaudeville team of Burns and Allen

INTRODUCED Balloon tires

SONGS "My Buddy" "Limehouse Blues" "Toot, Toot, Tootsie!" "Way Down Yonder in New Orleans" "Carolina in the Morning" "Chicago"

THE WORLD Mussolini marched on Rome and formed a Fascist government in Italy. ☐ The Irish Free State was established after negotiations between Britain and moderate elements of the Sinn Fein. ☐ Mahatma Gandhi was sentenced to six years' imprisonment for civil disobedience. ☐ The tomb of King Tutankhamen was discovered at Luxor, Egypt, by Howard Carter. ☐ Insulin was discovered by two Canadians, Frederick Banting and Charles Best.

THE UNITED STATES The twenties were starting to roar. Speakeasies and bootleggers operated in defiance of Prohibition. To prevent the smuggling of liquor, a "Prohibition navy" was formed. But the smugglers got through and some of the cargo found its way into the popular hip flask, carried by the nicest people. Cruise ships took the moneyed thirsty beyond the three-mile limit. ☐ The stock market boom began. ☐ Lt. Jimmy Doolittle flew a plane from Jacksonville, Florida, to San Diego, California, with only one stop. ☐ King Tut fever hit America; everything from fashions to phonograph cabinets started to look Egyptian. ☐ Striking coal miners clashed with nonunion workers in Herrin, Illinois; twenty-six persons died. ☐ Women began to smoke in public. Holding the fort for traditional good manners was Emily Post, whose first book of etiquette was published. Others tried to maintain standards: bathers in swimsuits considered too short and bare were arrested on Chicago's beaches for indecent exposure. ☐ Sixty thousand people owned radios, generally listening to them through earphones. There were over two hundred radio stations in America. Station WEAF, New York, carried the first sponsored program, with a discreet message from a real estate company. ☐ The *Saturday Evening Post* had 2,200,000 readers each week, paying 5¢ a copy, following the serial stories religiously. ☐ Bernarr MacFadden, publisher of *Physical Culture*, selected Charles Atlas as the world's most perfectly developed man.

SPORTS Big Bill Tilden continued to rule tennis, unbeatable at Wimbledon and Forest Hills. ☐ Walter Hagen became the first American golfer to win the British Open, while Gene Sarazen won the U.S. Open for the first time. ☐ Babe Ruth became an outfielder for his club, the Yankees.

ARTS AND ENTERTAINMENT Having won the Pulitzer Prize for *Anna Christie*, Eugene O'Neill was firmly established as the first American dramatist in the major European tradition. Reviewing a new play on Broadway, *Life* magazine critic Robert Benchley said, "*The Rotters* is no longer the worst play in town. *Abie's Irish Rose* has just opened." Despite Benchley's continuing battle ("America's favorite comedy, God forbid"), the show established a new record—five years—for Broadway runs that stood until the advent of *Oklahoma*. ☐ In popular music, Paul Whiteman was the "King of Jazz," controlling twenty-eight bands playing the East Coast of the United States. Rudy Vallee

53

established himself and crooning. Louis Armstrong joined King Oliver's band in New York, while Jelly Roll Morton moved from California to Chicago. ☐ Hollywood was rocked by a series of scandals. Fatty Arbuckle faced criminal charges for the 1921 rape and manslaughter of a young actress; he was tried three times, twice with hung juries, and finally was acquitted, but his career was ruined. Wallace Reid, a "nice family young man," turned out to be what was called a drug fiend, dying from a morphine overdose. Actress Mary Miles Minter's career also was ruined when leading man and director William Desmond Taylor was found dead under mysterious circumstances, his closet filled with feminine underwear marked MMM. Out of it all came the Motion Picture Producers and Distributors of America, which named a Presbyterian elder, Will H. Hays, its president, to establish and maintain a code which was to govern moviemaking for years to come.

☐ **1923**

"Day by day in every way I am getting better and better."
—*Catchphrase introduced by French self-improvement prophet* EMILE COUÉ, *who soon had everyone saying it after he opened autosuggestion clinics in the United States to cure mental and physical ills*

FOUNDED Aeroflot, Soviet airline; the first newsmagazine, *Time*; *College Humor*; the League of Composers, in New York, for performance of modern music

INTRODUCED Double-sided phonograph records, by Victor Red Seal; power-operated windshield wipers; the autogiro plane, by Juan de la Cuerva of Spain; cellophane, in the United States (1912 in Switzerland); a 2¢ black commemorative stamp as tribute to President Harding; console organs in vaudeville houses

SONGS "Yes, We Have No Bananas" "Barney Google"

"Charleston" "I Cried for You" "That Old Gang of Mine"
"Bugle Call Rag" "Swingin' Down the Lane"

DANCE STEPS The Charleston

FASHION Skirts remained conservative in length but waistlines were lowered to the hipbone. Small hats curved down on either side of the face.

THE WORLD Inflation in Germany went through the ceiling. The value of the mark dropped hourly until it was virtually worthless; the exchange rate reached 4 million marks to the dollar. Willy Messerschmitt established an aircraft factory in Germany. ☐ French and Belgian troops occupied the Ruhr to enforce German reparation payments. President Harding ordered withdrawal of American troops stationed in the Rhineland since the end of the war. ☐ The Munich "Beer Hall Putsch," led by Adolf Hitler, failed. Hitler was sentenced to five years in prison, served only one, dictating *Mein Kampf* to Rudolph Hess while there. ☐ Chaim Weizmann was named first president of the World Zionist Organization. ☐ A violent earthquake in Tokyo and Yokohama destroyed the centers of both cities; 120,000 died. ☐ Prince George of England, later King George VI, married Lady Elizabeth Bowes-Lyon. Also in England, adultery was made grounds for divorce. ☐ The United States refused to recognize the USSR unless foreign debts were paid and alien property restored.

THE UNITED STATES President Harding died in San Francisco on August 2, while returning from a trip to Alaska; Calvin Coolidge became president. Harding died shortly before his administration's worst scandal was fully exposed—Teapot Dome, involving bribery in turning over naval oil reserves to private interests. Hearings began in Washington. ☐ Gangsters Johnny Torrio and Al Capone parted company. Torrio had a force of seven hundred men controlling the sale of beer in Chicago; Capone controlled the suburb of Cicero, where he installed his own mayor, posted his agents in gambling establishments and in 161 bars. The expression "taking him for a ride" gained currency as the gangs disposed of rivals' members. In New York City alone, an estimated five thousand speakeasies (the word was new) opened. ☐ The Ku Klux Klan held a tri-

55

state conclave in Kokomo, Indiana, attended by 200,000. Oklahoma established martial law to combat lawlessness and the night-riding of the Klan. ☐ Flogging was abolished in Florida labor camps. ☐ The first nonstop transcontinental flight, New York to San Diego, was made in twenty-six hours, fifty minutes, by two army lieutenants. ☐ U.S. Steel, with efficiency stepped up, reduced the workday from twelve hours to eight, hired seventeen thousand additional workers, raised wages, still showed a large profit increase. The minimum-wage law for women and children was ruled unconstitutional. New England telephone operators earned an average of $12 weekly. Army privates got 67¢ a day. The wholesale price of beef was 12¢ to 17¢ a pound. ☐ Montana and Nevada enacted the first old-age pension payments—$25 per month. ☐ Aimee Semple McPherson's Angelus Temple in Los Angeles seated five thousand, was topped by a rotating cross visible for fifty miles; her own broadcasting station preached the Four Square Gospel.

SPORTS Golfer Bobby Jones won his first U.S. Open. ☐ Helen Wills became America's "Queen of the Nets," winning the U.S. singles tennis title. ☐ Jack Dempsey retained his heavyweight title in a short but vicious battle with Luis Firpo, "the wild bull of the Pampas"; Dempsey knocked Firpo down seven times in the first round and Firpo knocked Dempsey out of the ring into the press section; Dempsey finished off Firpo early in the second. ☐ Grantland Rice became famous writing about the Notre Dame football team's "four horsemen."

ARTS AND ENTERTAINMENT Eleonora Duse made her last visit to the United States, at 64, packing them in. She died on her way to a Pittsburgh performance on April 21. ☐ The Charleston, introduced in a black revue, was taken over by ballroom dancers and swept the country. King Oliver's Creole Jazz Band was big, playing "real jazz," the New Orleans sound; Oliver and Jelly Roll Morton made many recordings during the year. Bix Beiderbecke, one of the first white jazzmen, organized the Wolverines; Duke Ellington got his start at Barron's cabaret in Harlem. Blues singer Bessie Smith made her first recording, "Down Hearted Blues"; 780,000 copies sold in six months. ☐ Seven-year-old Yehudi Menuhin created a sensation playing the

Mendelssohn violin concerto in San Francisco. ☐ Radio stations WEAF, New York, and WJAR, Providence, were joined by wire to become the first network. ☐ In painting, German Expressionism began with Max Beckmann's *The Trapeze*. ☐ Westman Publishing Co., U.S. publishers of Handel's *Messiah*, won a plagiarism suit against the composers of the hit song "Yes, We Have No Bananas," claiming the opening bars were stolen from the opening bars of the "Hallelujah Chorus."

☐ **1924** "Keep cool with Coolidge"
—*Campaign slogan*

FOUNDED The Federal Bureau of Investigation; Wisconsin Senator Robert LaFollette's Progressive Party; two more New York tabloids, the *Daily Mirror* and *Daily Graphic*; *The Daily Worker*, a continuation of the Communist weekly, *The Worker*

INTRODUCED Kleenex, the first facial tissue; wireless photos, transmitted by RCA to London; an ice-cream-cone folding machine

SONGS "Lady Be Good" "Indian Love Call" "Rose Marie" "I'll See You in My Dreams" "Fascinating Rhythm" "I Want to Be Happy" "The Man I Love" "Somebody Loves Me" "Tea for Two" "California, Here I Come"

CRAZES Crossword puzzles, inspiring two young men to publish a book of them that included a pencil; it was the first publication of the firm of Simon and Schuster. ☐ The Mah-Jongg craze was stronger than ever.

FASHION Maternity clothes were shown for the first time. Most women had short hair, over which they wore cloches, helmetlike hats. Street shoes were low-cut pumps or oxfords. Hosiery was now beige silk or rayon. Skirts remained at mid-calf length. Evening pajamas were a new fashion.

THE WORLD Lenin died and the struggle for Soviet power began. ☐ In Italy, the Fascist party was firmly established

57

as the only one; trade unions were abolished. ☐ Two years after the discovery of King Tut's tomb at Luxor, the Egyptian government officially opened it. ☐ Leonardo da Vinci's *Last Supper* was saved from ruin when a "surgeon of art" set up scaffolding and, using a syringe, injected the mural with essence of petroleum, then a soft resin to draw the paint back to the plaster wall.

THE UNITED STATES Despite the Teapot Dome scandal of the Harding administration, Calvin Coolidge was elected for another term, defeating Democrat John W. Davis and Progressive Robert M. LaFollette. Of the 24 million votes cast, LaFollette polled a whopping 4 million. For the first time, election results were reported on radio. ☐ Nellie Taylor Ross of Wyoming and "Ma" Ferguson of Texas became the first women to be elected governor. ☐ Former Secretary of the Interior Albert B. Fall was indicted for bribery and conspiracy in connection with the Teapot Dome scandals. ☐ The Statue of Liberty was declared a national monument and the U.S. immigration bill excluded all Japanese. ☐ Salesmanship had become an American way of life. Advertising man Bruce Barton's book, *The Man Nobody Knows,* which became a great bestseller, lauded the profession and endorsed Jesus as the world's greatest salesman of all time. ☐ The year's spectacular crime was the kidnapping and murder of 13-year-old Bobby Franks by two Chicago youths, Richard Loeb and Nathan Leopold, both 19, who did it for thrills. Their attorney, Clarence Darrow, saved them from hanging; they received life sentences. ☐ The year's mystery, never solved, was the murder of movie mogul Thomas Ince aboard the yacht of William Randolph Hearst. Other guests on the cruise included Marion Davies, Charlie Chaplin, and Hollywood gossip columnist Louella Parsons. ☐ Ford manufactured its 10-millionth car. A Ford without self-starter cost $290. ☐ In Muncie, Indiana, the "Middletown" of a sociological study, 90 percent of all homes had electric irons, and both electric washing machines and vacuum cleaners were gaining acceptance.

SPORTS Knute Rockne's Notre Dame football team won nine out of nine games. University of Illinois star Red Grange, "the galloping ghost," was named All-American halfback. ☐ Finland's track star, Paavo Nurmi, won three Olympic events. Johnny Weissmuller won the top Olympic swimming honors and the fame that later brought him Hollywood triumph as Tarzan.

ARTS AND ENTERTAINMENT Texas Guinan opened the El Fay Club, where everyone was greeted with the salutation, "Hello, Sucker!" ☐ George Balanchine left Russia and became Diaghilev's principal choreographer in France. Kiki of Montparnasse (Marie Prin), who was to become the model for many artists working in Paris, sat for her first, Moise Kisling. ☐ Vladimir Horowitz, at 20, made a sensational European tour. Serge Koussevitzky was appointed chief conductor of the Boston Symphony. Attorney Paul Robeson, working in a law firm, sang spirituals arranged by Lawrence Brown, in Greenwich Village, New York; a concert tour resulted. ☐ Jazz history was made when George Gershwin's "Rhapsody in Blue" was presented as "symphonic jazz" by Paul Whiteman's orchestra at Aeolian Hall, New York, with the composer at the piano. *The New York Times* critic found it "trite, feeble, vapid, futile and fussy." Duke Ellington, already creating his own brand of music, organized a small jazz band. Louis Armstrong was playing at Roseland Ballroom on Broadway; according to trumpeter Rex Stewart, Louis wore an old-fashioned box-back jacket "but man, after he started playing, box-back coats was the latest style."

☐  "The business of America is business."
—PRES. CALVIN COOLIDGE

FOUNDED The annual Guggenheim Fellowships; *The New Yorker* magazine; Hebrew University in Jerusalem; the Atheists' Association; Chrysler Corporation; the Coolidge Foundation of the Library of Congress

INTRODUCED Dry ice; scarlet-fever antitoxin; electrically recorded phonograph records and the Orthophonic Victrola to play them on; dance marathons; the Leica camera;

the first motor hotel, the Motel Inn, in San Luis Obispo, California

FINALE   The Maxwell automobile

SONGS   "Show Me the Way to Go Home" "Don't Bring Lulu" "Always" "Collegiate" "Five Foot Two, Eyes of Blue" "Sometimes I'm Happy" "Yes, Sir, That's My Baby" "I Never Knew" "Only a Rose"

FADS   Flagpole-sitting and tree-sitting endurance contests

FASHION   The flapper arrived—straight, flat-chested dresses with hemlines above the knees and waistlines at the hips; snug-fitting cloche hats, strap pumps.

THE WORLD   In the Soviet Union, the strain between Stalin and Trotsky that started with Lenin's death resulted in Trotsky's dismissal from the chairmanship of the Russian Military Council. ☐ Paul von Hindenburg was elected president of Germany. Hitler reorganized the Nazi party, which had twenty-seven thousand members, and published the first volume of *Mein Kampf.* ☐ Roumania's Crown Prince Carol renounced his right to the throne and left the country with his mistress, Magda Lupescu.

THE UNITED STATES   Gen. Billy Mitchell, advocating a larger air force in opposition to his superiors, was court martialled, suspended for five years without pay, and resigned from the army. ☐ Ford cars, previously available only in black, were offered in "deep channel green" and "rich Windsor maroon." Among other popular models on the road were the Apperson, Buick, Franklin, Haynes, Locomobile, Oldsmobile, Overland. Luxury cars included the Auburn, Cord, Cunningham, Stutz, Cadillac V12 and V16, Packard, and Lincoln. ☐ For motorists, tourist homes and tourist courts were springing up. The roadsides were decorated with Burma Shave signs, little rhymes whose phrases were separated on series of small signs spaced to be read as one drove along (e.g., "Famous last words . . . for lights that shine . . . If he won't dim his lights . . . I won't dim mine . . . Burma Shave.") ☐ The Scopes "monkey trial" in Dayton, Tennessee, pitted Clarence Darrow against fundamentalist William Jennings Bryan when schoolteacher John Scopes defied the state law against teaching the theory of evolution. Darrow called it "the first trial of its kind since we stopped trying people for witchcraft." Scopes was found guilty and fined $100. ☐ The Florida land boom was at its height; there were twenty-five thousand real estate agents extolling the Eden "where the whispering breeze springs fresh from the lap of the Caribbean with the elusive cadence like unto a mother's lap." Miami's population grew from thirty thousand in 1920 to seventy-five thousand in 1925. ☐ Dog teams reached Nome, Alaska, with serum to combat a diphtheria epidemic. ☐ One of the most successful mail-order home-study campaigns of all time was launched by the U.S. School of Music with the headline, "They laughed when I sat down at the piano, but when I started to play . . ." Among other advertising slogans of the day: "Listerine ends halitosis," "I'll tell the world they satisfy" (Chesterfield cigarettes), "I'd walk a mile for a Camel," "Good to the last drop" (Maxwell House coffee).

SPORTS   Red Grange, captain of the Illinois football team, caused violent controversy when he left college to sign with a professional team, the Chicago Bears. He said he didn't like football enough to play for nothing; he was a millionaire in three years. ☐ Sportswriter Grantland Rice selected the first All-American team for *Collier's Weekly.* ☐ In New York, a new Madison Square Garden opened, considerably north of its original Madison Square location.

ARTS AND ENTERTAINMENT   The first Guggenheim Fellowship to a composer was awarded Aaron Copland. ☐ Josephine Baker, a skinny young black woman from St. Louis, made a hit in Paris in La Negre Revue with Sidney Bechet and Florence Mills. Her show-stopping entrance-costume was one pink flamingo feather. ☐ Paul Robeson went to England to star in Eugene O'Neill's *The Emperor Jones.* ☐ In Hollywood, Rin-Tin-Tin was a big star. Much bigger was Clara Bow, dubbed the "It Girl" by writer Elinor Glyn. "It" was the special magnetism the actress, the archetypal flapper, had. ☐ In jazz, Bessie Smith was "Empress of the Blues." The Charleston, which was first danced in cabarets, spread quickly, along with another dance, the Shimmy. Fifth Avenue matrons sought Negro maids who could teach them the Charleston. ☐ Harlem, where such stars as Cab Calloway were playing, became the chic place for New Yorkers to end an evening. ☐ Thin was in. When movie actress Barbara LaMarr died from a drug overdose, her studio, anxious to avoid scandal, attributed the death to stringent dieting. ☐ Arthur Murray married, and his wife, Kathryn, became his dance partner. ☐ George Bernard Shaw, 69 years old and a financial as well as literary success, received the Nobel Prize and commented, "The money is a lifebelt thrown to a swimmer who has already reached the shore in safety."

☐ **1926** "I forgot to duck."
—JACK DEMPSEY, *explaining his loss of the heavyweight title to Gene Tunney*

FOUNDED The Book-of-the-Month Club; the U.S. Army Air Corps; the National Broadcasting Company, the first real radio network, with WEAF, New York, as its key, plus nineteen affiliates joined by telephone lines

INTRODUCED The yo-yo; the cushioned, cork-centered baseball; 16mm movie film, introduced by Eastman Kodak

SONGS "One Alone" "Blue Room" "When Day Is Done" "Bye, Bye, Blackbird" "Mountain Greenery" "In a Little Spanish Town" "Birth of the Blues" "Someone to Watch Over Me"

FASHION Above-knee skirts added flared flounces. Shirtwaist dresses in cotton, never worn on the street before, were revolutionary, then quickly classics. Gum-chewing was popular but not fashionable.

THE WORLD Germany was admitted to the League of Nations. The Hitler youth organization was formed. ☐ Great Britain was paralyzed by a general strike for nine days; Parliament passed an act which made a general strike a criminal conspiracy against the nation. ☐ The man-eating leopard of Rudraprayag, blamed for 125 deaths, was captured. ☐ Hirohito became Emperor of Japan.

THE UNITED STATES U.S. troops landed to preserve order during a Nicaraguan revolt. ☐ The Florida land boom collapsed, following two destructive hurricanes. ☐ Evangelist Aimee Semple McPherson, at her peak, disappeared and a great hunt was launched. A month later, a $500,000 ransom note was delivered to her temple. Next day, Sister Aimee surfaced in Mexico but police were suspicious of her fuzzy tale of kidnapping and escape. It developed that she had run off with the operator of her temple radio station, and her days as prophet and healer were ended. ☐ The New York *Daily Mirror* reopened the unsolved 1922 murder of the Rev. Edward Hall and his paramour, Mrs. Eleanor Mills, found dead on an abandoned New Jersey farm. *Mirror* reporters gathered statements, including one from the eccentric owner of a nearby pig farm—Jane Gibson, but known to *Mirror* readers as the "Pig Woman." She implicated Reverend Hall's wife, her two brothers, and a cousin in the killing, and they were brought to trial. During the eighteen days of the trial, three hundred reporters filed 9 million words of copy. The accused were acquitted. ☐ Movie idol Rudolph Valentino died in New York and hysterical fans crowded to view his remains at a funeral parlor. ☐ Queen Marie of Roumania, accompanied by a retinue of press agents, toured the United States and was a smash hit. ☐ One of the nifty little cars was the Overland Whippet, with four-wheel brakes. In 1929, it became the Willys Whippet. ☐ Irving Berlin, the poor Jewish boy who made good, married heiress Ellin Mackay. ☐ Holeproof Hosiery, with large ads for beige, orchid, and sunburn shades, made silk stockings necessities rather than luxuries. Palmolive Soap promised to "keep that schoolgirl complexion" and Woodbury's Facial Soap countered with "the skin you love to touch." Dr. Seuss was the illustrator for an insecticide ad whose slogan, "Quick Henry, the Flit!" became a popular expression.

SPORTS The heroine of the year was American Gertrude Ederle, who became the first woman to swim the English Channel; her time was fourteen hours, thirty-one minutes. ☐ The Gene Tunney win over Jack Dempsey was on points, in ten rounds; the fight drew a million-dollar gate. ☐ Babe Ruth was dubbed the Sultan of Swat. Grover Cleveland Alexander, with all bases loaded, struck out Tony Lazerti in the seventh game of the World Series. ☐ In what was billed as the match of the century, French tennis star Suzanne Lenglen defeated America's Helen Wills. ☐ Golfer Bobby Jones won the British Open.

ARTS AND ENTERTAINMENT There now were 536 licensed radio stations in the United States. ☐ Jelly Roll Morton began recording with his Red Hot Peppers and Kid Ory joined the band; among the classics they cut were "Black Bottom Stomp," "Smoke House Blues," and "Jelly Roll Blues." Fletcher Henderson's ten-man band played regularly at the Roseland Ballroom in New York. Duke Ellington expanded his band to twelve pieces and started composing and arranging. ☐ The Dada movement in art came to an end. ☐ Puccini's *Turandot* had its American premiere at the New York Met. ☐ In film, Warner Brothers introduced talking movies—the sound was on recordings—in *Don Juan*, starring John Barrymore; real "talkies" came the following year. Harold Lloyd became the highest paid actor of the day, playing the cheerful American boy whose trusting nature perpetually landed him in trouble. Deadpan comedian Buster Keaton headed his own studio, writing and directing as well as starring in many of the films. ☐ Bing Crosby cut his first commercial recording, "I've Got a Girl," on the Columbia label. ☐ The novelty books of the year were Milt Gross' *Nize Baby* and *Dunt Esk!*, picturing New York tenement life, complete with Yiddish dialect humor. Sinclair Lewis declined the $1,000 Pulitzer Prize for *Arrowsmith*. Dutch physician Theodore Van de Velde caused a stir with his book, *Ideal Marriage*, urging men to learn techniques for bringing about female orgasm. ☐ Mystery writer Agatha Christie was reported missing in England and more than ten thousand people took part in the search. She turned up eleven days later but never explained what happened. ☐ *The* party took place on stage after a performance of Earl Carroll's *Vanities*, when a nude model climbed into a bathtub filled with champagne and men lined up to fill their glasses from the tub. In the investigation that followed Carroll denied there had been any illegal wine in the tub and went to jail for perjury. ☐ Dancer Martha Graham, who had been a

64

student of Ruth St. Denis and Ted Shawn, gave her first concert of solos and trios in New York.

| | **1927** | "I do not choose to run." |

□ **1927** "I do not choose to run."
—PRES. CALVIN COOLIDGE, *announcing that the Republicans would have to find another candidate for 1928*

FOUNDED The Academy of Motion Picture Arts and Sciences; the Literary Guild

INTRODUCED Talking pictures, with Al Jolson in *The Jazz Singer*; the Theremin, the first electronic musical instrument, named after its inventor, Lev Theremin; Chanel #5 perfume; the iron lung; hydraulic shock absorbers for cars; the transatlantic radio telephone; handset telephones, replacing wallset transmitters

SONGS "My Heart Stood Still" "My Blue Heaven" "Let a Smile Be Your Umbrella" "Blue Skies" "Make Believe" "S'Wonderful" "Ol' Man River" "Varsity Drag"

FASHION Everything in women's clothes was dead straight, not a curve in sight. French couturier Gabrielle Chanel startled the fashion world by accessorizing her simple, elegant suits with fake jewelry.

THE WORLD Charles A. Lindbergh made the first solo, nonstop transatlantic flight, from Roosevelt Field, New York, to Le Bourget airport in Paris in thirty-three hours, twenty-nine minutes, thirty seconds, and was hailed as a hero all over the world. He was mobbed in Paris, given the French Legion of Honor, and returned home to a huge New York ticker tape parade that weighed in at eighteen hundred tons of paper dropped. He received fifty-five thousand Western Union telegrams, one of them signed by seventeen thousand people; it was 520 feet long, carried by ten messenger boys. □ The German economic system collapsed. Volume II of *Mein Kampf* and the program of Hitler's Nazi party were published. □ Socialists rioted in Vienna when Nazis were acquitted of a political murder. ☐ Leon Trotsky was expelled from the Communist Party in Moscow. ☐ Slavery was abolished in Sierra Leone. ☐ U.S. consulates in China were looted by nationalists, and a thousand Marines landed to protect American lives and property. ☐ On September 14, near Nice, France, dancer Isadora Duncan's trailing scarf caught in the rear wheel of her Bugatti automobile and strangled her.

THE UNITED STATES Sacco and Vanzetti were executed, setting off protest demonstrations in many countries. Heywood Broun and Edna St. Vincent Millay were among the writers arrested in U.S. protest parades. ☐ The words "racket" and "racketeering" entered the language. In Chicago, fake labor unions collected heavy "dues" from proprietors of cleaning and dyeing shops. ☐ After producing the 15-millionth Model T, Ford closed its factories for six months and reopened to unveil the Model A, spending $1,300,000 on ads in a six-month period. On unveiling day, 100,000 people flocked to showrooms in Detroit; mounted police were called out in Cleveland. ☐ Although Packard's sales were only a fraction of Ford's, the elegant car was owned by Joseph Stalin, President Coolidge, and nine royal families. ☐ There were 23 million cars on U.S. roads and with them came a blooming of hot-dog stands, filling stations and garages, and chicken-dinner restaurants. ☐ The interurban trolley was vanishing and railroads abandoned branch lines as busses and trucks took over their functions. ☐ New Orleans was saved from total flooding by destruction of the levee below the city. Mississippi Valley floods inundated twenty thousand square miles and left 700,000 homeless. ☐ A Negro sharecropper's annual income, after paying the landlord and the landlord's store, was about $350 a year. ☐ The tabloids went wild with the juicy Snyder-Gray murder case. Housewife Ruth Snyder and corset salesman Judd Gray were convicted of murdering her husband, Albert. The papers faked photos in covering both the trial and the execution, which took place the following year. Perhaps the dead low in tabloid journalism was the coverage of the intimate life of 50-year-old Daddy Browning and his 15-year-old "Peaches." ☐ Children's court Judge Benjamin Lindsey created a stir when he advocated companionate or trial marriages as well as legalization of birth control. ☐ Pilot Roscoe Turner set up an airline known as the Alimony Special; it had one route—Los Angeles to Reno, the quickie-divorce haven. ☐ A piano could be bought for less than $300, a vacuum cleaner for $28.95, a refrigerator for $87.50, and a washing machine for $97.50. ☐ Real estate was big; half a billion dollars were spent on advertising land during the year. In another type of ad, a young woman who was "often a bridesmaid, never a bride," had halitosis, a misfortune caused by failure to use Listerine.

SPORTS Jack Dempsey attempted to regain his lost title in a return bout with Gene Tunney. A total of 104,942 people paid more than $2,600,000 to see the fight and an estimated 50 million listened to Graham McNamee describe the match on radio. The famous "long count" occurred when the referee refused to start counting Tunney's fall until Dempsey retired to a neutral corner. This gave Tunney an extra four seconds; he regained control and won a ten-round decision. ☐ In baseball, the New York Yankees won 110 out of 154 games played; Babe Ruth had his greatest home-run year, hitting sixty of them, two during the World Series against the Pittsburgh Pirates. ☐ René Lacoste defeated Bill Tilden in the U.S. tennis finals.

ARTS AND ENTERTAINMENT Ten-year-old Yehudi Menuhin, playing Beethoven's violin concerto, made a spectacular Carnegie Hall debut. Dmitri Shostakovich wrote his first and second symphonies. ☐ Bing Crosby joined the Paul Whiteman band as one of the Rhythm Boys. ☐ Quiz books were popular, *Ask Me Another* being the most successful. The publishing phenomenon of the year was Sinclair Lewis' *Elmer Gantry*, which sold 200,000 copies in its first ten weeks. ☐ Architect Le Corbusier designed the Monzies Houses at Garches, France. Sculptor Gutzon Borglum began to carve the enormous faces of Washington, Jefferson, Lincoln, and Theodore Roosevelt in the rock of Mt. Rushmore, South Dakota. ☐ Television, already demonstrated in Europe, was demonstrated by RCA in a telecast from Washington, D.C., which was received in New York. Still many years away from practical use, television became a popular topic of conversation and subject for futuristic movies.

"A chicken in every pot, a car in every garage."
—*Republican* HERBERT HOOVER's *presidential campaign slogan*

FOUNDED   Mickey Mouse, who made his debut in a cartoon feature, *Steamboat Willie*

INTRODUCED   Safety plate-glass windows for cars; the teletype; the Sanforizing process, to control fabric shrinkage; hardwater soap; the world's first shopping center, Suburban Square in Ardmore, Pennsylvania; packaged potato chips; a popular monoplane for business corporations, the Stimson Detroiter, seating pilot and five passengers; the moving electric-light messages around the New York Times building in Times Square; color motion pictures, exhibited by George Eastman in Rochester, New York

SONGS   "Crazy Rhythm" "Makin' Whoopee" "You're the Cream in My Coffee" "Button Up Your Overcoat" "I Can't Give You Anything but Love" "Let's Do It" "Lover Come Back" "Sweet Sue"

FASHION   Chanel established herself firmly, making her suits, with easy little jackets, classics that are still around. The fashions seen everywhere were the epitome of the flapper—boyishly straight, with long waists, pleated skirts. Hair was shingled; small hats sat low at the nape of the neck.

THE WORLD   The first Five-Year Plan was initiated in the USSR. Leon Trotsky was banished to Central Asia. ☐ Chiang Kai-shek was elected president of China. ☐ The Kellogg-Briand Peace Pact, signed by fifteen nations in Paris, outlawed war and agreed that international differences should be sought by pacific means.

THE UNITED STATES   It was a hectic election year, with Herbert Hoover, the Republican, running against Al Smith, whose Catholicism was thought by many to be a threat. Political rumor had it that the Pope would come to America and take over. The Socialist party nominated Norman Thomas, and Communist William Z. Foster was the Workers Party candidate.

Hoover swept in with 444 electoral votes to Smith's 88, and a wit was reported to have cabled the Pope, "Unpack." ☐ Eternal youth was the talk of the day, after Serge Veronoff's book, *The Conquest of Life*, raised the possibility of rejuvenation through gland transplants. ☐ In gangland, gambler Arnold Rothstein was shot and killed by person or persons unknown. ☐ It was the era of the great ocean liners; 437,000 people went to Europe by ship. The dirigible *Graf Zeppelin*, with twenty passengers and thirty-eight crew members, flew from Freidrichshafen, Germany, to Lakehurst, New Jersey. The first airplane night coach with sleeping facilities appeared for transcontinental trips. ☐ The summer was a sizzler and, to prove it, someone fried an egg on the steps of the Capitol in Washington. ☐ The economy and the stock market soared. RCA stock, which had not yet paid a dividend, sold at 120 and, in a six-month period, rose to 400. ☐ Amelia Earhart became the first woman to fly the Atlantic, making the flight in a trimotored Fokker with Wilmer Stutz, pilot, and Louis Gordon, mechanic. ☐ Near Los Angeles, St. Francis Dam collapsed, killing 450.

SPORTS Gene Tunney retired from the ring, undefeated. ☐ At the Olympics, Sonja Henie won the figure-skating competition; Johnny Weissmuller established a new record for the 100-meter freestyle swim. ☐ Helen Wills won the U.S., Wimbledon and French women's tennis titles. ☐ Ty Cobb retired from the Philadelphia Athletics, batting .323 in his last season.

ARTS AND ENTERTAINMENT Pianist Vladimir Horowitz made his American debut, with the New York Philharmonic, under its new conductor, Arturo Toscanini, whose daughter, Wanda, he later married. Ravel's *Bolero*, which premiered in Paris, caused a near riot with its insistent beat. ☐ Bessie Smith recorded "Poor Man's Blues" and Fats Waller broke out of Harlem to play downtown at places like the Kentucky Club. ☐ They were still dancing the Charleston and Shimmy, and a new craze, the Black Bottom, was added. At a "buck dancing" contest for Broadway performers, Bill Robinson was first; Fred Astaire, third. ☐ George Gershwin's *An American in Paris* premiered, played by the New York Philharmonic, with Walter

Damrosch conducting. □ Al Jolson's record of "Sonny Boy" sold 12 million copies in its first four weeks. □ The National Broadcasting Company split into two semi-independent radio networks, the Blue Network, with WJZ, New York, as its center, and the Red Network, with WEAF, New York, as its center. □ General Electric's radio station WGY in Schenectady was awarded the first license for experimental television broadcasting. □ John Held, Jr.'s drawings were appearing in a Hearst paper's daily comic strip and *College Humor,* picturing the flapper as part-ruffled innocence, part-hardbitten sophistication —rolled stockings, long cigarette holder, short skirt, boyish bob. Her Joe College boyfriend was slick-haired, wore puffy pants and raccoon coat. □ Kurt Weill's *Threepenny Opera* opened in Berlin, and Paul Robeson scored a triumph in London singing "Ol' Man River" in *Showboat.*

1929

"I know of nothing fundamentally wrong with the stock market or with the underlying business or credit structure."
—NATIONAL CITY BANK CHAIRMAN CHARLES MITCHELL, *two days before the market crash. (The day after it,* PRESIDENT HOOVER *said,* "The conditions are fundamentally sound.")

FOUNDED The Seeing Eye Foundation; the Columbia Broadcasting System; the Limited Editions Book Club; the New York Museum of Modern Art

INTRODUCED The airplane automatic pilot; the Motion Picture Academy Awards; airmail service between North and South America; blind instrument air flight, first accomplished by Lt. James Doolittle

SONGS "Ain't Misbehavin'" "Stardust" "Moanin' Low" "Tip Toe Through the Tulips" "Singin' in the Rain" "St. James Infirmary" "The Pagan Love Song" "Happy Days Are Here Again" "I'll See You Again"

FADS Bridge-playing was a madness, with many devotees converted to fiendish commitment.

FASHION Hemlines, still short in front, swooped downward in back, particularly for late-day wear. Coco Chanel introduced the look of rows and rows of fake pearl necklaces. The fashionable female figure was shaped by a flat-topped all-in-one corselet but the bosom was about to reappear. Philippe de Brassière, a former wartime flying ace, promoted a chest halter which many others have claimed to have invented but which bears his name. D. J. Kennedy of England patented protective breastpads for use in sports, which gained acceptance as cosmetic falsies.

THE WORLD Leon Trotsky was expelled from the USSR. ☐ Hitler's German SS, with Himmler as its Reichsfuhrer, was started. ☐ Arabs attacked Jews in Palestine, following disputes over Jewish use of the Wailing Wall in Jerusalem. ☐ The *Graf Zeppelin* completed a round-the-world trip. The German ship *Bremen* set a new record on her maiden voyage, crossing from Cherbourg to New York in four days, seventeen hours, forty-two minutes.

THE UNITED STATES Herbert Hoover was inaugurated as the 31st president of the United States, fated to carry the blame, if not the responsibility, for the Great Depression. ☐ The U.S. Workers Party changed its name back to Communist Party. ☐ The year which was to bring the stock market crash started with boom. While investors bought on margin, consumers bought on the installment plan; 90 percent of all washing machines, 80 percent of radios, refrigerators, and vacuum cleaners, 70 percent of furniture, and 60 percent of all cars were bought on time payments. Radio sales reached $842,545,000; by now 10 million families owned radios. ☐ Chain stores and supermarkets boomed, too. A & P, which had 400 stores in 1912, now had more than 15,000; J. C. Penney had 2,660. ☐ The Waldorf-Astoria Hotel on Fifth Avenue, New York City, was torn down to make way for what was to be the world's tallest building, the Empire State. ☐ Air travel had the railroads so worried that the Pennsylvania Railroad offered an air-railroad combination trip coast-to-coast in forty-eight hours: by train from New York to

Columbus, Ohio; plane to Airport, Oklahoma; car to the Atchison, Topeka and Santa Fe sleeping car in Clovis, New Mexico; car to Portair, New Mexico, for a flight to Glendale, California. □ On February 14, a group of Chicago gangland killers wearing police uniforms gunned down seven rivals in a garage, in what became known as the Saint Valentine's Day Massacre. □ A birth control clinic in New York was raided by police on a complaint brought by the DAR. Two doctors and three nurses were arrested and the case histories of patients confiscated. □ A juvenile court judge in Indiana asserted that automobiles, of which 83 percent now were closed, were "houses of prostitution on wheels." Of thirty female defendants brought before his court, nineteen had committed the sex offense in a car. *Factors in the Sex Life of 2,200 Women*, by Katherine B. Davis, was published. It was the heyday of sex adventure and confession magazines, the biggest of the confession books being *True Story*, with more than 2 million readers monthly. □ Albert B. Fall, Secretary of the Interior under Harding, was sentenced to a year's imprisonment and fined $100,000 for accepting a bribe in the leasing of the Elk Hills (Teapot Dome) naval oil reserve. □ Hero Charles A. Lindbergh married Anne Morrow, daughter of the U.S. ambassador to Mexico. □ The stock market crash that was to start an era of unemployment and depression came in October. Thirty billion dollars in paper value was wiped out between mid-October and mid-November and the owners of millions of shares held on 10 percent margin were wiped out with it. The collapse came on October 24, Black Friday. The stock of Union Cigar went from $113 to $4 in a single day, and the company's president fell or jumped from a ledge of a New York hotel. One commentator said, "In Wall Street, every wall is wet with tears." Optimistic Morgan partner, Thomas Lamont, said, "There has been a little distress selling on the Stock Exchange." □ The market for consumer goods was glutted; 90 percent of the nation's wealth now was in the hands of 13 percent of the people. Farmers, textile workers, coal miners, all lacked income sufficient to buy their minimal needs. It was a dark time for makers of hairpins and corsets, but a glorious time for the cosmetic industry. The beautician had arrived; for every adult woman in the country, there were sold annually a pound of face powder, eight rouge compacts; there were fifteen hundred brands of face cream on the market. If all the lipsticks sold in the year were placed end to end, they would have reached from New York to the divorce mills of Reno.

SPORTS Philadelphia awarded the $10,000 Edward W. Bok prize—an award previously given to scientists, philanthropists, and the like—to Connie Mack, manager of the Athletics baseball club, for distinguished service to that city.

ARTS AND ENTERTAINMENT There were 618 radio stations in the nation, many broadcasting at all hours. Radiomakers had their own programs—the "General Electric Symphony," the "Philco Hour," the "Stromberg Carlson Hour." □ Asked to define his art, Fats Waller said, "What's jazz, lady? If you don't know, I can't tell you." Duke Ellington and his orchestra were playing at New York's Cotton Club. □ Radcliffe Hall, the author of *The Well of Loneliness*, a gentle novel about lesbianism, was taken to court on obscenity charges; the banning of the book later was overturned.

 **1930** "American business is steadily coming back to a normal level of recovery."
—JULIUS H. BARNES, *head of the National Business Survey Conference.* (PRESIDENT HOOVER *agreed:* "We have passed the worst.")

FOUNDED The Institute for Advanced Study at Princeton
INTRODUCED Airline stewardesses, who replaced male "couriers" on Boeing Air Transport's eighteen-passenger biplane flights from Chicago to San Francisco; power brakes, by Cadillac; photoflash bulbs; free-wheeling, allowing cars to coast when the foot was off the throttle; "Baffle Ball," the first coin-operated pinball machine; the Latex rubber process, which quickly was applied to manufacture of improved condoms; Scotch tape; commercially marketed quick-frozen foods

SONGS "I Got Rhythm" "Three Little Words" "Time on My Hands" "Walkin' My Baby Back Home" "Body and Soul" "Embraceable You" "Something to Remember You By" "On the Sunny Side of the Street"

CRAZES Miniature golf; backgammon; on college campuses, goldfish-swallowing

FASHION Women's hemlines came down with prices; daytime clothes were three inches below the knee, evening clothes swept the ground. Longer hair and permanent waves were replacing bobbed hair. The boyish look gave way to softer, figure-revealing fashions; the natural feminine shape, with brassiere to help it along, was in. Small-brimmed hats, worn on the back of the head, had nose veils.

THE WORLD The Nazis gained 107 seats in the German elections; a Nazi became government minister in Thuringia. □ France began building the Maginot Line, designed to protect her from German military aggression. □ Mahatma Gandhi began his march to the sea, in India. □ The planet Pluto was discovered by C. W. Tombaugh.

THE UNITED STATES The Great Depression was on in earnest. Businessmen were desperate. Five million Americans were unemployed, compared to 3 million in 1929. President Hoover asked for $150 million for construction of public works to help the situation. The unemployed demonstrated in every major city, demanding unemployment insurance. Police attacked a crowd of thirty-five thousand in New York and fifteen thousand engaged in a melee with police in Cleveland. American fashion buyers did not attend the Paris openings; there were not enough American customers for the expensive clothes. □ Bootlegging and gangsterism were at their height, despite the efforts of 2,836 Prohibition agents. Chicago was the undisputed crime capital; a bootlegging ring exposed there involved 31 corporations and 158 persons selling 7 million gallons of whiskey to speakeasies; volume was estimated at $50 million. Al Capone controlled the sale of beer and liquor to ten thousand Chicago-area speaks, seeming above the law as he rode about in an armored car, went to the theater attended by eighteen tuxedo-garbed guards. There were five hundred gang murders in Chicago during the year, one of them being Jake Lingle, who led a double life as a reporter for the *Chicago Tribune* and as an associate of gangsters; he was shot to death in a crowded train station at midday. □ With money tight, people turned to an inexpensive diversion, miniature golf, which became a national craze; there were thirty thousand of the tiny courses in operation by the end of the year, many paying taxes on sites abandoned for the building no one could afford. Contract bridge assumed worldwide craze proportions; riding the wave was Eli Culbertson, who took his wife Josephine and two others as a team to England to play against a British team, raising money for the trip by taking orders for a book not yet written; his team clobbered the British in a 200-hand match at Almack's Club, London, and he made his fortune with the book, presenting the Culbertson system. □ Betting on the Irish Sweepstakes became the favorite get-rich-quick fad for Americans. The country went mad for Tarzan, as the Ape Man starred in comic strips, movies, and daily radio shows. □ The word of the day was "technocracy," the potential absolute domination of man by technology. □ Franklin D. Roosevelt won reelection as governor of New York. □ Judge Joseph F. Crater, a justice of the New York City Supreme Court, vanished on August 6, never to be seen again. The disappearance inspired vaudeville humor, with acts interrupted by loudspeaker announcements: "Judge Crater, call your office." □ Albert Einstein arrived in the United States for a visit. When aggressive reporters frightened him, his wife sent them a note: "Professor Einstein is not eccentric. He is not absentminded. He dislikes dirt and confusion. Politically, we are Socialists."

SPORTS Gallant Fox won the Triple Crown—Derby, Preakness, and Belmont—with jockey Earle Sande up for all three rides. □ Bobby Jones won golf's first grand slam—the British amateur and open and U.S. amateur and open tournaments. □ Mildred "Babe" Didrikson gained national attention, winning the baseball and javelin throws at an AAU meet in Dallas.

ARTS AND ENTERTAINMENT Louis Armstrong went to Los Angeles, charmed them all, and made the first of many

75

records with Lionel Hampton: "Memories of You." ☐ John Masefield became Britain's poet laureate. ☐ The Chrysler Building, an Art Deco masterpiece, became the world's tallest building, 1,048 feet to the top of its delicate spire. Samuel Hoffenstein, a poet of the day, wrote, "Behold I saw the Chrysler building rise/ the most mighty phallus that has yet essayed the skies." ☐ People tuned each weeknight to "Amos and Andy" for a much-needed fifteen minutes of laughs. Americans owned 13,750,000 radios. ☐ The silent films were completely dead when ads for the film *Anna Christie* shouted "GARBO TALKS!" Ninety million went to the movies each week. ☐ Sinclair Lewis became the first American to win a Nobel Prize. ☐ That most American of painters, Grant Wood, painted "American Gothic." ☐ Dancer Martha Graham presented *Lamentations*, a seminal work in her career. ☐ A copy of James Joyce's *Ulysses*, on its way to Random House in New York, was seized by customs agents as obscene. Boston banned all books by Leon Trotsky. ☐ Although television was only experimental, radio station WEEI, Boston, televised daily programs to the few receivers that existed.

☐   **1931**   "The only occasion when traditions of courtesy permit a hostess to help herself before a woman guest is when she has reason to believe the food is poisoned."
—EMILY POST

FOUNDED The Group Theater; *Ballyhoo*, a magazine whose circulation quickly rose as it ridiculed everything troubling people

INTRODUCED "The Star Spangled Banner" as the official national anthem of the United States; the Ford Tri-Motor airplane, the durable "Tin Goose," which was to fly for more than forty years; the electric dry shaver; air-conditioned trains, on the B & O; the electron microscope

SONGS "Minnie the Moocher" "Mood Indigo" "Goodnight, Sweetheart" "Dancing in the Dark" "I Found a Million

Dollar Baby in the Five-and-Ten-Cent Store" "Of Thee I Sing" "That's Why Darkies Were Born"

FASHION The women's hat of the year was the Empress Eugenie, a small, tilted number with brim turned up on one side and trimmed with plumes. ☐ Men's sportswear featured baggy knickers, high wool socks, saddle shoes, soft shirts, and homburg hats.

THE WORLD In Spain, the civil guard withdrew its support of King Alfonso XIII, who left the country without abdicating; the Second Republic took over. ☐ An explosion on the Manchurian railway served as a pretext for Japan to begin occupation of Manchuria. ☐ Triggered by bankruptcy of the Credit Anstalt in Austria, Central European finances collapsed; German banks closed for a month. ☐ Great Britain abandoned the gold standard; the pound fell more than a dollar in value. ☐ The German Nazi party, now 800,000 strong, gained financial support from Fritz Thyssen and other captains of industry. In England, Oswald Mosley formed a new party along Fascist lines. ☐ Rachmaninov's music was banned in the USSR as decadent. ☐ Auguste Piccard and his assistant, Charles Kipfer, made the first flight into the stratosphere, rising in a helium-filled balloon to an altitude of 51,793 feet above Augsburg, Bavaria.

THE UNITED STATES President Hoover declared a one-year moratorium on war debts owed to the United States. ☐ Gangster Al Capone, finally nabbed on a charge of income-tax evasion, was sentenced to eleven years in prison; he was released in 1939, died in 1941. "Legs" Diamond, another gangster of note, was slain while he slept in an Albany, New York, boarding house. ☐ The Depression deepened. U.S. Steel cut wages by 10 percent. An estimated 188,000 migrants were on the road— hoboes hopping freight trains, eating canned beans, no place to live. Banks started to close, wiping out depositors' savings; 305 closed in September, 522 in October. A total of 1,300 closed during the year, the most sensational being the Bank of the United States, which had 400,000 depositors. There were 10 million unemployed, and the apple-selling, breadline years had arrived. ☐ Nine young black men were accused by two white women of raping them on a freight train. At the trial in Scottsboro, Alabama, eight of the young men were sentenced to death by an all-white jury. The Scottsboro case caused world concern, the validity of the accusations being dubious. After years in prison, all of the Scottsboro Boys were finally vindicated. □ Investigating conditions of miners in "Bloody Harlan" County, Kentucky, writers Theodore Dreiser, John Dos Passos, and others were indicted for criminal syndicalism to overthrow the government. □ The body of Starr Faithfull, a beautiful young socialite who, it was said, had been corrupted by her prominent uncle at an early age, was found on a Long Island beach. The murder, never solved, inspired John O'Hara's 1935 novel, *Butterfield 8*. □ The Empire State Building on Fifth Avenue, New York, opened; at 1,250 feet, 102 stories, it ended the Chrysler Building's brief reign as the world's tallest. The building of Rockefeller Center in New York began. The George Washington Bridge, joining New York and New Jersey, became the world's longest suspension span. □ Rumor had it that the United States would go off the gold standard, and those who could afford it hoarded gold.

SPORTS Knute Rockne, Notre Dame coach, was killed in a plane crash. □ Glen Campbell established a new auto speed record of 246 mph. □ Rogers Hornsby of the St. Louis Cardinals set a record when he hit three home runs in a single game.

ARTS AND ENTERTAINMENT In July, CBS inaugurated the first regular schedule of television broadcasting. New York's Mayor Jimmy Walker officiated at the telecast, Kate Smith sang "When the Moon Comes Over the Mountain," George Gershwin played "Liza," and the Boswell Sisters sang "Heebie Jeebie Blues." □ Milton Berle was a smash in a solo vaudeville act at New York's Palace. □ In Harlem, they were dancing the Lindy Hop. Eddy Duchin was playing at New York's Central Park Casino. In the Midwest, the Casa Loma orchestra was making semi-swinging sounds. Brilliant jazz cornetist Bix Beiderbecke died of lobar pneumonia, traceable to alcoholism. □ Coloratura soprano Lily Pons made her debut at the New York Metropolitan Opera, singing *Lucia di Lammermoor*. On Broadway, Fred Astaire danced with Tilly Losch in *The Band Wagon*.

☐ In a spectacular $8 million art purchase, American millionaire Andrew Mellon acquired twenty paintings from the Hermitage Museum in Leningrad; included were paintings by Van Eyck, Rembrandt, Velazquez, Botticelli, and Raphael. ☐ Some great entertainment careers were about to start. Dorothy Lamour was chosen Miss New Orleans. Clark Gable started working in Hollywood.

☐ **1932** "I'm afraid and every man is afraid. I don't know, we don't know, whether the values we have are going to be real next month or not."
—CHARLES SCHWAB *of Bethlehem Steel*

FOUNDED The London Symphony Orchestra, by Sir Thomas Beecham

INTRODUCED Unemployment insurance, in Wisconsin; the movie-house double bill; bank night at the movies, in Colorado; Pablum pre-cooked cereal; full-color movie cartoons, with Disney's *Flowers and Trees*; Radio City Music Hall and the world's longest permanent chorus line, the precision-dancing Rockettes; the Ford V-8; Polaroid glass, developed by Edwin H. Land

SONGS "Brother, Can You Spare a Dime?" "I'm Getting Sentimental Over You" "Night and Day" "Let's Have Another Cup of Coffee" "April in Paris" "Mimi" "Isn't It Romantic?"

FADS Marathon dancing, a sad fad. Couples shuffled around a dance floor for days, competing for prize money that went to the last survivors. The longest, for a prize of $1,000, lasted twenty-four weeks, five days.

FASHION Bosoms were in. *Vogue*, which announced that spring fashions would feature curves, carried a brassiere ad for a garment that "beautifully emphasizes the uplift bust." Dorothy Shaver of Lord & Taylor, New York, began to promote American designers, particularly Claire McCardell, whose original, totally

79

American designs included jersey sheath dresses and blue denim as a fashion fabric.

THE WORLD Adolf Hitler, who had polled 13 million votes, losing to Von Hindenburg in the German elections, refused the offer to become vice chancellor; he did become a German citizen, though. The Nazis won 230 seats in the Reichstag, to become the strongest party in Germany. ☐ The Soviet Union started its second Five-Year Plan. ☐ The Japanese, continuing their undeclared war on China, occupied Shanghai. Manchuria, renamed Manchukuo, became a Japanese puppet state. The United States protested Japanese aggression and said it would recognize no territorial gains made. ☐ In India, Gandhi's Congress party was declared illegal and he was arrested again.

THE UNITED STATES It was the worst year of the Depression; 12 million were unemployed. Veterans of World War I organized a "bonus march" on Washington to demand immediate payment of money due them at a later date. They camped out at Anacostia Flats while Congress debated, then defeated, a bill to pay them. When they refused to budge from their makeshift town, troops, headed by Gen. Douglas MacArthur, attacked them, then destroyed their tents and huts; the Bonus Marchers disbanded. ☐ Congress established the Reconstruction Finance Corporation to rebuild the economy via loans to business, on the theory that the money would trickle down to the people. ☐ The U.S. Botanical Gardens ceased being a source of table flowers for government officials. ☐ In April, a tabloid headline announced BABY DEAD and everyone who saw it knew it referred to the infant son of Charles and Anne Lindbergh, kidnapped from his crib six weeks earlier. The crime brought J. Edgar Hoover and his FBI to prominence and triggered passage of the Lindbergh Kidnapping Law, which made the crime a federal offense. ☐ Amelia Earhart made a solo flight across the Atlantic, the first by a woman. ☐ Ford's new V-8 was an instant success and, with its speed and quick acceleration, became the favorite getaway car of such gangsters and bank robbers as Clyde Barrow and John Dillinger. A more expensive, racier car still on the road was the Stutz Bearcat. ☐ Compared to pre-crash 1929, American industry was operating at less than half the volume, total wages paid were 60 percent less, dividends 57 percent less. A survey in Buffalo indicated that, out of fifteen thousand canvassed, 31 percent could not find jobs and more than half were working only part-time. Cotton was 5¢ a pound; wheat, 32¢; farmers were desperate. ☐ Three thousand unemployed marched on Ford's River Rouge plant, asking for jobs. Police fired on the demonstrators with pistols and machine guns, killing four. More than thirty thousand attended the common funeral a few days later. ☐ Jimmy Walker, New York City's colorful, handsome, and popular mayor, was forced to resign early in the year by scandal and news of corruption. He fled to Europe, accompanied by actress Betty Compton, leaving behind an irate Mrs. Walker. She later divorced him and he married Miss Compton. ☐ President Hoover reduced his own salary and those of the vice president and cabinet officers but he couldn't seem to do anything right. When the Democrats nominated Franklin D. Roosevelt as their candidate for the presidency, an adviser told Roosevelt that to win, "all you have to do is stay alive until the election." Columnist Walter Lippmann disagreed, writing that, while Roosevelt had made a good governor and might make a good cabinet officer, he "simply does not measure up to the tremendous demands of the office of President." Roosevelt swept into office, winning 22,821,857 popular votes to Hoover's 15,761,841. The Communist Party candidate drew the largest in its U.S. history: 102,991. ☐ The crime of the year became known as the Massie Case. Thalia Massie, wife of a naval lieutenant, was raped in Honolulu; Massie and his mother-in-law took it on themselves to kill a Hawaiian who had been accused of the attack. Clarence Darrow defended the killers, pleading temporary insanity, got them off with a ten-year sentence which was commuted, under pressure from navy brass, to one hour in custody. The case aggravated relations between Americans and Hawaiians.

SPORTS Lou Gehrig hit four home runs in one day, a new record. ☐ Jack Sharkey defeated Max Schmeling in a fifteen-

81

round decision. ☐ Babe Didrikson took the Olympic gold medals in the 80-meter hurdles and javelin throw.

ARTS AND ENTERTAINMENT   The Chicago Symphony, strapped for funds, gave no performances during the year. ☐ *Of Thee I Sing,* with book by George S. Kaufman and Morrie Ryskind and music and lyrics by George and Ira Gershwin, became the first musical to win a Pulitzer Prize. ☐ Duke Ellington was hailed as a serious jazz composer and the first "Negro musician of distinction." ☐ Sculptor Alexander Calder caused a stir with the first exhibition of what he called "mobiles," structures moved by air currents. ☐ The Nicholas Brothers were a popular vaudeville acrobatic tap-dance team. Adele Astaire retired as her brother Fred's dance partner to become Lady Cavendish. ☐ The popular saying originated with Popeye: "I yam what I yam."

☐   **1933**   "We have nothing to fear but fear itself."
—FRANKLIN DELANO ROOSEVELT *in his March 4 inaugural address*

FOUNDED   The New Deal "alphabet agencies": NRA, TVA, SEC, AAA, PWA, CCC; the Experiment in International Living; the Newspaper Guild

INTRODUCED   Legal drinking in the United States, with ratification at year's end of the Twenty-First Amendment, repealing Prohibition; polyethylene; FDR's "fireside chats," radio talks to the nation; the first U.S. aircraft carrier, *Ranger*; radioactive isotopes, produced by Irene Joliot-Curie and Frederic Joliot; the Boeing 247 plane, capable of cruising at 189 mph with a payload of ten passengers and baggage; the singing telegram; the term "G-Men," when Machine Gun Kelly, about to be arrested by FBI agents, shouted, "Don't shoot, G-Men!"; the drive-in movie theater, in a four-hundred-car parking lot in Camden, New Jersey (by 1958, there were four thousand drive-ins around the country); the first woman cabinet member, Secretary of Labor Frances Perkins

SONGS "Smoke Gets in Your Eyes" "Stormy Weather" "Who's Afraid of the Big, Bad Wolf?" "Easter Parade" "Boulevard of Broken Dreams" "Lover" "Inka Dinka Doo" "I Cover the Waterfront"

FADS Jigsaw puzzles

FASHION Women's hair was worn shoulder-length, softly curled (or what passed for softly curled via permanent waving). Hats were important, an especially popular style being a kind of wreath with a hole in the middle. Sandals were popular and pumps had openings at the toes.

THE WORLD Adolf Hitler became chancellor of Germany, appointed by President von Hindenburg. In the subsequent elections the Nazis won 92 percent of the vote. Hermann Göring was named Prussian prime minister and head of police; Joseph Goebbels, Minister of Propaganda and Enlightenment. Hitler kept his promises. Within a few months, he had secured, legally, dictatorial powers. The Reichstag fire, blamed on a Communist, launched the Hitler horrors. Books were burned, labor unions were suppressed, political parties were dissolved, freedom of speech and press were suspended, boycott of Jews and Jewish business began, and concentration camps were set up. The refugee exodus started. ☐ The Spanish republic, attacked from the left and right, was defeated in the elections and succeeded by a rightest coalition under Gil Robles. ☐ Japan occupied China north of the Great Wall. ☐ The United States recognized the USSR and resumed trade with that country. It also voted independence for the Philippines. ☐ Vidkun Quisling, whose name would become a curse word in World War II, organized a Nazi party in Norway.

THE UNITED STATES An attempt by one Joseph Zangara to assassinate FDR as he drove through Miami, Florida, failed, but Mayor Anton J. Cermak of Chicago, who was riding with the president-elect, was fatally wounded. ☐ When Roosevelt took office, 25 percent of the labor force, close to 14 million people, were unemployed. "Hoovervilles," shantytowns, occupied vacant lots; apple-sellers stood on street corners. There were a million transients on the road, 200,000 of them children; 1,500 passed through Kansas City each day and other cities had similar counts. ☐ The banking system was in collapse. On inaugural day, Roosevelt declared a "bank holiday," calling Congress into special session to pass an emergency banking bill. ☐ During the first hundred days, Roosevelt pressured Congress to pass much of the basic legislation of the New Deal: The Agricultural Adjustment Act (AAA), to support farm prices; the Civilian Conservation Corps (CCC), to hire young men for work in national parks; the Federal Deposit Insurance Corporation (FDIC), to insure bank deposits; the Emergency Relief Administration, for direct relief to the unemployed; and the National Industrial Recovery Act (NRA), to increase purchasing power and spread work via industry codes. The sum of $500 million in cash was given to the destitute during the first three months. ☐ On stores, cars, and windows of homes, stickers with the NRA eagle symbol and the slogan We Do Our Part began to appear. ☐ One of Roosevelt's earliest—and most popular—moves was modification of the Volstead Act, to permit sale of 3.2 percent beer and wine. Repeal came later, when Utah became the thirty-sixth state to ratify the Twenty-First Amendment on December 5. ☐ In September, 2,000 rural schools failed to open, 1,500 schools and colleges suspended activities, and 200,000 teachers were unemployed. ☐ The American Federation of Labor, with 4 million members, voted a boycott of German goods. ☐ Wiley Post became the first person to fly solo around the world. British planes flew over Mount Everest. Richard E. Byrd began his second South Pole expedition. ☐ The U.S. went off the gold standard. ☐ Fiorello H. La Guardia defeated New York's Tammany Hall organization to become the feisty and popular mayor. ☐ Albert Einstein came to the United States, settling in Princeton, New Jersey. ☐ The U.S. dirigible *Akron* crashed, killing seventy-two. ☐ The Chicago World's Fair opened, marking "A Century of Progress." Of the myriad national and industrial exhibits, the undisputed winner was the midway performance of Sally Rand; crowds surged to see her come down velvet steps wearing nothing but the giant fans she waved deftly. She claimed she had never made money until she took off her pants. ☐ Woolworth heiress Barbara Hutton married her first title, Prince Alexis Mdivini.

SPORTS   Primo Carnera knocked out Jack Sharkey in the sixth round to take the heavyweight title.

ARTS AND ENTERTAINMENT   Among those fleeing the Hitler regime were painters Paul Klee and Wassily Kandinsky, conductor Fritz Busch and his violinist brother Adolf, Bruno Walter, and composer Arnold Shoenberg. ☐ A total of 80 million Americans went to the movies each week, paying 25¢ for adults, 10¢ for children, to see double features and have a crack at the door prizes. ☐ The Ballet Russe de Monte Carlo toured the country; another dance event was the U.S. visit of Uday Shankar with his Hindu dance group. ☐ The popular art triumph of the year was Walt Disney's cartoon, *The Three Little Pigs,* along with its song, "Who's Afraid of the Big, Bad Wolf?" Busby Berkeley's incredible musical movie extravaganzas burst on the world in the "By a Waterfall" number in *Footlight Parade.* Fred Astaire and Ginger Rogers danced together for the first time in *Flying Down to Rio.* ☐ Kate Smith was the highest-paid woman on radio, making $3,000 a week. ☐ The sex picture was confused: While the Hays Office forbade movies to show a woman's nipples or the inside of her thigh, Dr. Robert Dickinson published *Human Sex Anatomy,* the first serious modern book to contain illustrations of positions for intercourse; and James Joyce's *Ulysses,* previously banned as obscene, was permitted entry to the United States after a court ruled it a serious work.

☐  "I suppose that taking care of people runs against the American grain—against the feeling that everyone ought to hustle for himself. But there comes a time when people can't hustle anymore."
—DR. EDWARD TOWNSEND, *originator of the Townsend Old Age Pension Plan*

FOUNDED   Two industries-to-be, with the appearance of Shirley Temple in *Little Miss Marker,* and the birth, on May

28, of the Dionne Quintuplets; the Catholic Legion of Decency; the Glyndebourne Festival in England

INTRODUCED The first sulfa drug, sulfanilamide; Muzak; fluorescent lighting; the first successful electrically operated phonograph attachment for radios—RCA Victor's Duo, Jr., at $16.50; the variable pitch airplane propeller; Little Big Books, small, pulpy, plump books for children and non-readers; the *Zephyr*, the first streamlined, diesel-powered train; The De Soto Airflow, a teardrop-shaped streamlined car; free dishes at the movies; the Soap Box Derby; the pipeless Hammond organ

SONGS "Blue Moon" "Stars Fell on Alabama" "All Through the Night" "You're the Top" "On the Good Ship Lollipop" "Anything Goes" "I'll Follow My Secret Heart" "Cocktails for Two"

FASHION Seersucker summer suits for men made their first appearance. For women, Paris couturière Vionnet created the cowl neckline.

THE WORLD In Germany, with the death of President von Hindenburg, Hitler consolidated the presidency with his office of chancellor, and was thenceforth known as "Fuehrer." □ China's Communists started their Long March, 6,000 miles from the south to the north, led by Mao Tse-tung: 100,000 started the trek; 20,000 finally reached Yenan in October 1935. □ In the USSR, the Great Purge started, following the assassination of Stalin's associate Kirov; the purge would end, three years later, with almost a third of Party members expelled or eliminated. □ Leopold became King of the Belgians after the death, in a mountaineering accident, of his father, King Albert. □ In England, while Oswald Mosley drew crowds for Fascist mass meetings, Winston Churchill warned the nation of the German air menace. □ Trotskyites among Communists outside the Soviet Union formed the anti-Stalin so-called Fourth International.

THE UNITED STATES With liquor legal, hotels and restaurants burst forth with cocktail lounges, taprooms, chromium fittings, and bright modern furniture. Speakeasies converted to restaurants or bars and grills, depending on their former degree of elegance, and bootleggers started looking for new rackets. During the year, 35 million barrels of beer and 42 million gallons

86

of hard liquor were consumed. ☐ Skiing took off in the United States with the introduction of mechanical ski lifts, improvements in skis, boots, and poles, and the introduction of more fashionable ski clothing. ☐ The FBI rode high when it eliminated Public Enemy Number One, bank robber John Dillinger, gunning him down outside a Chicago movie house after he had been fingered by "the lady in red." Pretty Boy Floyd was slain and Dillinger's sidekick, Baby Face Nelson, became Public Enemy Number One. Bonnie and Clyde, after a reign of terror including bank robberies and killings, were shot to death in their stolen Ford V8. ☐ President Roosevelt founded the Warm Springs Foundation to fight infantile paralysis; the organization developed into the March of Dimes. ☐ Led by United Mine Workers president John L. Lewis, seventy thousand coal miners went on strike. There were sit-down strikes by Woolworth clerks, hosiery workers in Philadelphia, and automobile workers. ☐ A vast dust cloud, a thousand miles wide, swept through the Midwest and Southwest, darkening cities at midday. The storms killed livestock, destroyed crops, and drove people from their land. The great Depression migration to California began as families left their devastated farms in Kansas, Texas, and Oklahoma, the state which gave to all of the migrants the name "Okies." ☐ Henry Ford restored the $5-a-day wage, reduced during the Depression's worst days, to 47,000 of his 70,000 workers. Purchasing power was up 25 percent and the number of business failures dropped. "Only fifty-eight banks folded during the year," records say. Typical 1934 wages and earnings were: a lawyer, $4,218; a doctor, $3,282; a civil service employee, $1,284; an electrical worker, $1,559; a construction worker, $907. Airline pilots were big earners, making an average of $8,000 a year. ☐ Here's what the Depression dollar could buy: a mink coat was $585; silk stockings, 69¢; a man's Stetson hat, $5; a Ford V8, completely equipped, $585 and a Chrysler sedan $995; a six-room house with two-car garage in Detroit, $2,800 and a 12-room villa in Westchester, New York, $17,000. Sirloin steak was 29¢ a pound, butter, 28¢ a pound, and potatoes, 2¢. Milk was 10¢ a quart. A sixty-day, eleven-country European tour was $495 and up. ☐ Evangeline Booth was elected head of the

87

worldwide Salvation Army. □ Writer Upton Sinclair ran for governor of California, won the Democratic nomination, but lost the election.

SPORTS Max Baer became world heavyweight champ, knocking out Max Schmeling in the eleventh round. Young Joe Louis won his first fight, against Jack Kracken. □ Red Grange retired from professional football to become a coach and, later, a radio and TV commentator.

ARTS AND ENTERTAINMENT The Catholic Legion of Decency added its voice in protest against indecent movies, issuing a regular proscribed list which some Americans quickly found to be a handy guide to movies they hadn't thought to see. □ Lincoln Kirstein brought George Balanchine from France to the United States, inviting him to found a school of ballet. The school became the forerunner of the New York City Ballet company. □ A modern opera, *Four Saints in Three Acts,* with music by Virgil Thomson and book by Gertrude Stein, opened in Hartford, Connecticut, then in New York. □ In Hollywood, John Barrymore appeared on a set so drunk he couldn't remember a word of the script; it was the beginning of his failing memory and health. □ Schoolchildren were subjected to lessons on James McNeill Whistler when his *Portrait of My Mother* showed up on a purple 3¢ stamp. □ The Dorsey Brothers, Tommy and Jimmy, formed a band that quickly became popular. Jazz clarinetist Benny Goodman organized a band to play at a nightclub. □ Veloz and Yolande were the top dance team. □ Henry Miller's *Tropic of Cancer* was published in Paris; Ezra Pound commented, "At last, an unprintable book that is fit to be read." □ A Parisian baker was hauled into court for making his wife wear a chastity belt. An amateur researcher in medieval history, he had seen one in the Cluny Museum and had it copied, velvet lining and all.

"If Fascism came to America, it would be on a program of Americanism."
—"KINGFISH" HUEY LONG, *popularist senator from Louisiana and virtual dictator of the state*

FOUNDED The U.S. Social Security System, by act of Congress; the first federal hospital for narcotics addiction, Lexington, Kentucky; Alcoholics Anonymous; the New York Drama Critics Circle

INTRODUCED 35mm Kodachrome film; beer in cans; loyalty oaths, in nineteen states; radar; parking meters (municipalities loved them and they caught on quickly); the Wagner Industrial Labor Relations Law; transpacific air service, by Pan American

SONGS "Begin the Beguine" "The Music Goes Round and Round" "I Got Plenty of Nothin'" "It Ain't Necessarily So" "Just One of Those Things" "Cheek to Cheek" "When I Grow Too Old to Dream" "Red Sails in the Sunset"

FADS Little Audrey stories ("Little Audrey laughed and laughed because *she* knew . . .")

GAMES Monopoly, acquired from its inventor by Parker Bros., a hit from the start and a durable favorite (70 million sets have been sold to date)

DANCES The rumba, very fashionable

FASHION The look was extremely slim, fabrics soft; dresses had self-scarves at the neck. Hair was short but softly waved, the hat always tipped over the right eye. Plain pumps were in. American designer Vera Maxwell introduced the idea of complete coordination with her "weekend wardrobe." □ From ski clothes came snowsuits for children and the end of leggings and long wool stockings.

THE WORLD Germany annexed the Saar territory. Hitler renounced the Versailles Treaty and ordered reintroduction of compulsory military service. The Nuremberg Laws virtually outlawed Jews. The Luftwaffe was formed. □ Italy invaded Ethiopia. Emperor Haile Selassie fled, appealed to the League

89

of Nations, which declared Italy the aggressor but did little else. ☐ In Spain, the moderate and left parties formed the Popular Front. ☐ Persia changed its name to Iran.

THE UNITED STATES "Kingfish" Huey Long, senator from Louisiana and former governor of the state, was assassinated by Dr. Carl A. Weiss, Jr. in the state capitol at Baton Rouge. ☐ The federal government provided jobs for writers, composers, actors, artists, and musicians through the Works Progress Administration (WPA). Jackson Pollack, Moses Soyer, Ben Shahn, and many others survived with such projects as murals in post office buildings, earning $94.90 a month. The federal music projects employed eighteen thousand musicians while they were in operation. ☐ The Supreme Court voided President Roosevelt's NRA of 1933. ☐ In San Francisco, a general strike supported the cause of twelve thousand striking longshoremen. ☐ Hurricanes struck southern Florida for ten days. ☐ Amelia Earhart made a solo flight across the Pacific, from Hawaii to California. ☐ The elegant French liner *Normandie* made its maiden voyage. With a first-class dining room longer than Versaille's Hall of Mirrors and the first motion-picture theater aboard a ship, it was the epitome of luxury. ☐ In a sensational trial in Flemington, New Jersey, Bruno Richard Hauptmann was convicted of kidnapping and killing the Lindbergh baby and was sentenced to death. ☐ William Randolph Hearst instructed the editors of his papers (he had thirty-three) to refer to the New Deal as the "raw deal." A survey revealed that Hearst and Mae West had the highest salaries in the nation. ☐ Kids sported toy G-Man badges. ☐ Someone shot gangster Dutch Schultz, who refused to name his slayer before expiring. ☐ Ma Barker and her four thug sons were done in by the law. ☐ Comedian Will Rogers and aviator Wiley Post were killed when Post's plane crashed in a fog in Alaska. ☐ The 726-carat Jonkers diamond arrived in New York City from England by registered mail, at a cost of 35¢. ☐ The $4 million navy dirigible *Macon* fell into the Pacific and sank off the California coast; all but two aboard were rescued. ☐ Only 10 percent of American farms were electrified. ☐ Bandleader Ozzie Nelson married his vocalist, Harriet Hilliard.

SPORTS The first nighttime major league baseball game was played in Cincinnati. ☐ Track star Jesse Owens, a sophomore at Ohio State, broke three world track records and equalled a fourth. ☐ Babe Ruth retired from active play.

ARTS AND ENTERTAINMENT In popular music, the Benny Goodman band was hired by the National Biscuit Company for a three-hour dance marathon on radio every Saturday night. It was the group's big break. With the recording of "King Porter Stomp," Goodman and the band arrived, ushering in the Swing Era. Tommy Dorsey left the Dorsey Brothers band to his brother Jimmy and formed his own group. Bing Crosby's kid brother, Bob, assumed leadership of the Bobcats, a big band that played Dixieland style. ☐ Jazz, along with music of Jewish origin, was banned on German radio. ☐ Contralto Marian Anderson, having established herself in Europe, began a successful American tour with a concert in Town Hall, New York. Wagnerian soprano Kirstin Flagstad made her American debut at the New York Metropolitan Opera. ☐ Actress Bette Davis upset all of Hollywood by attending the formal Academy Awards event in an informal checkered dress. Checkered dresses were the latest style when she won the Best Actress award for her role in *Dangerous*.

The horse and wagon for home deliveries of milk was giving way to small trucks. Many milkmen resisted the changeover (the horses were smarter than trucks and knew the route) and some diehards held out until the late forties, when the dairies retired either the deliverers or their nags.

1936

"You look better than you did four years ago."
—FRANKLIN DELANO ROOSEVELT, *in speeches, as he campaigned for reelection*

FOUNDED The Ford Foundation; *Life* magazine, using the name of a defunct publication

INTRODUCED Tampax, the first tampons; the Douglas DC-3, a two-engined plane that became the backbone of commercial aviation (thirty-five years later, more than eight hundred were still in operation)

LAST TIME The final public hanging in the United States, in Owensboro, Kentucky

SONGS "Pennies from Heaven" "De-lovely" "Is It True What They Say about Dixie?" "I Can't Get Started with You" "Whiffenpoof Song" (revised version) "I'm an Old Cowhand" "There's a Small Hotel" "The Way You Look Tonight"

CRAZES *Gone With the Wind;* not only was everyone reading Margaret Mitchell's Civil War novel, the women were wearing Gone With the Wind dresses, men Gone With the Wind bow ties; homes sported Gone With the Wind bookends and little girls dressed Scarlett O'Hara dolls. ☐ The scavenger hunt was almost a certainty for party guests, who would arrive to find the host and hostess armed with lists of improbable items that teams of guests would have to round up by evening's end (an elk's tooth, a taxi, a monkey wrench, a copy of *Moby Dick*). It made party-giving a snap: no conversation, just feed them and send them hunting.

FASHION Shoulders of women's dresses and suits were widened and padded, under the influence of Hollywood designer Adrian. This year, the dowager Queen Mary, who had been loyal to one hat style since 1913, was only one of millions of women wearing turbans; open-crown turbans were especially popular. Culottes were a daring new look.

THE WORLD German troops occupied the demilitarized Rhineland, violating the Locarno Pact; England and France did nothing to stop them. ☐ Italy, under Mussolini, seized Addis Ababa and the Ethiopian War ended. ☐ Edward VIII succeeded to the throne but abdicated before he was crowned "to marry the woman I love," an American divorcée, Wallis Warfield Simpson. The romance captured the hearts of sentimentalists, brought George VI to the throne, and converted the erstwhile king into the Duke of Windsor. ☐ The Popular Front won the Spanish election but a group of generals led by Francisco Franco revolted, and the Civil War was on. ☐ Chiang Kai-shek declared war on Japan. ☐ In France, with the emergence of the anti-fascist French Popular Front, Socialist Leon Blum became premier.

THE UNITED STATES With 80 percent of the press against him, Roosevelt swept to victory over Alfred Landon by an electoral vote of 523 to 8, winning every state but Maine and Vermont and changing the old saw from "As Maine goes, so goes the nation" to the wags' "As Maine goes, so goes Vermont." ☐ Drew Pearson and Robert Allen, in their "Washington Merry-Go-Round" newspaper column, coined the expression "nine old men" to describe the conservative Supreme Court. ☐ German Bund societies, pro-Nazi groups, drew members from German-Americans, some of whom thought they were joining social organizations. ☐ Bruno Richard Hauptmann, kidnapper of the Lindbergh baby, was electrocuted. Richard Loeb, imprisoned for the 1924 Leopold-Loeb murder of Bobby Franks, was slain by a fellow inmate. ☐ Dr. Alexis Carrel, aided by Charles Lindbergh, created an artificial heart. ☐ Boulder Dam on the Colorado River was completed, creating Lake Mead, the world's largest reservoir. ☐ The Civilian Conservation Corps taught thirty-five thousand illiterates to read. ☐ Trailers attached to cars, a new mode of living and vacationing, became popular. There were 160,000 on the road. ☐ The Triborough Bridge, joining Manhattan and two other New York City boroughs, Queens and the Bronx, was opened. ☐ As the year ended, automobile workers, led by Walter and Victor Reuther, staged a sit-down strike in an effort to unionize the industry.

SPORTS American track star Jesse Owens won three events at the summer Olympics in Berlin and was a member of the winning American relay team; his 100-meter record of 10.3 seconds was equalled but unbeaten for twenty-five years and his broad jump of 26 feet, 5 inches also stood for twenty-five years; Chancellor Adolf Hitler refused to shake hands with the Negro champion. ☐ Samuel Reshevsky, 25-year-old Polish-born chess genius, won the 1936 American chess tournament. ☐ Joe Louis, who had won twenty-two straight fights, suffered a setback when he was knocked out by Max Schmeling in his try for the championship.

ARTS AND ENTERTAINMENT   Arturo Toscanini conducted his last season with the New York Philharmonic, packing Carnegie Hall for each of a series of farewell concerts. ☐ The big-band era and swing music were firmly established. The bands were playing in theaters, ballrooms, nightclubs, hotels, and on radio, records, and college-campus one-night stands. Benny Goodman made his New York debut at the Hotel Pennsylvania. Artie Shaw opened at the Lexington Hotel. In a tiny New York club, The Famous Door, Count Basie drew attention. ☐ Josephine Baker, the toast of Europe, appeared in the *Ziegfeld Follies* but failed to make it with American audiences. ☐ *Gone With the Wind* was published in June at the unbelievably high price of $3. More than a million copies were sold within the first six months; the book ruled the bestseller list for two years. ☐ Actress Mary Astor's personal diary became news when her husband produced it in a court battle for custody of their daughter. Among the ten lovers mentioned, one of the most athletic appeared to be a "George," who turned out to be Broadway playwright and director George S. Kaufman. Even the sedate *New York Times* ran a headline, "Warrant Out for Kaufman," but Public Lover Number One failed to appear in court. ☐ Zsa Zsa Gabor was Miss Hungary. Shirley Temple signed a contract that would pay her $5,000 a week.

The Cunard liner *Queen Mary*, largest ship afloat, made her maiden voyage.

☐  "I see one-third of a nation ill-housed, ill-clad, and ill-fed."
—FRANKLIN D. ROOSEVELT *in his second inaugural address*

FOUNDED   The Baseball Hall of Fame at Cooperstown, New York; the NBC Symphony, created for Arturo Toscanini's radio concerts; the Israel Philharmonic Orchestra at Tel Aviv

INTRODUCED   Nylon, created at Dupont by Wallace Carothers

FINALE The *Literary Digest,* a magazine which had conducted a 1936 pre-election poll of telephone owners and predicted that Landon would win the presidency in a landslide, folded.

SONGS "Bei Mir Bist Du Shoen" "A Foggy Day" "In the Still of the Night" "The Lady Is a Tramp" "The Dipsy Doodle" "Where or When" "Nice Work If You Can Get It" "Thanks for the Memory"

NEW GAMES Canasta, imported from Argentina; Inky Pinky rhyming riddles

DANCES The Big Apple; the shag; the Susie Q; trucking

FASHION Schiaparelli introduced the color, Shocking Pink; Wally Simpson's wedding costume, a floor-length cocktail dress with fitted jacket, wrist-length gloves, high-heeled sandals, and small skullcap, all in "Wallis blue," was promptly copied by American fashion houses. Teen-age girls wore gored skirts, Sloppy Joe Shetland wool sweaters, and multicolor-striped "sharpie" socks. Standard footwear for high school and college students, both male and female, was saddle shoes in black or brown and white.

THE WORLD Japan seized the Chinese cities of Peking and Nanking. Chiang Kai-shek united with the Communist leaders Mao Tse-tung and Chou En-lai to fight the invaders. The U.S. gunboat *Panay* was sunk in the Yangtze River; Japan apologized for the "accident." ☐ In England, George VI and Elizabeth were crowned. ☐ The Duke of Windsor made Mrs. Simpson his duchess in a widely publicized wedding in France; her trousseau included eighty dresses, forty hats. ☐ Spain's Loyalist government moved to Barcelona; German or Italian bombers destroyed the town of Guernica. ☐ In the USSR, the purges and trials continued, with a group of generals accused of working on behalf of Germany.

THE UNITED STATES President Roosevelt started his second term. Isolationism was the prevailing mood of the country; in a Gallup Poll, 70 percent said they thought the United States had erred in entering World War I. Some felt differently: volunteers began leaving for Spain to fight for the Loyalists with the American Abraham Lincoln Brigade; a total of four thousand

95

Americans had gone by the end of the Civil War; half of them returned. ☐ The United Auto Workers won the strike started the previous year against General Motors, gaining a 5¢-per-hour wage increase. A relatively new labor weapon, the sit-down strike, was much in the news. On Memorial Day, a strike against Republic Steel became violent; four workers were killed, eighty-four injured in a battle with company "goons." ☐ The U.S. Supreme Court ruled in favor of a minimum wage for women. ☐ President Roosevelt sought to overcome conservative domination of the Supreme Court by packing it—enlarging it to fifteen. The issue became so hot that a skywriter flew over a Washington ball game with the message, "Play the Game, Don't Pack the Court." FDR failed in his effort. ☐ The German dirigible *Hindenburg* burst into flames while landing at Lakehurst, New Jersey. The catastrophe, described in a memorable on-the-spot radio broadcast, effectively ended the era of the airship for passenger travel. ☐ Amelia Earhart and her navigator disappeared in mid-Pacific during an around-the-world flight and were never found. Howard Hughes piloted a plane from Los Angeles to New York in seven hours, twenty-eight minutes. ☐ During a New York City newspaper strike, the city's "Little Flower," Mayor Fiorello La Guardia, made use of his regular Sunday radio reports to the city's citizens to read the news to adults and the funnies to the kids. A less popular mayor, Jersey City's boss, Frank Hague, proclaimed, "I am the law." ☐ One of the reigning beauties was Hope Chandler, a nightclub girl who was to become the elegant Mrs. David W. Hearst. ☐ The Golden Gate Bridge, spanning the entrance to San Francisco Bay, was opened to traffic. ☐ The debutante of the year was Gloria Baker, who wore a strapless white gown at her coming-out party. Professional party-giver Elsa Maxwell gave a ball at which society guests came dressed as their pet hates. ☐ A Ford convertible sedan cost $959.

SPORTS Joe Louis, the "Brown Bomber," knocked out heavyweight champion James J. Braddock to win the title. ☐ Joe DiMaggio of the Yankees became the American League batting champion for the first time. ☐ Walter Hagen retired from active golf competition.

ARTS AND ENTERTAINMENT Blues singer Bessie Smith died following an auto accident in Mississippi; a white hospital to which she had been taken had refused to admit her. ☐ Benny Goodman, now billed as the "King of Swing," caused near riots at New York's Paramount Theater when he opened there. Teen-aged fans lined up from 6:00 A.M., danced in the aisles and up onto the stage in a frenzy of swing passion. The words "Swing it, Mr. Goodman" were chalked on sidewalks. ☐ The Big Apple, the dance rage, was a strenuous variation on the square dance, with one couple "shining" in the center. The dancers, who called themselves "alligators," "jitterbugs," or "cats," jived, did the Susie Q and the shag, a bouncy step, and trucked on down, waving a finger and shaking the head. Pecking, a chickenlike head motion, was part of it. ☐ Woody Herman formed a band during the year. ☐ At the Paris Exposition, Picasso exhibited his enormous, passionate commentary on war, *Guernica*. ☐ On Broadway, young innovator Orson Welles and his Mercury Theatre burst on the scene, startling audiences with a modern-dress version of Shakespeare's *Julius Caesar*, in which the familiar characters were transformed into contemporary totalitarians.

☐  "This is the second time in our history that there has come from Germany to Downing Street peace with honor. I believe it is peace for our time."
—BRITISH PRIME MINISTER NEVILLE CHAMBERLAIN, *on his return from the dismemberment of Czechoslovakia at Munich*

FOUNDED The March of Dimes, raising funds to combat infantile paralysis; the Society for the Preservation and Encouragement of Barber Shop Quartet Singing in America; the National Organization for Decent Literature

INTRODUCED A treatment for gonorrhea, with newly discovered sulfa drugs; the Jefferson-head nickel, replacing the buffalo; flexible drinking straws; a self-propelled combine to cut, thresh, and clean grain

SONGS "My Reverie" "Flat-Foot Floogie" "A Tisket, A Tasket" "Music Maestro, Please" "Jeepers, Creepers" "Our Love Is Here to Stay" "This Can't Be Love" "You Must Have Been a Beautiful Baby"

FADS Bingo, which grew into an American way of life; knock-knock jokes

FASHION The shirtwaist look was back again; for evening, women wore long, slinky gowns with bolero jackets. Claire McCardell introduced an important new look—monastic dresses hanging loosely from the shoulders, with fullness caught in at the waist with a cord belt. Fox scarves were big.

THE WORLD Hitler occupied Austria, proclaimed the "Anschluss," the Austrian union, and declared himself Germany's war minister. Attacks on Jews worsened, climaxing in the "Crystal Night" destruction of Jewish synagogues, homes, and shops. ☐ In Spain, the Franco forces drove toward the coast. ☐ British, French, German, and Italian diplomats met in Munich, Germany, and agreed to cede Czechoslovakia's western provinces to Germany. Anthony Eden resigned from the British Foreign Office in protest. Churchill called it the worst defeat in English history. ☐ English friends helped the endangered Sigmund Freud, a Jew, to leave Austria for England.

THE UNITED STATES A new Wages and Hours Bill provided for a 40¢-an-hour minimum wage, a maximum work week of forty-four hours. Child labor was prohibited. The Committee for Industrial Organization was expelled from the American Federation of Labor (AFL) and became the Congress of Industrial Organizations (CIO), with mine leader John L. Lewis as its president and Amalgamated Clothing Workers president Sidney Hillman as vice president. ☐ During the Munich crisis, CBS news commentator H. V. Kaltenborn delivered eighty-five extemporaneous broadcasts in eighteen days, sleeping in the studio and never leaving his post. ☐ Radio's Father Coughlin, after ranting against Jews as being Communists, was dropped by many stations and forced off the air by his Catholic Church superiors. Under the auspices of the America First Committee, Charles A. Lindbergh toured the country, condemning the concept of U.S. intervention in Europe and recommending alliance with Germany. ☐ An obscure pilot, Douglas G. Corrigan, achieved instant celebrity as "Wrong-Way" Corrigan when he flew from New York to Dublin, without passport or permit, made it in a little more than twenty-eight hours, and claimed he had really been headed for California. Howard Hughes and a crew of four set a round-the-world flight record, making it in three days, nineteen hours, in a monoplane. ☐ The country was covered with trailer camps, trailer parks—and trailers. ☐ A generation of curious kids got a quick answer to their questions when *Life* magazine published an issue carrying photos taken from the movie *Birth of a Baby.* The issue was banned in thirty-three cities, copies were confiscated by police, and *Life* publisher Roy Larsen was arrested. ☐ Every little girl who liked dolls had or wanted a Shirley Temple doll; 6 million of them were sold during the year.

SPORTS Joe Louis knocked out Germany's Max Schmeling in the first round. ☐ Eddie Arcaro rode his first Derby winner, Lawrin. ☐ Bobby Feller of the Cleveland Indians struck out eighteen men in a game with the Detroit Tigers. ☐ Don Budge took the tennis grand slam.

ARTS AND ENTERTAINMENT Orson Welles' "Mercury Theatre of the Air" presented *War of the Worlds* so realistically on radio that people who tuned in late thought the simulated news bulletins about the Martian attack were real; they rushed to roofs and out on streets armed with guns, canes, brooms, hammers, and monkey wrenches to fight off the invaders. The panic was greatest in the New York–New Jersey area, where the green men were supposedly attacking the 15-mile Pulaski Skyway bridge. ☐ Aaron Copland's ballet, *Billy the Kid,* premiered; so did Gian Carlo Menotti's opera, *Amelia Goes to the Ball.* ☐ Kate Smith revived a song Irving Berlin had written in 1917 and made "God Bless America" something of a national anthem. ☐ Seven million schoolchildren marched into assembly each week to listen to Walter Damrosch's "Music Appreciation Hour" on radio. ☐ Swing was in. In what may well have been the first jazz festival, twenty-five big bands played six hours for twenty-three thousand jitterbugs at New York's Randall's Island. The swing vocabulary grew; swing fans were "hep cats" who "cut a rug" dancing, as Benny Goodman played his "licorice stick." Among the most important "canaries" starring with the big bands were Helen O'Connell, Marian Hutton, Martha Tilton, Ella Fitzgerald, Mildred Bailey, and Billie Holiday. □ The Musician's Union won a six-day, instead of seven-day, week for members. "Paramount News" featured couples dancing the Lindy Hop at the Harvest Moon Ball. Arthur Murray Dance Studios were teaching an English export, the Lambeth Walk. □ One of the talked-about books of the year was *Fashion Is Spinach,* by Elizabeth Hawes, a completely original fashion revolutionary who advocated comfort and natural lines in clothing years before the message got through to most of the crowd. □ Walt Disney's first full-length film, *Snow White and the Seven Dwarfs,* was a smash and had everyone whistling "Whistle While You Work." The most-quoted dialogue of the year was an imitation of Charles Boyer, "Come wiz me to the Casbah," which he didn't actually say to Hedy Lamarr in their film *Algiers.* □ And people quoted the final line of *Blockade,* a film about the Spanish civil war, when Henry Fonda, as the film's hero, turned to the movie audience and asked, "Where is the conscience of the world?"

1939

"I cannot forecast to you the action of Russia. It is a riddle wrapped in a mystery inside an enigma."
—WINSTON CHURCHILL, *speaking over BBC about the Nazi-Soviet pact a month after the start of World War II*

FOUNDED Little League Baseball, three teams, in Williamsport, Pennsylvania; the first Blue Shield surgical plan, in California

INTRODUCED The first commercial home-television receiver, marketed by Allen B. Dumont; synthetic detergents; the first helicopter, built by Igor Sikorsky; the Volkswagen "Beetle," in Germany; the self-winding watch; paperback books, with ten titles at 25¢ each, distributed through 100,000 newsstands by Pocket Books

FADE-OUT Running boards on automobiles were headed for oblivion.

SONGS "Deep Purple" "Moonlight Serenade" "Over the Rainbow" "Three Little Fishies" "I'll Never Smile Again" "Hold Tight, Hold Tight" "Beer Barrel Polka" "All the Things You Are" "In the Mood"

FADS Telephone booth-packing, on college campuses; unbleached canvas beer jackets with jokes, drawings, friends' autographs India-inked on, worn by both sexes on high school and college campuses

DANCING Jitterbugging; the Lindy

FASHION Babushkas, large scarfs folded into triangles and worn, tied under the chin, in place of hats; pillbox hats with detachable wimples. The popular hairdo for women had a pompadour on top, a rolled puff on either side of the head, and back hair curled at shoulder length.

THE WORLD World War II began on September 1, when Germany invaded Poland; Great Britain and France, as Poland's allies, declared war on Germany September 3. Poland quickly collapsed and was divided between Germany and the Soviet Union. The British, anticipating German air raids, evacuated women and children from London. The Soviet Union invaded Finland. ☐ In Spain, Loyalist resistance practically ceased and the civil war ended with recognition of the Franco dictatorship by Britain and France. ☐ President Roosevelt signed a bill enabling France and Britain to purchase U.S. arms. ☐ The disabled German battleship *Graf Spee* scuttled itself off Uruguay to prevent seizure by the enemy.

THE UNITED STATES Great Britain's King George and Queen Elizabeth visited the United States during the summer, were entertained at the White House by Marian Anderson, Lawrence Tibbett, and Kate Smith, then treated to an American-style hot dog picnic at FDR's Hyde Park, New York, home. ☐ Sixty nations participated in the spectacular "World of Tomor-

row" at the New York World's Fair. The April 30 opening ceremonies were telecast over NBC's experimental channel. General
Motors' "Futurama" was a hit; so was Billy Rose's "Aquacade,"
featuring beautiful girls swimming to music. Dinner at the elegant French Pavilion cost almost $10. ☐ The Nazi regime pre-
sented its Grand Cross decoration to Henry Ford and a medal
to Charles Lindbergh. ☐ During the year 3,400,000 passengers
travelled by air. Pan American Airways started regular flights
between the United States and Europe with its amphibious
Dixie Clipper. Air travel was well-established and the era of
record flights to popularize planes came to an end with the start
of the war. ☐ Hatred of FDR ran high in business circles; a
salesman could write orders by presenting a card that read, "If
you don't give me an order, I'll vote for him again." Mrs.
Eleanor Roosevelt was the focus of both jokes and admiration as
she turned up in unexpected places, serving as her husband's
eyes and ears. ☐ The "Deb of the Year," Brenda Frazier, came
out at the Ritz Hotel in New York at a $50,000 party for fifteen
hundred guests. ☐ After serving twenty-three years for the
crime he claimed he did not commit, former labor leader Tom
Mooney was pardoned by the governor of California.

SPORTS For the second year in a row, the New York
Yankees won the World Series in four straight games. Yankee
Lou Gehrig retired because of ill health. ☐ Bobby Riggs was
the male tennis champion at Wimbledon and Forest Hills, and
Alice Marble took the women's titles at both. ☐ In active sports,
skiing, long popular in Europe, caught on in the United States;
special snow trains and busses were jammed.

ARTS AND ENTERTAINMENT After a widely publicized search and screen-testing of Hollywood's biggest female
stars, a virtually unknown British actress, Vivien Leigh, was
chosen to play Scarlett O'Hara in the film *Gone With the Wind*.
Clark Gable, who was to be Leigh's Rhett, married actress
Carole Lombard. ☐ The Daughters of the American Revolution
barred black contralto Marian Anderson from giving a concert
in its Washington, D.C., Constitution Hall. At Mrs. Roosevelt's
suggestion, Secretary of the Interior Harold Ickes made the
Lincoln Memorial available and the noted singer gave an open-

air concert before seventy-five thousand persons, including distinguished government figures. The *Washington Post* reported, "The crowd roared its acclaim for the colored girl" (she was 37). ☐ Gian Carlo Menotti's opera *The Old Maid and the Thief* received its world premiere on an NBC radio broadcast. ☐ British pianist Myra Hess organized luncheon concerts at London's National Gallery; they continued right through the blitz. ☐ Anna M. Robertson achieved fame as Grandma Moses, following an exhibition of her primitive paintings. ☐ On radio, Buck Rogers and his co-pilot, Wilma Deering, were favorites of children. Macy's, in New York City, was mobbed by twenty thousand people when it advertised Buck Rogers disintegrator guns. CBS aired "Ballad for Americans," a folk ballad, with Paul Robeson and Burgess Meredith in the large cast. ☐ The big bands rode high; dancing hit a peak it was not to see again until disco days. The two-year-old Glenn Miller band caught on, to become the most popular dance band for the next few years. Trumpeter Harry James left the Benny Goodman band to form his own; when someone asked him the name of the band's great, skinny little singer, James said, "Not so loud. He considers himself the greatest vocalist in the business"; the name was Frank Sinatra. Jack Teagarden left Whiteman and formed his own band. The Ink Spots, a black quartet, skyrocketed to fame with a recording of "If I Didn't Care," featuring the tenor-soprano voice of Bill Kenny and the sonorous spoken second chorus of Hoppy Jones. ☐ The Federal Theatre Project of the WPA was disbanded following unfavorable testimony before the House Un-American Activities Committee. The project had employed more than thirteen thousand actors.

 **1940**

"We shall defend our Island whatever the cost may be . . . We shall fight in the fields and in the streets, we shall fight in the hills. We shall never surrender."

—PRIME MINISTER WINSTON CHURCHILL,
before Parliament, in June

FOUNDED The Selective Service System, the first peacetime draft in U.S. history; I Am an American Day, by act of Congress

INTRODUCED Nylon stockings, which made a brief appearance before the fiber was diverted to military use; Tyrothricin, the first miracle drug for humans; the Boeing Stratoliner, the first four-engine, pressurized U.S. plane, which became the World War II Flying Fortress bomber

SONGS "The Last Time I Saw Paris" "Fools Rush In" "A Nightingale Sang in Berkeley Square" "How High the Moon" "Cabin in the Sky" "Tuxedo Junction" "When the Swallows Come Back to Capistrano"

FASHION In a real revolution for men, waist-length outer jackets, formerly worn only as work clothing, were adopted for sportswear. Women's long hair was caught up in snoods, colorful open-work crocheted nets. Playsuits, one-piece shorts and top plus separate skirt, were a sports favorite.

THE WORLD Germany's blitzkrieg continued, with Nazi forces invading Denmark, Belgium, Holland, Norway, and Luxembourg within less than two months. In May, Winston Churchill became Britain's Prime Minister and told Parliament and, via radio, the nation, "I have nothing to offer but blood, toil, tears and sweat." British forces were driven from the Continent and Britain marshalled everything that could float for the heroic rescue of 300,000 British and French soldiers at Dunkirk. □ Italy declared war on Britain and France, an act which caused FDR to say, "The hand that held the dagger has struck it in the back of her neighbor." Italy moved on the Balkans, attacking Greece and Yugoslavia. Bulgaria, Roumania, and Hungary came under German control. □ France surrendered to Germany in June. Just before the end, Gen. Charles de Gaulle was secreted to London, from which he broadcast to France saying, "France has lost a battle but not the war," and urging Frenchmen to rally to him in England. ☐ Heavy bombing of England by the Luftwaffe began; 4,558 Britons were killed during the first month of the blitz. Americans, pinned to their radios, safe in their homes, heard the nightly broadcasts of Edward R. Murrow describing the devastation of the blitz, opening each time with, "This . . . is . . . London." ☐ The United States leased naval bases in Newfoundland and the Caribbean to Great Britain. ☐ Leon Trotsky, living in Mexico, was assassinated by a presumed Stalinist agent.

THE UNITED STATES A new law required alien residents to register. The new Selective Service Act required draft registration of all men 20 to 36. The U.S. Army ranked seventeenth in the world in manpower and modern weapons. There were two black officers in the army. ☐ Fifty overaged destroyers, "the mothball fleet," were given to England. ☐ A rumpled Hoosier, Wendell Willkie, whom Harold Ickes dubbed "the barefoot boy of Wall Street," challenged the champ, FDR, in his run for an unprecedented third term. Roosevelt won by 27 million votes to Willkie's 22 million and Communist Earl Browder's 48,000. ☐ Pan American's Yankee Clipper flew from New York to Lisbon, Portugal, in eighteen hours, thirty-five minutes. Subsequent flights became famous as the most desirable escape route for European refugees. ☐ Adolescents suddenly found themselves an important new entity known as the teenage market when American producers of everything from clothing to books realized the profit potential of catering to their tastes. ☐ The 6-year-old Dionne Quintuplets made the cover of *Life* in their First Communion dresses. Magazine cover girl Jinx Falkenburg became the first Miss Rheingold, smiling from beer ads in magazines and on billboards. ☐ Fiorello La Guardia, coping with one of New York's perennial problems, said, "There is no Republican way or Democratic way to clean the streets."

ARTS AND ENTERTAINMENT Two French schoolboys discovered the Lascaux caves, containing prehistoric wall paintings estimated to be between fourteen thousand and twenty-eight thousand years old. ☐ Stephen Foster's "Jeannie with the

Light Brown Hair" and "Camptown Races" were the top tunes heard on radio, as broadcasters decided not to renew their ASCAP licenses, thus barring performance of all works not in the public domain. The boycott lasted for a year, starting in October 1940. ☐ American music was enriched as notable refugees continued to arrive from Europe; among them were Stravinsky, Bartok, Hindemith, Milhaud, Kurt Weill, and Oskar Straus. ☐ Swing continued to rule popular music. At New York's Manhattan Center, Benny Goodman, Glenn Miller, Count Basie, Glen Gray, Les Brown, Guy Lombardo, and some twenty other big bands played to six thousand fans without letup from 8:00 P.M. to 4:00 A.M. ☐ Agnes de Mille's ballet *Rodeo* premiered. ☐ F. Scott Fitzgerald died in Hollywood. ☐ The first color-TV broadcast in history was transmitted by CBS but commercial application was still years away. ☐ A quiet hero of the French Resistance was couturier Lucien Lelong, who headed the Syndicate, the official organization of the couture. When the conquering Germans demanded that records and export information be shipped to Vienna, which they planned to make the new fashion center, Lelong stalled, holding long conferences to solve the myriad problems he explained existed. He stalled for four years, probably saving his city's 112,000 skilled needlecraft workers from deportation and slave labor.

☐ **1941**   "Yesterday, December 7, 1941, a date that will live in infamy, the United States of America was suddenly and deliberately attacked by naval and air forces of the Empire of Japan."
—PRES. FRANKLIN D. ROOSEVELT, *December 8, asking Congress to declare a state of war*

INTRODUCED   Gasoline rationing; tire rationing; Savings Bonds and Savings Stamps; the aerosol spray

SAVED Muzak, a failing business, which got back in the black by piping brisk tunes into defense factories

SONGS "Bewitched, Bothered and Bewildered" "Jersey Bounce" "I Got It Bad and That Ain't Good" "Buckle Down, Winsocki" "Blues in the Night" "Chattanooga Choo Choo" "There'll Be Bluebirds Over the White Cliffs of Dover" "Green Eyes" "Amapola"

FASHION Women's suits were broad-shouldered, mannish, set off by elaborate hats which sat high on the head, often dripping with veiling. Hemlines had risen again and were a little below the knee. In Paris, the women of the German occupying forces were known as "grey mice" for the somber colors of their clothes; to set them apart, Parisians wore wild colors and any kind of outrageous hat they could devise.

THE WORLD World War II continued and by year's end the United States was inevitably drawn in. ☐ German air attacks almost totally destroyed the British House of Commons and the town of Coventry. ☐ The war moved on to Africa, where the British attacked and the Germans counterattacked. In one of the war's odd sidelights, Nazi bigwig Rudolph Hess flew a plane to Scotland, parachuted down, said he was looking for the Duke of Hamilton (who was not expecting him), and was taken prisoner. ☐ In June, the Germans invaded Russia and penetrated deeply. They were thrown back at Moscow but advanced to the outskirts of Leningrad, which they blockaded but never succeeded in taking (Leningrad held out for nine hundred days). A second try for Moscow failed when the snow began to fall, as it had on Napoleon's forces in 1812. ☐ Hitler ordered a policy of genocide as "the final solution" to the Jewish problem. The systematic murders disposed of some 6 million Jews by war's end and extended to an estimated 4 million other religious and political undesirables. ☐ Japanese troops landed in Indochina; Hong Kong surrendered to Japan. Japanese assets in the United States were frozen by the government.

THE UNITED STATES President Roosevelt initiated a program of Lend-Lease to Great Britain, later extended to the USSR, appropriating $50 billion in goods and services. The

United States shipped to England more than a million tons of food and 952 tanks. Putting together "bundles for Britain" became a community project in many American cities and towns. ☐ The Manhattan Project, a top-secret, intensive atomic research program which was to culminate in the atom bomb, began in Chicago and Los Angeles. ☐ German and Italian assets in the United States were frozen, consulates closed, and Nazi propaganda organizations shut down. ☐ The America First Committee was prominent among groups questioning the country's drift toward war. One of its spokesmen, Charles Lindbergh (Alice Roosevelt Longworth was another), called FDR a warmonger; speaking in Iowa, Lindbergh asserted that three groups were pushing the country toward war: the British, the Jews, and the Roosevelt administration. ☐ In August, Roosevelt and Churchill met secretly aboard a battleship in the Atlantic and drafted the eight principles of the Atlantic Charter. ☐ The Pacific situation worsened and on December 7, Japanese warplanes attacked the port of Pearl Harbor, Hawaii, as well as the Philippines, Wake Island, and Guam. The Pearl Harbor attack destroyed 19 ships, including all but one U.S. battleship, and cost 3,457 lives. The United States declared war on Japan the following day. On December 11, Italy and Germany, as Japan's allies, declared war on the United States.

SPORTS Joe Louis knocked out Red Burman in five rounds, Gus Forzaio in two, Abe Simon in thirteen, Tony Musto in nine, Buddy Baer in seven, Billy Conn in thirteen, and Lou Nova in six. ☐ Whirlaway, ridden by Eddie Arcaro, won the triple crown. ☐ Joe DiMaggio hit safely in fifty-six consecutive games. Lou Gehrig died.

ARTS AND ENTERTAINMENT The Shostakovich Seventh Symphony, written during the seige of Leningrad, was recorded and sent to the United States for radio presentation, inspiring Carl Sandburg to remark, "This wonderful sound comes enclosed in a tomato can." ☐ The National Gallery of Art opened in Washington, D.C., a gift to the nation from Andrew W. Mellon. ☐ James Joyce died; Virginia Woolf committed suicide. F. Scott Fitzgerald's unfinished *The Last Tycoon* was published posthumously. ☐ Hollywood's Rita Hayworth was

108

dubbed "the Love Goddess." ☐ Mrs. Roosevelt announced that, because the president was so busy, no formal White House functions would be held.

☐ **1942** "I shall return."
—GEN. DOUGLAS MAC ARTHUR, *on leaving Corregidor in the Philippines on presidential orders*

FOUNDED WACS, the U.S. Women's Army Corps; WAVES, the U.S. Woman's naval organization; SPARS, the women's branch of the U.S. Coast Guard; The Armed Forces Radio Service

INTRODUCED ENIAC, the first "electronic brain," or automatic computer; silicone; the word "antibiotic"; penicillin, discovered fourteen years earlier by Alexander Fleming; rocket warfare, with launching of the pilotless German V-1 missiles; the Bazooka, named after comedian Bob Burns' homemade musical instrument; V-mail, microfilmed overseas mail to and from GIs

REACTIVATED *Stars and Stripes,* U.S. armed forces daily newspaper, not published since the end of World War I

SONGS "Deep in the Heart of Texas" "Praise the Lord and Pass the Ammunition" "That Old Black Magic" "Don't Sit Under the Apple Tree" "I've Got Spurs That Jingle Jangle Jingle" "White Christmas" "I Left My Heart at the Stage Door Canteen"

FASHION The armed forces had first claim on fabric and leather; women's fashions were straight, short, and narrow; men's trousers were cuffless; canvas shoes supplemented leather ones. Women defense workers who wore slacks for work started wearing them on the street as well. Claire McCardell introduced her "popover," a surplice-wrapped "kitchen dinner dress." Shoes had either sensible "Cuban" heels or the new wedged soles. There was no rubber for babies' pants.

THE WORLD American forces surrendered to the Japanese at Bataan and Corregidor; Japan invaded the Malay Peninsula, Burma, Siam, Singapore, and the island bases of New Guinea, New Britain, and the Solomons. Gen. Douglas MacArthur, who had left the Philippines for Australia, was named Supreme Commander of the Southwest Pacific area. Following its first show of strength at the naval battles of the Coral Sea and Midway, in August, the United States started its counterattack on Guadalcanal in the Solomon Islands. Lt. Col. James H. Doolittle led a squadron of B-25 bombers in a short raid on Tokyo and other coastal cities, more psychological than strategic in purpose. □ In the European theater of war, forces under American Gen. Dwight D. Eisenhower, Commander in Chief of the Allied armies, invaded North Africa, taking on "the Desert Fox," Germany's Gen. Erwin Rommel. □ The air war strengthened as Allied planes raided France daily; the Germans bombed Bath, Exeter, and London, and a thousand Allied bombers raided Bremen. Germany moved into unoccupied France but failed to hold Stalingrad in the Soviet Union. Norwegian Fascist leader Quisling became premier of his country under Nazi domination and his name became a synonym for traitor. □ Meeting in Washington, representatives of the United States, Britain, China, and twenty-two other Allied nations pledged to make no separate peace with the enemy.

THE UNITED STATES The government transferred 100,000 Japanese-Americans from the West Coast to inland internment camps. □ War factories, known as "defense plants," stepped up to maximum production. A West Coast industrialist, Henry J. Kaiser, developed a technique for turning out a complete ship every four days, the famous Liberty Ships. □ New government alphabet agencies appeared—the WPB (War Production Board), OWI (Office of War Information), WMP (War Manpower Commission). □ The French liner *Normandie,* being refitted as a troop transport in New York, burned at her pier, possibly the victim of saboteurs; she lay there, at a sharp list, throughout the war. □ Rationing went into effect—food, clothing, gasoline—all under the OPA (Office of Price Administration). Americans began figuring costs of food in ration stamps instead of dollars. Rents, wages, and prices were frozen. □ Air-raid sirens were installed in U.S. cities and blackout rehearsals began. ☐ Father Coughlin's weekly publication, *Social Justice*, increasingly anti-Semitic, was banned from the mails. ☐ World War I aviation ace Capt. Eddie Rickenbacker and seven men, whose plane had been forced down in the Pacific, were found by a rescue crew after drifting twenty-three days on a life raft.

SPORTS Joe Louis knocked out challenger Buddy Baer in one round, later disposed of Abe Simon in six, then went off to join the army.

ARTS AND ENTERTAINMENT Film star Carole Lombard was killed in an air crash while on a bond-selling tour. Twenty-two percent of Hollywood's movie population was in the armed forces and new leading men emerged to see the movies through the war. The comedy team of Abbott and Costello was a smash in movies. So were the singing Andrews Sisters. ☐ New York radio station WNEW listed the big bands, in order of popularity, as Harry James, Glenn Miller, Tommy Dorsey, Jimmy Dorsey, Vaughn Monroe, Benny Goodman, Woody Herman, Kay Kyser, Charlie Spivak, Sammy Kaye. Well down on the list came Count Basie and Artie Shaw. RCA Victor originated the Gold Disc for superselling phonograph records, presenting the first to Glenn Miller for "Chattanooga Choo Choo." ☐ Composer Aaron Copland wrote *Lincoln Portrait*. ☐ An important new literary figure appeared in France when Albert Camus published *The Stranger*. ☐ Columnists Drew Pearson and Robert Allen, who wrote the popular "Washington Merry-Go-Round" column, were lured from the Washington *Times Herald*, where they each earned $35 weekly, to the *Washington Post*, with an offer of $100 a week. ☐ The Armed Forces Radio Network was started by GIs in Alaska, who built a radio station to kill time, then wrote Hollywood stars asking them to record messages. In a year, there were 306 stations in forty-seven countries.

 **1943**   "The Jewish residential district no longer exists."
—*Report to Himmler on the liquidation of the Warsaw ghetto by* ss GEN. JUERGEN STROOP

FOUNDED   The Pulitzer Prize for music, won by William Schuman; the American Broadcasting Co., formerly NBC's Blue Network; *Esquire* magazine's Jazz Poll, won by Louis Armstrong

INTRODUCED   Postal zoning in 178 American cities; pay-as-you-go income tax (payroll deductions); streptomycin; The Pentagon, the world's largest office building; gremlins, destructive imps who played havoc with air force planes and war-plant production

SONGS   "Pistol Packin' Mama" "People Will Say We're in Love" "Mairzy Doats" "Comin' in on a Wing and a Prayer" "Do Nothin' Till You Hear from Me" "Oh, What a Beautiful Mornin'" "One for My Baby" "Surrey with the Fringe on Top" "As Time Goes By"

FASHION   Claire McCardell, now credited with creating the first American look for women, showed halter dresses with little boleros, bloomer playsuits, and ballet slippers for street wear.   Attention was on a noisy, short-lived young men's style, the zoot suit with the reet pleat. Zoot Suiters favored long, single-button jackets, full-legged trousers that narrowed at the ankle, long chains, and broad-brimmed fedoras.

THE WORLD   Allied forces finally secured Guadalcanal in January. The Pacific balance was turning as U.S. forces landed in New Guinea and twenty-two ships of a Japanese convoy were destroyed in the Battle of the Bismarck Sea. □ The British and American armies linked up in Africa and drove the Axis powers from that continent. Early in July, U.S., British, and Canadian forces invaded Sicily and proceeded North. Italy's Premier Benito Mussolini resigned, escaping to the German lines. Heavy Allied fighting with German forces continued in Italy, which declared war on its former ally. □ On the Eastern Front, the Germans were experiencing a rerun of the Napoleonic wars.

The USSR had retaken two-thirds of the territory lost to the Germans; facing a Russian winter without warm clothes and with inadequate arms, the German army at Stalingrad was destroyed and the army of General von Paulus collapsed. Hundreds of thousands of Germans were taken prisoner. ☐ Jews in the Warsaw ghetto were massacred. ☐ Germany continued to bomb London; the Allies retaliated with heavy raids on Berlin and the industrial Ruhr. German women were conscripted.

THE UNITED STATES The federal government was spending money at five times the rate it had spent during World War I. Many women filled jobs abandoned by men in the war factories; others enlisted in the WACS, WAVES, SPARS, and the air force auxiliary, the WASPS. ☐ Recycling of materials was at full tilt as Boy Scouts and Girl Scouts collected waste paper, aluminum foil, and tin cans which civilians carefully saved. Hoarders of food, tires, shoes, and other items in short supply ranked second to Nazis and Japanese as villains. ☐ Bond rallies helped raise money for the war. At one bond auction in New York, Jefferson's Bible and Jack Benny's violin were among the items up for bid, the latter going for one million dollars. ☐ The huge migration into Northern factories of Southern blacks created tensions that erupted in race riots in Detroit and New York. ☐ The FBI again rode high, this time as the nemesis of spies instead of gangsters. Among its triumphs was the capture of Nazi spies and saboteurs who landed on Long Island and near Jacksonville, Florida. ☐ The Supreme Court, in a case brought by Jehovah's Witnesses, ruled that children need not salute the flag in school if it were against their religion. ☐ An infantile paralysis epidemic killed nearly twelve hundred and crippled thousands more in the United States. Penicillin, although in short supply, was used to combat a number of acute infections at home as well as in the war zones.

ARTS AND ENTERTAINMENT Leonard Bernstein, at 25 assistant conductor of the New York Philharmonic, was called in to replace ailing Bruno Walter and met with instant acclaim. ☐ Skinny, appealing young Frank Sinatra opened at New York's Paramount Theatre, inspired frenzied outbursts, screaming, and fainting among teenage "bobby soxers." ☐ Big musicals and

113

patriotic dramas dominated films. Topical war-news books became bestsellers; so did former presidential candidate Wendell Willkie's *One World*, written after FDR had sent him on a round-the-world trip. □ Jackson Pollack had his first one-man show, in New York. □ A Pan American Clipper, carrying entertainers to perform for GIs, crashed in Lisbon's Tagus River with the loss of twenty-four lives, including singer Tamara; radio singer Jane Froman was among the survivors. Actor Leslie Howard, flying from Lisbon to London, died in a plane shot down by the Germans over the Bay of Biscay. □ Charlie Chaplin, 54, married Eugene O'Neill's 18-year-old daughter, Oona; it was generally agreed the marriage would not last. Earlier he was sued for child support in a paternity suit brought by Hollywood starlet Joan Barry; although blood tests indicated that Chaplin could not be the father, a jury decided that he was. Chaplin's lawyer, Jerry Geisler, answering a charge that Charlie had taken Miss Barry to New York, said that would have been unnecessary, since he could have engaged in sex with her in California "for as little as twenty-five cents and carfare." The scandal, on top of Chaplin's reputed radical politics, finished his U.S. film career. □ The glamour photo of the year was of model Chili Williams posing in a polka-dot two-piece swimsuit. For woman-hungry GIs, however, there was no substitute for the cheesecake shot of the shapely Betty Grable, the pin-up of choice for ships' lockers and barracks walls.

On college campuses, students who would have been swallowing goldfish or dancing at proms a few years before, turned to politics, joining those who were serious about it. It was a risky diversion, there being only four possible positions according to the rules of student politics: Left Wing, Liberal, Trotskyite, or Fascist.

1944

"Nuts!"
—U. S. GEN. MC AULIFFE, *in answer to a German surrender ultimatum when his troops were besieged at Bastogne, Belgium, during the Battle of the Bulge*

FOUNDED The World Bank

INTRODUCED The ranks of five-star general and admiral, four having previously been tops; the G.I. Bill of Rights, a broad educational and financial aid program for veterans; synthetic quinine; the German V-2, the first ballistic missile to be used in warfare; Kilroy

SONGS "Rum and Coca-Cola" "Ac-cent-tchu-ate the Positive" "Besame Mucho" "Don't Fence Me In" "Swinging on a Star" "Bell Bottom Trousers" "Trolley Song" "Long Ago and Far Away" "Spring Will Be a Little Late" "I'll Be Around"

NEW WORD "Gobbledygook," coined by Texas Representative Maury Maverick to characterize the involved rhetoric of government reports

FASHION Rayon was the fabric of blouses and hose, with silk and nylon assigned to military use. Women turned to leg makeup, smelly but inexpensive, using eyebrow pencil to draw a simulated seam up the back of the leg. *Life* ran a photo of Wellesley students in jeans, with the tails of white shirts hanging over them; many readers were outraged.

THE WORLD The air war in Europe grew fiercer as the Allies began daylight bombing of the Continent, the RAF bombed Berlin, and the Germans loosed the unmanned V-2 rocket on England. □ The long awaited D Day Allied landing on the Continent came on June 6, when Allied forces hit the Normandy beaches with Gen. Dwight D. Eisenhower as Supreme Commander. They moved on into southern France, then broke through the German's defensive Siegfried Line. Paris was liberated on August 25; General de Gaulle and Allied troops entered the city. □ The final German offensive came in December, in what became known as the Battle of the Bulge. General

115

Patton's Third Army rescued beseiged American troops and the drive was stopped just before the year's end. To the East, the Russians took Minsk and 100,000 Germans, crossed into Poland, and invaded Yugoslavia. □ An attempt to assassinate Hitler failed in July; the conspirators, a group of generals and high officials, were executed. Field Marshal Rommel, the Desert Fox, was implicated and given a choice by Hitler of trial or suicide; he chose the latter. □ In the Pacific, Americans retook the Solomon Islands, landed in New Guinea, and returned to the Philippines; the Battle for Leyte Gulf in the Philippines in late October remains the greatest naval action ever fought and is remembered for the enormous losses (sixty-eight Japanese ships, twenty-one U.S. ships) and the Japanese kamikaze pilots.

THE UNITED STATES   Representatives of the Allied nations met at Bretton Woods, New Hampshire, and established the World Bank, which went into operation in June 1946. The framework for the United Nations was established during a conference of delegates from the United States, Britain, the Soviet Union, and China at Dumbarton Oaks near Washington. □ FDR was elected for a fourth term, running with Harry S. Truman as the vice presidential candidate and handily defeating Republican Thomas E. Dewey. □ Montgomery Ward chairman Sewell Avery, refusing to comply with a court order to recognize a striking union or to budge from his office, was carried, chair and all, from the premises when the plant was seized by the government. □ With most popular brand cigarettes allocated to the armed forces, Americans smoked some odd tobacco, packaged under such names as Spuds and Rameses. Driving could be hazardous, provided enough ration stamps were available for gas; cars, all prewar models, were showing their age, and tires, subjected to repeated retreading, tended to blow out for no apparent reason. The national speed limit was 45 mph. □ The worst circus fire in history occurred when the nonfireproofed canvas tent of the Ringling Brothers and Barnum and Bailey Circus caught fire during a performance in Hartford, Connecticut. The fire and resulting panic took 163 lives and injured 261.

ARTS AND ENTERTAINMENT   Band leader Glenn Miller, who had organized a band for the armed forces, was killed on a flight from England to France. ☐ Martha Graham presented *Appalachian Spring*, to a score by Aaron Copland. ☐ Newspaper comic strips were as popular as ever but the wriest laughter was for the war cartoons of Bill Mauldin, with his weary GIs, Willie and Joe, and for George Baker's stumblebum private, Sad Sack. ☐ Abstractionist painter Piet Mondrian died; the last of his geometric works was *Broadway Boogie*. ☐ Overseas and on the home front, drawings showed up on the sides of buildings, in latrines, on billboards, sidewalks, fences—wherever a GI set foot: a bald head, startled eyes, and long nose peering over a fence, accompanied by the mysterious legend that seemed to make sense to everyone—"Kilroy was here."

☐ **1945** "I am a soldier and I'm sure no one thinks of me as a politician."
—GEN. DWIGHT D. EISENHOWER *on his return from Europe*

FOUNDED The United Nations; independent Vietnamese republic; *Seventeen*, the first magazine to recognize teenagers as a lucrative market

INTRODUCED The atom bomb; fluoride, first used in the municipal water supply of Grand Rapids, Michigan; 45 rpm records; ballpoint pens (they could write under water), at $25 each, then duplicated by Macy's, New York, at the bargain price of $11; the first glass-dome railroad car

SONGS "Laura" "June Is Bustin' Out All Over" "It Might as Well Be Spring" "If I Loved You" "On the Atchison, Topeka and Santa Fe" "These Foolish Things" "Personality" "Symphony"

FASHION Teenage girls, who used to wear children's clothes until they were old enough to switch to grownup fashions, now had styles of their own. One manufacturer who moved into the market early sold 8 million teen garments during 1945.

THE WORLD In February, Roosevelt, Churchill, and

Stalin met at Yalta, in the Crimea, to settle the Polish question, plan for Germany's unconditional surrender, and arrange for the first United Nations conference. □ While Eisenhower's forces moved in on Germany from the west, the Russian army was moving in on a wide eastern front. By April 25, Berlin was completely surrounded by the Russians, Eisenhower having stopped his forces fifty-five miles short of that city. The war in Italy ended April 29 and the German surrender came on May 7. Hitler is believed to have committed suicide in his Berlin bunker; Goebbels and his wife poisoned their six children before killing themselves. □ On April 12, less than a month before V-E Day, President Roosevelt died of a cerebral hemorrhage and Harry S. Truman became president. Truman, Churchill, and Stalin met for the Potsdam Conference in July. But on July 25, in a huge Labor landslide, Churchill was out of office and a new Prime Minister, Clement Atlee, replaced him at Potsdam. □ The United Nations Conference on International Organization opened on April 25 in San Francisco, with forty-six nations present. Selected as UN Secretary General for the conference was Alger Hiss. □ In the Pacific war, following heavy conventional bombing of Japan's chief cities, an American B-29 released the first atomic bomb on the city of Hiroshima on August 6, killing or maiming half the city's population; three days later, a second bomb was dropped on Nagasaki, killing approximately forty thousand. Japan substantially surrendered on August 14; the formal surrender came on September 2, aboard the battleship *Missouri*. □ General MacArthur was assigned the task of occupying Japan and rehabilitating the Japanese. General Tojo attempted suicide but failed; he and five other former high Japanese officials were found guilty of war crimes and executed. □ The World Zionist Congress demanded the admission of one million Jews into Palestine. The Arab League—Egypt, Syria, Iraq, Saudi Arabia, Jordan, Yemen, and Lebanon—was formed to oppose the creation of a Jewish state.

THE UNITED STATES Americans went through a schizophrenic year—deep mourning for FDR, the only president many young adults had known; then the hysterical celebration of V-E Day, when strangers embraced and wept with joy; then the stunned reaction to the A-bomb, which few understood beyond the fact that the tiny atom had been split and the population of a major city had been decimated; then the exhausted realization, with the Japanese surrender, that the war was over. □ A U.S. Army bomber crashed into the Empire State Building in New York, killing thirteen. □ The country returned to Standard Time, after the Daylight Time of the war. The Stage Door Canteen on Broadway in New York closed, after having entertained 3,200,000 servicemen. □ The Surplus Property Board, custodian of war supplies no longer needed, announced the availability of 10 million pounds of contraceptive jelly, just one item among $90 billion worth of leftover goods to be disposed of on the civilian market. □ Rationing of tires, meat, and butter ended in November. Price controls remained.

ARTS AND ENTERTAINMENT Pianist Vladimir Horowitz made a rare contribution to the war effort—a piano transcription of "The Stars and Stripes Forever" in which he sounded like Sousa's entire band, piccolo and all. The memory of the performance lingers on, along with recordings, but Horowitz stopped performing it when the war ended. □ The combination of the war, the increased use of recordings instead of live music on radio, and a tax on dance floors brought the era of the big bands and, for many years, ballroom dancing, to an end. □ Ernie Pyle, popular war correspondent, was killed by a Japanese sniper while observing the U.S. landing on Okinawa. □ Dutch painter Hans van Meegeren, accused of collaborating with the Nazis for selling rare masterpieces of Dutch painter Jan Vermeer to Hermann Göring, revealed that he had painted the Old Masters himself, grinding his own properly aged paints. He proved his claim by painting an "original" Vermeer in prison, was tried for forgery instead of treason, sentenced to a year in prison but died before he could serve the time.

☐ 1946

"Wanted, Congressman candidate with no previous political experience to defeat a man who has represented the district in the House for 10 years. Any young man, resident of the district, preferably a veteran, fair education, may apply for the job."
—*Advertisement run by a local California Republican group and answered by Richard M. Nixon*

FOUNDED The Atomic Energy Commission

INTRODUCED The Kaiser and Frazer cars; the seven-passenger Jeep station wagon; synthesized cortisone; strapless wired bras; electric clothes dryers; electric blankets; automatic transmission for automobiles

SONGS "There's No Business Like Show Business" "Zip-a-Dee-Doo-Dah" "La Vie en Rose" "I Don't Know Enough About You" "How Are Things in Glocca Morra?" "They Say It's Wonderful" "Come Rain or Come Shine" "The Girl That I Marry" "Shoofly Pie and Apple Pan Dowdy"

FASHION Women's suits featured jackets with peplums, wide lapels, and slim skirts to a bit below the knee. Shoes had sling backs or were little-girl-like with ankle straps. Short "topper" coats were flared, thigh length. On college campuses, coeds wore neat black flats as replacements for saddle shoes; sweaters were tucked into narrow, knee-length skirts. Each young college man had a tuxedo. Men found the crew cuts they had worn in the services comfortable and easy and they became the standard civilian style.

THE WORLD Englishman William Joyce, who had broadcast from Germany to England during the war as "Lord Haw Haw," was tried and hanged for treason. In Nuremberg, Germany, high Nazi officials were brought before the International Military Tribunal for war crimes and crimes against humanity. Ten, including Göring and von Ribbentrop, were condemned to death (Göring killed himself two hours before the scheduled execution); Hess and Funk received life sentences. ☐ The

League of Nations disbanded and assigned its assets to the new United Nations, which met in New York. A Norwegian, Trygve Lie, was elected the first Permanent Secretary General. ☐ East Germany's Social Democrats merged with the Communists. ☐ In Japan, power was transferred from the Emperor to an elected assembly; General MacArthur ordered a purge of extreme nationalists. ☐ The strain in East-West relations was already being felt when Winston Churchill, speaking in Fulton, Missouri, described the wall of secrecy behind which the Soviet government operated: "From Stettin in the Baltic to Trieste in the Atlantic, an iron curtain has descended across the continent." ☐ The Philippine Islands became self-governing, independent of the United States.

THE UNITED STATES Housing, which had been at a standstill during the war, was at a premium as veterans married and the baby boom started. Alert builders began constructing homes in batches—developments—concentrating on economical, small houses that could be expanded to fit growing families and incomes. The ranch house, with expansion attic, became standard. ☐ It was a year of strikes—coal miners, railroad engineers, and trainmen, truck drivers, licensed seamen—and by year's end, some 14,600,000 workers lost 108 million workdays in strikes. President Truman seized the mines, then ended the threatened rail strike by seizing the railroads. ☐ The atom bomb was tested on Bikini Atoll, whose some three hundred inhabitants were resettled on other islets. For some reason, the tiny island gave its name to a scanty French swimsuit fashion, whose designer felt that the frivolous garment and the horrendous bomb shared his "concept of the ultimate." ☐ Among war veterans who decided to enter politics, two of those to succeed on the first try were California Republican Richard M. Nixon, who defeated liberal Democrat Jerry Voorhis, whom he called "a friend of the Communists," and Massachusetts Democrat John F. Kennedy. ☐ Earl Browder was ousted as national chairman of the Communist Party, succeeded by the more militant William Z. Foster. ☐ The Supreme Court ruled that "Jim Crow" segregation of blacks on interstate busses was unconstitutional. In July, in accordance with a 1944 Court ruling, blacks voted in Mississippi's Democratic primaries for the first time. ☐ John D. Rockefeller, Jr., presented to the United Nations a six-block area along the East River, above 42nd Street in New York City, as a site for its headquarters.

SPORTS The Brooklyn and Cincinnati National League teams played a nineteen-inning scoreless baseball game at Ebbets Field, Brooklyn, called because of darkness after four hours, forty minutes.

ARTS AND ENTERTAINMENT Sales of phonograph records soared, with companies selling 78 rpm discs at a rate ten times that of 1936. American Federation of Musicians president James C. Petrillo tried to force radio stations to replace records with live music so that more instrumentalists would be employed. He failed when Congress passed legislation stopping his move. ☐ *The New Yorker* devoted a full issue, for the first time, to a single report: John Hersey's *Hiroshima*. Albert Einstein ordered a thousand copies. ☐ The Salzburg music festival resumed in Europe. ☐ Pablo Picasso began working in pottery at Vallauris. ☐ A New York judge ruled Edmund Wilson's *Memoirs of Hecate County* obscene. When the Supreme Court failed to reverse the decision, the book could not be bought anywhere. ☐ W. C. Fields, who hated Christmas as well as dogs and children, died on Christmas Day. ☐ Pierre Balmain opened his own couture house in Paris, inviting Gertrude Stein and Alice B. Toklas, for whom he had made nice warm suits while he was still with Lucien Lelong. At the opening, Stein whispered to Toklas, "We are the only people here wearing Balmain clothes but we must never let anybody know, for we are not great advertisements for the world of fashion." ☐ Also not great advertisements for the world of fashion were the tubular wool jersey dresses women were running up for themselves. They took no sewing skill; a dress length of jersey was hemmed at one end, slit at the sides at the other to make armholes, then sewn at the top, leaving room for a head to go through, of course.

 **1947**

"Groucho Marx is prettier, Sonny Tufts is a more gifted actor, Connie Mack a better rassler, and the Princeton Triangle Club has far superior female impersonators."
—*Sports writer* RED SMITH *on Gorgeous George, the TV wrestler with peroxided, marcelled hair and mincing act*

FOUNDED The U.S. Department of Defense, unifying the army and navy commands; The U.S. Air Force as an independent service; Americans for Democratic Action

INTRODUCED Blacks in major league baseball, with the signing of Jackie Robinson by the Brooklyn Dodgers; Edwin Land's one-shot Polaroid self-developing camera; tubeless automobile tires; the Douglas DC-6 airplane; wraparound car windows, on the Studebaker; credit cards for railroad and airplane travel

SONGS "Tenderly" "Almost Like Being in Love" "Come to the Mardi Gras" "Ballerina" "Open the Door, Richard" "There But for You Go I" "Too Fat Polka" "Managua, Nicaragua" "Old Devil Moon"

FASHION Paris designer Christian Dior introduced the New Look, the most dramatic fashion change in years—full skirts reaching to below the calf, bosoms and hips emphasized, waists small, with waist-nipping foundation garments for those who couldn't make it naturally. Women howled with fury, asserting they were not about to throw out perfectly good wardrobes. Within weeks they had done so, happy to toss aside practical wartime carryovers in favor of feminine, fabric-wasting, swoopy fashions. Within a few weeks after the Dior showing, American manufacturers had sold a million dresses copied from the Dior originals.

THE WORLD Arabs and Jews rejected a British proposal for dividing Palestine into Arab and Jewish zones to be administered by a trusteeship. The UN later announced a Palestinian partition plan, with Jerusalem under UN trusteeship. ☐ Gen. George C. Marshall called for a European Recovery Program which became known as the Marshall Plan. ☐ England's Prin-

123

cess Elizabeth married Philip Mountbatten. ☐ India became an independent nation, no longer a British colony, and was partitioned into India and Pakistan.

THE UNITED STATES   President Truman appointed Gen. George C. Marshall as secretary of state, to succeed James F. Byrnes. ☐ General concern over the spread of Communist ideology was reflected in President Truman's order to examine the loyalty of all government employees. The House Investigating Committee on Un-American Activities—the Dies Committee—claimed to have collected a file of a million "fellow travelers, liberals, dupes, Communists." ☐ Congress overrode President Truman's veto of the Taft-Hartley Labor Act. ☐ A "Friendship Train" toured the country, collecting some two hundred carloads of food for the displaced persons in war-devastated Europe. ☐ For the first time, people reported seeing strange flying objects. A U.S. army recruiting ad showed an artist's rendition of a rocket-driven vehicle, not yet built, that was expected to journey as much as 200,000 feet above the earth, reaching speeds as high as 1,700 mph ☐ General Electric Co. used dry ice to seed cumulus clouds in New Hampshire and succeeded in producing rain. ☐ Jukeboxes were a flourishing industry; 80 million of them consumed five billion nickels a year. Magazines were flourishing, too; thirty-eight of them had circulations of more than a million. ☐ Arrow shirts cost $3.25 to $4.75; an imported briar pipe, $3.50 to $15; a Telechron electric alarm clock was $4.50 to $6.50; Smith Brothers' Cough Drops, 5¢; and a fedora by Adam Hats $7.50 for "the man who can pay $12 for a hat." ☐ Perle Mesta, a plump widow backed by an Oklahoma oil fortune, was Washington's outstanding hostess, managing to hook the biggest fish in Washington's social and political swim through the simple device of giving wonderful parties. ☐ Henry Ford died, leaving $600 million.

SPORTS   At Yankee Stadium, "the House that Ruth Built," nearly sixty thousand fans saluted the ailing Babe at special ceremonies. ☐ Jack Kramer dominated men's tennis, winning at Wimbledon and Forest Hills and leading the American Davis Cup team to victory over the Australians. ☐ Babe Didrikson

Zaharias became the first American to win the British women's amateur golf championship.

ARTS AND ENTERTAINMENT Maria Callas made her operatic debut in Verona and became an instant star. Margaret Truman made her singing debut with the Detroit Symphony. ☐ Cellist Pablo Casals vowed not to play in public as long as Franco remained in power in his native Spain. ☐ In jazz, bebop was the new sound. The flamboyant Dizzy Gillespie and Thelonious Monk who, with Charlie Parker, invented it, caused consternation with off-beat presentation of their basically serious music. ☐ TV was growing, although anyone who owned a set was pretty much guaranteed a steady stream of visiting friends and neighbors. "Meet the Press" moved over from radio and "Howdy Doody" dug in for a long run. The best comedy acts were the wrestling matches. A World Series game was telecast to Washington, Philadelphia, New York, and Schenectady. ☐ A new genre of mystery novel appeared with *I, the Jury*, Mickey Spillane's brutal and somewhat incredible first book.

A Bedouin boy named Muhammed the Wolf, seeking a goat that had strayed, found a cave in a cliff on the western shore of the Dead Sea and, in the cave, what became known as the Dead Sea Scrolls, dating from 22 B.C. to A.D. 100. ☐ Thor Heyerdahl set sail to Polynesia from Peru on a balsa raft to test his theory of prehistoric immigration.

□ 1948

> "I want to say to you at this time that during the next four years there will be a Democrat in the White House and you're looking at him."
> —PRES. HARRY S. TRUMAN, *on a whistle-stop campaign tour*

> "It defies all common sense to send that roughneck, ward politician back to the White House."
> —REPUBLICAN SENATOR ROBERT A. TAFT *on Truman's November victory*

INTRODUCED Supersonic rocket planes; LP phonograph records; transistors; aureomycin and chloromycin; fitted bed sheets; Velcro; the double-decked Boeing Stratocruiser plane; wraparound bumpers for cars

SONGS "Nature Boy" "Buttons and Bows" "So in Love with Love" "It's So Peaceful in the Country" "My Darling, My Darling" "On a Slow Boat to China" "All I Want for Christmas Is My Two Front Teeth"

FASHION The New Look was firmly established but somewhat modified; skirts were a bit shorter, waistlines less pinched. Another look entirely came with big dolman sleeves, called batwings.

THE WORLD The Cold War deepened. Tito's Yugoslavia was expelled from the World Communist Organization. The USSR, taking advantage of Berlin's isolation within the Soviet zone, cut off roads and railways to the city, which was under joint Soviet, British, U.S., and French rule. The Western Powers organized an airlift, which operated from June 1948 to May 1949, using an average of a thousand planes a day to shuttle in supplies. □ Korea divided, with the Republic of Korea in the south choosing Syngman Rhee as its president. The Communists in the north formed the Korean People's Republic and claimed authority over the entire country. □ Mahatma Gandhi, apostle of nonviolence, died in India from an assassin's bullet. □ Israel became a state, with Chaim Weizmann as president and David Ben-Gurion as premier.

THE UNITED STATES   Anti-Communism was in the air. William Z. Foster, national chairman of the Communist Party, and eleven other party leaders were indicted for conspiring to overthrow the government. Foster's case was dropped when he became ill; the others were convicted in 1949 and sentenced to prison terms. ☐ The House Un-American Activities Committee reported finding microfilm copies of important documents in a pumpkin on the farm of Whittaker Chambers, who had already accused former State Department official Alger Hiss of giving the documents to him. ☐ The Senate appropriated additional funds for "Voice of America" broadcasts to combat anti-American broadcasts from the Soviet Union. ☐ Defying the pollsters, Harry S. Truman defeated the shoo-in candidate, Thomas E. Dewey, to the surprise of everyone but the feisty president. He won despite the defection of Democratic votes to States Rights Party candidate Strom Thurmond, the Progressive Party's Henry A. Wallace, and the perennial Socialist candidate, Norman Thomas. ☐ Two jet-propelled P-80 Air Force planes covered the distance from New York to Washington in 27 minutes; the same flight had taken 194 minutes in 1918, when airmail service was introduced. In New Mexico, test rocket missiles reached 78 miles above the earth, hitting 3,000 mph. ☐ The cost of living rose. Rent control was extended for an additional year. For the first time a cost-of-living increase was written into a contract in a settlement between the UAW and General Motors. ☐ Congress enacted legislation to admit 205,000 European refugees within the following two years and passed the Foreign Assistance Act, setting up the Marshall Plan, with a fund of over $6 billion to rehabilitate Europe and China.

SPORTS   The horse of the year was Citation; he won the Triple Crown, with Eddie Arcaro up, then galloped unchallenged through the Pimlico Special as the only horse in the race. ☐ Bob Mathias won the decathlon at the summer Olympics and Dick Button, the men's figure skating gold medal at the winter games. ☐ The Army-Navy football game ended in a 21–21 tie.

ARTS AND ENTERTAINMENT   1948 is generally accepted as marking complete public acceptance of television.

127

There were four networks—CBS, NBC, ABC, and Dumont Television. During the year twenty-five new stations started up and 140,000 sets a month were being produced. Coaxial cables linked stations across much of the country. TV's first major star was Milton Berle; everyone tuned in to Uncle Miltie on Tuesdays.
□ RCA's answer to Columbia's 33 rpm LP records were its 45 rpm entries, made with a large hole in the middle and still playing only four minutes per side. Irving Kolodin thought the idea was "as if someone had perfected the automobile hand crank."
□ In publishing, paperback books were gaining strength; 135 million were sold during the year.

Newspapers and magazines were filled with advance publicity on the remarkable new rear-engine Tucker automobile, whose prototype model was the most photographed automobile since the Model T. The four-door, six-passenger Tucker was to retail for $1,000. Only fifty of the cars were ever built.

1949

"There is only one thing worse than one nation having the atomic bomb; that's two nations having it."
—HAROLD C. UREY, *Nobel Prize chemist*

FOUNDED The Department of Welfare and Education, with a Cabinet post to go with it

INTRODUCED Cortisone for treatment of arthritis; Minute Rice; a hardtop with a convertible look, introduced by Buick

SONGS "Some Enchanted Evening" "Why Can't You Behave" "Mule Train" "Rudolph, the Red-Nosed Reindeer" "Younger than Springtime" "It's a Big, Wide, Wonderful World" "Baby, It's Cold Outside" "Riders in the Sky"

FAD Pyramid clubs

PASTIME Canasta, again popular

FASHION Women were making their own—full-circle felt skirts, made by cutting a waist-sized hole in the center of a table-sized piece of felt, adding a waistband and zipper. Also popular: the gamine haircut; mother-daughter dresses, usually trimmed with lace and rick-rack; Poses (pronounced pose-ease), tiny, adhesive-backed breast covers worn with a prayer.

THE WORLD The Chinese Communists emerged the victors in the civil war and took power; Mao Tse-tung was chairman; Chou En-lai, premier. Chiang Kai-shek and the Nationalist government fled to Formosa (Taiwan). ☐ Israel was admitted to the UN. ☐ The USSR exploded its first atomic bomb. ☐ After some 227,000 airlift flights, East Germany lifted the Berlin blockade. ☐ Siam changed its name to Thailand.

THE UNITED STATES Russian expansionism was feared. Eleven leaders of the American Communist Party were convicted and jailed for advocating the overthrow of the U.S. government by force. Alger Hiss, former State Department official, went on trial for perjury after denying the testimony of Whittaker Chambers that linked him to Communist activities. The Hiss case provided the first major press exposure for California Representative Richard M. Nixon. ☐ Ordinary people started being psychoanalyzed. ☐ Inflation was serious and the minimum wage was raised from 40¢ to 75¢ an hour. Vowing to whip inflation, President Truman attacked "the six-cent nickel candy bar." An average two-bedroom house cost $10,000, a gallon of gas 25¢, a quart of milk 25¢, a Cadillac $5,000. A steelworker earned $3,000 a year, a dentist $10,000, a high school teacher $4,700. ☐ Following his inauguration, President Truman presented a program of legislation he called the "Fair Deal." ☐ Aviator William P. Odom flew nonstop, solo, from Honolulu to Teterboro, New Jersey, 5,300 miles, in thirty-six hours. A few months later, after establishing a new speed record at the air races in Cleveland, he was killed when his plane crashed into a house in Berea, Ohio. A Pan American double-decker Stratocruiser set a New York–London record of nine hours, sixteen minutes. ☐ Tokyo Rose, American-born Iva Toguri D'Acquino, who had broadcast popular music, alluring chatter, and Japanese propaganda to American troops during the war, was convicted of treason, sentenced to ten years in prison. Axis Sally, Mildred E. Gillars, who had broadcast to GIs in Europe from Germany, was sentenced to ten to thirty years. ☐ Atlantic City's

Million Dollar Pier was almost destroyed by fire. ☐ The weather was awful: 290 tornadoes hit the country; blizzards in the West stranded livestock; floods hit New England, New Jersey, and New York; temperatures that fell to 14 degrees in Southern California destroyed a fifth of the citrus crop. ☐ Religion made a comeback. Billy Graham burst upon the scene, drawing 300,000 people to his Los Angeles crusade and converting 6,000. Norman Vincent Peale's *A Guide to Confident Living*, Fulton J. Sheen's *Peace of Soul*, and Fulton Oursler's *The Greatest Story Ever Told* all made the bestseller list. ☐ Pyramid clubs shook the social scene. An in-person substitute for outlawed chain letters, they called for "members" to pay a dollar to attend a coffee-and-doughnut party, then attend a second, bringing two recruits. In theory, after twelve days the pot to a member, who would have given one party in the process, would be $2,048. The clubs folded because of decreasing mathematical probability, but before they died, friendships and marriages were made, people had invited their bus drivers and bosses to gatherings in order to meet their quotas, and lonely souls who hadn't been to a party in years had been dragged into a glorious social whirl. ☐ A steel strike involving 500,000 workers was settled when the companies agreed to worker's pension demands.

SPORTS The New York Yankees won the World Series under first-year manager Casey Stengel. ☐ Joe Louis retired, undefeated, as heavyweight champion; Ezzard Charles defeated Joe Walcott, Gus Lesnevich, and Pat Valentino to become the new champion.

ARTS AND ENTERTAINMENT Model Robin Roberts brought suit against Humphrey Bogart for tearing a giant stuffed panda out of her hands at the El Morocco nightclub. Bogie said the panda was his; she said he had given it to her; the case was dismissed. Ingrid Bergman filed for divorce from her husband, Dr. Peter Lindstrom, having found romance with Italian film director Roberto Rossellini; her unconventional behavior, including premarital pregnancy, scandalized Hollywood, which ostracized her. ☐ A widely criticized Cultural and Scientific Conference for World Peace was held at the Waldorf-Astoria Hotel in New York, with Soviet and American creative people coming together, among them Dmitri Shostakovich, Norman Mailer, Arthur Miller. ☐ Cool jazz, a progression from bebop, started with the recordings of a group led by Miles Davis. The word "cool" quickly came to mean sophisticated, good, and a bit stand-offish. ☐ Victoria de los Angeles made her New York singing debut. Britain's Sadler's Wells Ballet made its first U.S. visit, with the dazzling young Margot Fonteyn. Margaret Truman made her Washington debut, singing with the National Symphony Orchestra; *Washington Post* critic Paul Hume found Miss Truman "still too much of a vocal beginner to appear in public." ☐ The musical *South Pacific* opened with a million-dollar advance sale and Arthur Miller's *Death of a Salesman* with a $600 advance at its Philadelphia tryout; both were smash hits. ☐ President Truman's inauguration was the first to be televised. There were a million TV sets in the country. Faye Emerson's low necklines were one of the features being watched. ☐ On Christmas Eve, Dick Tracy and Tess Trueheart finally said "I do."

☐ 1950

"I have in my hand a list of two hundred and five names that were known to the Secretary of State as being members of the Communist Party and who are nevertheless still working and shaping the policy in the State Department."
—SEN. JOSEPH MC CARTHY, *speaking before a Republican Women's Club in Wheeling, West Virginia*

FOUNDED The National Council of Churches, with 32 million members

INTRODUCED Antihistamines; the Diner's Club credit card for use in restaurants; Miltown, the first popular tranquillizer; Xerox copying; Orlon

SONGS "From This Moment On" "If I Were a Bell" "Music! Music! Music!" "Tennessee Waltz" "I've Never Been in Love Before" "It's So Nice to Have a Man Around the

House" "It's a Lovely Day Today" "Tzena, Tzena, Tzena" "Chattanoogie Shoe Shine Boy" "C'est Si Bon" "Goodnight, Irene"

FASHION Serious-minded suits with easy skirts to calf-length were basic wardrobe items. Bonnie Cashin introduced a layered look of mix-and-match separates for the adventuresome. Carefully cut slacks were worn for sportswear but not street wear. Ballet shoes were favorites of young women. For men, the suburban coat—half coat, half jacket—was new.

THE WORLD War began between North and South Korea. The UN Security Council, with the Soviet delegation absent, approved armed intervention on the side of the South. General MacArthur was named commander of the UN forces. Seoul was taken by North Korea, retaken by UN forces and, with a powerful assist from American warships and planes, the North Koreans were pushed back to the 38th Parallel. China threw in 850,000 volunteers. ☐ Great Britain recognized Israel and the People's Republic of China. Jawaharlal Nehru became India's first prime minister. ☐ The Roman Catholic Church marked Holy Year and pilgrims descended on Rome in what became the first big tourist year since the war.

THE UNITED STATES Following the start of the Korean War, President Truman was granted emergency powers, and sixty-two thousand reservists were called up for active duty. ☐ Red fever was rampant. When a short circuit stalled a New York subway train, 1,000 passengers stampeded, many of them shouting, "The Russians!" FBI director J. Edgar Hoover claimed there were 55,000 Communists and 500,000 fellow travellers in the country. Rep. Richard Nixon asserted that "traitors in the high councils in our own government have made sure that the deck is stacked on the Soviet side." ☐ Alger Hiss was found guilty of perjury in his second trial, sentenced to five years in prison. The Senate appointed a special committee to investigate Senator McCarthy's charges that Communists had infiltrated the government. Political cartoonist Herblock coined the word "McCarthyism," using it as a label on a barrel of tar. ☐ Over President Truman's veto, Congress passed the Internal Security Act, compelling "Communists and totalitarians" to register with the

Department of Justice and denying them passport privileges. ☐ An assassination attempt on President Truman by two Puerto Rican nationalists led him to remark that "a president has to expect these things." ☐ When Truman authorized continued work on the hydrogen bomb, leading physicists protested; Albert Einstein said that "annihilation of any life on earth has been brought within the range of technical possibilities." ☐ Six hundred sightings of strange craft and flying objects were reported by citizens who had seen them with their own eyes; the U.S. Air Force spent $50,000 investigating. ☐ Bandits wearing Halloween masks held up the Boston express office of Brink's, taking $2,775,000, more than a million of it in cash. The bandits kept a low profile for more than six years; then one squealed a week before the statute of limitations expired. ☐ At mid-century, the U.S. population was 150,697,000; 24,300,000 were aged 5 to 14. There were 44 million automobiles, 43 million telephones. During the year American companies sold 250,000 automatic dishwashers, 750,000 garbage disposal units, 1,700,000 washing machines, 6 million gallons of gin, 12 million pounds of aspirin, 750 million pounds of hot dogs, and 2 million bicycles. The average weekly wage in industry was $60.53, an all-time high; 85 percent of farms were electrified. ☐ Less than a year after being reelected mayor of New York City, William O'Dwyer resigned, as news broke of political racketeering, featuring underworld leader Frank Costello. O'Dwyer accepted an appointment as U.S. ambassador to Mexico from President Truman, whom he had loyally supported. ☐ Elizabeth Taylor married for the first time; the groom was Nicky Hilton. Rita Hayworth married Prince Aly Khan, in Monte Carlo.

SPORTS Retired champion Joe Louis attempted a come back but was defeated in a fifteen-round fight by Ezzard Charles. ☐ Connie Mack retired as manager of the Philadelphia Athletics; he had spent sixty-seven years in baseball, fifty of them with the Athletics.

ARTS AND ENTERTAINMENT The Federal Communications Commission resolved a dispute between CBS and RCA, both of which had developed color TV systems, in favor of CBS, whose system was compatible with existing black-and-

133

white sets. □ An exciting new magazine, *Flair,* edited by Fleur Cowles, was filled with such innovations as die cuts, accordian inserts, lift-out sections, and offbeat art; it was a wonder, but lasted only twelve issues, killed by its high production costs. □ Benny Goodman and the NBC Symphony Orchestra premiered a work for clarinet by Aaron Copland. Gian Carlo Menotti's opera *The Consul* opened on Broadway, played 269 performances, and won the Pulitzer Prize. □ The Congressional Redhunt hit the entertainment world with force. Two members of the "Hollywood Ten" started jail terms. The group of movie writers, claiming Fifth Amendment rights, refused to answer questions on their political affiliations before the House Un-American Activities Committee. □ *Washington Post* music critic Paul Hume incurred the wrath of the president when he noted of Margaret Truman's Constitution Hall concert that "she is flat a good deal of the time . . . still cannot sing with anything approaching professional finish." With paternal fury, Truman shot off a letter to Hume, saying he hoped to meet him some day and "when that happens, you'll need a new nose, a lot of beef steak for your black eyes and perhaps a supporter below. Pegler, a guttersnipe, is a gentleman alongside of you." News of the letter leaked out. Miss Truman graciously commented that Mr. Hume had a right to write as he pleased and that she was certain her father wouldn't use such language.

□ **1951**　"I killed more people tonight than I have fingers on my hands and I shot them in cold blood and I enjoyed every minute of it. They were Commies."
—*Mike Hammer,* MICKEY SPILLANE'S *fictional detective, in* One Lonely Night, *which sold 3 million copies*

FOUNDED The first U.S. Reactor Testing Station, generating electricity from atomic energy, in Idaho
INTRODUCED Bank credit cards, by Franklin National

Bank, New York; cross-country direct long-distance dialing; power steering, on Buick and Chrysler cars; commercial color television.

SONGS "Getting to Know You" "Unforgettable" "Too Young" "Come on-a My House" "Love Is the Reason" "Shrimp Boats" "I Talk to the Trees" "On Top of Old Smoky" "Hello, Young Lovers"

FASHION The poodle haircut—short, skull-hugging, and curled, was in. Capezio, which had been making dance shoes for professionals for years, found itself in the fashion business, making colorful versions of ballet shoes for street wear.

THE WORLD Armistice talks failed in Korea. ☐ Winston Churchill formed a new government and became Britain's prime minister for a second time. ☐ The United Nations occupied its permanent headquarters in New York.

THE UNITED STATES The Twenty-Second Amendment to the Constitution, limiting the presidency to two terms, was passed. ☐ Americans sat glued to their television sets as daytime TV got up its first real steam with the airing of the astounding, juicy, sometimes funny testimony before Sen. Estes Kefauver's Committee to Investigate Organized Crime in Interstate Commerce. Underworld character Frank Costello's expressive hands became stars when he refused to permit his face to appear on camera. ☐ England's Princess Elizabeth made her first visit to the United States. ☐ World War II ended officially for the United States with the signing of treaties with Japan and Germany. ☐ Julius and Ethel Rosenberg, accused of supplying atom-bomb secrets to Russia, were sentenced to die by electrocution; they were executed in 1953. Two halves of a Jello box, purportedly used for spy-to-spy identification, were main exhibits. ☐ There were 400,000 pounds of penicillin and 350,000 of streptomycin produced in the United States. ☐ President Truman dismissed Gen. Douglas MacArthur from his post as Commander in Chief of the American Army in Korea for publicly challenging the policies of his civilian superiors. MacArthur advocated bombing and invasion of China. On his arrival home, MacArthur was greeted with wild ticker-tape parades and was invited to address both houses of Congress, to whom he gave his "Old soldiers never die, they just fade away" speech, then retired to private life as president of Sperry-Rand. ☐ Transcontinental television was inaugurated; the first telecast was of the September 4 opening of the Japanese Peace Treaty conference in San Francisco. ☐ Engineers were kings of the job market. "Even the worst student has three job offers," a college counsellor said, remarking on the four thousand corporations that were deploying talent scouts to college campuses. ☐ In California, people started building fallout shelters in their backyards and others around the country followed suit. ☐ American Telephone and Telegraph became the first corporation to have a million shareholders. ☐ Americans bought some 8 million automobiles. ☐ The postwar building boom was at its height. Levittown, named after its builder, sprang up in what had been a potato patch on Long Island; by 1951, it contained 17,447 two-bedroom houses with expansion attics, venetian blinds, washing machines, and two chests of drawers; they sold for $7,990—$90 down, $58 a month to cover purchase and insurance. In Chicago, architect Mies van der Rohe designed Lake Shore Drive Apartments, two twenty-six-story buildings walled entirely in glass.

SPORTS   Joe DiMaggio retired from baseball at the end of the season, with a lifetime batting average of .325. ☐ For the second year in a row, the U.S. tennis team lost the Davis Cup to Australia. ☐ Jersey Joe Walcott was outpointed by Ezzard Charles in March, then gained the heavyweight crown by knocking Charles out in the seventh round in a July return bout.

ARTS AND ENTERTAINMENT   Black singing star Josephine Baker was refused service at Sherman Billingsley's snooty New York Stork Club. Black scholar W. E. B. Du Bois was brought to trial for not registering as a subversive and was acquitted. "A great silence has fallen on the real soul of this nation," he said. Writer Dashiell Hammett was held in contempt and jailed for five months after refusing to provide information concerning former Communist acquaintances. ☐ 190 million phonograph records were sold, 10 percent of them classical. The sale of 120,000 sets of Bach's *Goldberg Variations* in a three-month period indicated growing interest in the classics. ☐ On commission from NBC-TV, Gian Carlo Menotti wrote *Amahl* *and the Night Visitors,* which was presented on Christmas Eve in the first of what became a traditional series of holiday telecasts. ☐ Paperback books continued to grow in importance; 231 million of them, mostly at 25¢ each, sold during the year.

☐ **1952** "Television is a triumph of equipment over people, and the minds that control it are so small that you could put them in the navel of a flea and still have enough room besides for a network vice-president's heart."
—COMEDIAN FRED ALLEN

FOUNDED The Commonwealth of Puerto Rico, formerly a United States territory

INTRODUCED Commercial jet flight, with the British Comet; Cinerama, a new type of three-dimensional motion picture projection; Holiday Inns, with the opening of the first, in Memphis, Tennessee; the tranquillizer Reserpine; atomic-powered submarines, with the dedication of the keel of the *Nautilus*; the word "egghead," applied to intellectual presidential candidate Adlai Stevenson; LSD

DIED Steam locomotives for New York Central passenger trains

SONGS "Anywhere I Wander" "Hi-Lili, Hi-lo" "I Hear a Rhapsody" "High Noon" "You Belong to Me" "Love Is a Simple Thing" "Wish You Were Here" "Cry" "I Saw Mommy Kissing Santa Claus" "Lullaby of Birdland" "Kiss of Fire"

SENSATION George Jorgensen, who returned to the United States from a trip to Sweden as Christine Jorgensen, having undergone sex-change surgery

FASHION The influence of Dior's 1947 New Look was still evident in narrow waists, uplifted or supplemented bosoms, and bouffant skirts filled out with crinoline petticoats, scratchy but

137

feminine, rolled and stored in torn stockings when not in use. ☐ Men's neckties had narrowed.

THE WORLD Following a coup d'etat led by Lt. Col. Gamal Abdel Nasser, King Farouk of Egypt was forced to abdicate. ☐ King George VI of England died and was succeeded by his elder daughter, who became Queen Elizabeth II. ☐ Prime Minister Churchill announced that the British had produced an atomic bomb. ☐ Israel and Germany agreed on restitution to surviving Jews for damages done by the Nazis. ☐ Sixteen thousand persons succeeded in escaping from East Berlin to West Berlin. ☐ Chinese Premier Chou En-lai visited Moscow. The Chinese levelled charges of germ warfare in Korea against the United States.

THE UNITED STATES The Supreme Court ruled, for the first time, on the inherent constitutional powers of the president when it decided that President Truman's order for government seizure and operation of striking steel mills was unconstitutional. ☐ A potato shortage developed and, with price ceilings still in effect, a black market developed. Later in the year, price ceilings were removed from most fresh and processed meats and vegetables. ☐ American scientists exploded a hydrogen bomb in the Marshall Islands; the resultant hole was a mile in diameter, as much as 175 feet deep. The Eniwetok Atoll, a battle site of World War II, disappeared. ☐ The Republican and Democratic national conventions, both held in Chicago during July, were televised for the first time. Gen. Dwight D. Eisenhower was the Republican choice, Richard M. Nixon his running mate. The Democratic choice was Illinois Governor Adlai E. Stevenson. Stevenson's image of intellect and integrity turned out to be a political handicap and the popular Eisenhower, running with the slogan "I Like Ike," won in a landslide. ☐ Just before the election, a question arose on an $18,000 Nixon fund. He went on TV and delivered a triumphant speech, in which he spoke of the family dog Checkers, a gift, and said, "We're going to keep it." He also noted that his wife Pat didn't have a mink coat—"Just a plain old Republican cloth coat." Eisenhower and the rest of the country ate it up. ☐ President-elect Eisenhower's announced cabinet was described as "eight millionaires and a plumber." Keeping a campaign promise that he would go to Korea if elected, he made a three-day trip. ☐ America turned green when chlorophyll, derived from plants, was introduced in some ninety products, most of which were supposed to improve the breath and body odors of people and their pets. Chlorophyll chewing gum, mints, toothpaste, deodorants, and dog food sold by the carload. The bonanza faded after the American Medical Association pointed out that grazing goats live on chlorophyll and are not noted for their pleasing aroma. ☐ Astrologer Jeane Dixon predicted that a young Democrat would become U.S. president in 1960 and would be assassinated in office. ☐ Willie Sutton, the bank robber who had eluded the cops and the FBI for years, finally was caught. Asked why he robbed banks, he replied, "That's where the money is." ☐ Dr. L. Lasagna administered LSD to a group of volunteers in Boston in a series of scientific tests.

SPORTS Rocky Marciano became heavyweight champion, knocking out Ezzard Charles in the thirteenth round. Middleweight and welterweight champion Sugar Ray Robinson made a try for the triple crown, taking on Joey Maxim, but failed; in the extreme temperature of the evening, referee Ruby Goldstein collapsed and had to be replaced. ☐ Australian Frank Sedgman won the Wimbledon and United States tennis titles; tiny American Maureen (Little Mo) Connolly won both women's titles. ☐ Dick Button took both the U.S. and Olympic figure skating titles.

ARTS AND ENTERTAINMENT Charlie Chaplin, harassed by the FBI and the Internal Revenue Service, left the United States with his family and settled in Switzerland. ☐ An optimistic movie tycoon, one of many dismayed by dwindling movie audiences, thought people would be back at the box offices in six months. "People will soon get tired of staring at a plywood box every night," he said. Plastic TV sets came on the market. ☐ Veterans' groups picketed Columbia Pictures' film version of Arthur Miller's *Death of a Salesman* because Miller had refused to issue an anti-Communist statement. The sentiment expressed was that the play's protagonist, Willy Loman, was a rotten salesman, not the victim of a hard-hearted system.

□ The Boston Symphony made its first European tour. Gershwin's *Porgy and Bess* also made a European tour, under government sponsorship. □ The Revised Standard Version of the Bible, the result of fifteen years' work by thirty-two scholars, made history by selling well over a million copies in the first few weeks after publication.

□ **1953**

"I thought that what was good for the country was good for General Motors and vice versa."
—SEC. OF DEFENSE CHARLES WILSON, *explaining to a Senate confirmation hearing why he had not yet divested himself of General Motors stock*

FOUNDED The Ford Foundation's Fund for the Republic, to help fight restrictions on freedom of thought and expression

INTRODUCED A rocket-powered U.S. plane able to fly 1,600 mph; the 35mm Stereo-Realist camera at $159, which came and went with the rest of the 3-D fad; liquid rouge; Dacron-cotton blends for wash-and-wear men's shirts and women's summer clothing; a model of the DNA molecule

RETIRED The last of the double-decker buses on New York's Fifth Avenue

SONGS "It's All Right with Me" "No Other Love" "Vaya Con Dios" "April in Portugal" "Song from Moulin Rouge" "Your Cheatin' Heart" "How Much Is That Doggie in the Window?" "No Two People" "Eh, Cumpari"

FADS Droodles, introduced by Roger Price; three-dimensional (3-D) movies and still photography

GAMES Scrabble, a twenty-year-old game which suddenly caught on

FASHION Bermuda shorts, worn with knee socks, were in for men and women. For women, the extremely short Italian haircut, carefully cut to look casual and windblown, was chic. American designer Bonnie Cashin introduced blanket ponchos and soft wool jersey dresses with self-hoods. ☐ Dacron suits became a popular convenience for men.

THE WORLD Joseph Stalin died. Malenkov took over as premier and Khrushchev as first secretary of the Communist Party, a new office replacing Stalin's more powerful one of general secretary. Police head Beria emerged as a dangerous rival for power; in June he was arrested, executed. ☐ Yugoslavia proclaimed a new constitution and Marshal Tito was elected president. He visited London. ☐ Queen Elizabeth's coronation was held in London. ☐ An armistice was signed in Korea in July. ☐ Mount Everest, the world's highest peak, was scaled by Edmund P. Hillary, a New Zealander, and the Sherpa, Tenzing Norkay. ☐ Fidel Castro was jailed after an attempt to overthrow the Batista dictatorship in Cuba. He was sentenced to fifteen years, was granted amnesty in 1955.

THE UNITED STATES Dwight D. Eisenhower was inaugurated president. ☐ Sen. Joseph R. McCarthy's Permanent Investigating Subcommittee accelerated its investigations, probing ruthlessly into possible Communist connections of prominent Americans. Sentiment was sharply split between those who viewed him as an earnest anti-Communist and those who thought him a dangerous demagogue. The House Un-American Activities Committee also stepped up its inquiries. Former President Truman rejected a subpoena to appear in answer to charges by Att. Gen. Herbert Brownell concerning Truman's appointment of the late Harry Dexter White. ☐ The General Electric Company announced that all Communist employees would be fired. The U.S. Communist Party was ordered to register with the Department of Justice as an organization controlled by the Soviet Union. ☐ Social Security coverage was extended to an additional 10,500,000 workers. ☐ The 1953 dollar was estimated to be worth 52¢ compared to 1935–39. ☐ First reports appeared suggesting a connection between cigarette-smoking and lung cancer. ☐ Pizza, previously available only in a limited number of Italian eateries, began to catch on as an American snack or meal.

SPORTS The New York Yankees took the World Series from the Brooklyn Dodgers to become the first team to win five world championships in a row. ☐ Native Dancer won the Belmont Stakes and the Preakness but a long shot, Dark Star, won the Kentucky Derby. ☐ Rocky Marciano knocked out Joe Walcott in the first round and Roland LaStarza in the eleventh. ☐ Maureen Connolly again swept the women's tennis field.

ARTS AND ENTERTAINMENT The New York Metropolitan Opera produced Igor Stravinsky's opera, *The Rake's Progress*. ☐ Finnish-born architect Eero Saarinen received the architectural award of merit for distinguished design. ☐ Following on *Cinerama*, moviemakers, fighting to recapture customers lost to television, went mad with 3-D. Audiences entering theaters were handed special cardboard-encased colored glasses through which they could see, with stereoptican effect, such forgettable films as *Bwana Devil*. ☐ Live theater on TV was at its best. When the "Hallmark Hall of Fame" presented *Hamlet*, it was estimated that more people saw it on the tiny screen than had seen it in its 350-year history. Arthur Godfrey fired singer Julius LaRosa from his show, saying that LaRosa "lacked humility." ☐ Pianist-comedian Victor Borge started a record run for a one-man show; it opened on Broadway October 2 and ran until 1956. ☐ For people who found themselves victimized by others' choices of pop music in jukeboxes, a happy alternative was a peculiar hit record; drop a coin in the jukebox and out came the restful number—"Three Minutes of Silence."

Thirty-six-year-old Massachusetts Senator John F. Kennedy married 24-year-old Jacqueline Bouvier. ☐ American biologist James Watson and British biochemist Francis Crick formulated a theory regarding the structure of the DNA molecule that accounted for the known properties of the gene and its ability to transmit information.

 **1954**

FOUNDED The U.S. Air Force Academy at Colorado Springs, Colorado

INTRODUCED Commercial color-television shows; *Sports Illustrated*, a new Time-Life magazine; *Confidential*, a magazine filled with sensational fact and innuendo about celebrities; Cinemascope, a wide-screen movie projection system; Academy Award presentations on TV

FINALE The Packard Motor Company went out of business.

SONGS "Baubles, Bangles and Beads" "Fanny" "Hernando's Hideaway" "Mister Sandman" "Smile" "Three Coins in the Fountain" "Young at Heart" "The Man That Got Away" "I Love Paris" "Hey, There" "Shake, Rattle and Roll"

DANCE CRAZE The Cuban mambo, introduced a few years earlier by bandleader Perez Prado

FASHION Dior dropped the waistline to hip level and ready-to-wear makers followed; skirts remained full. Coco Chanel reopened her couture house, reintroduced her easy, crochet-edged cardigan suits and they once again were copied for the masses. Most popular look was the slim, snug-fitting, unbelted sheath dress, often worn with short bolero. Hats were small.

THE WORLD Gamal Abdel Nasser became premier and military governor of Egypt. France sent troops to quell trouble in Algeria. ☐ The Soviet Union announced that tourists were welcome. ☐ After sixty-eight years in Indochina, the French withdrew, acknowledging defeat after Dien Bien Phu fell to Communist guerillas. ☐ Britain's Comet jet plane was grounded, following a series of accidents, and commercial jet flight was postponed for another four years.

THE UNITED STATES Signing of the Espionage and Sabotage Act authorized the death penalty for such activities during peacetime. The Communist Control Act outlawed the Communist Party in the United States. Membership in the Party was sufficient grounds for deportation of aliens, the Supreme Court ruled, upholding a 1950 law. ☐ Racial segregation in public schools was declared unconstitutional by a unanimous Supreme Court decision. Schools were instructed to end the practice "with all deliberate speed." ☐ Sen. Joseph McCarthy took on the U.S. Army, accusing certain officers of promoting Communists to higher posts. Edward R. Murrow's TV program, "See It Now," presented a report that discredited McCarthy's investigations, an extraordinarily bold move at the time. The army engaged Boston lawyer Joseph N. Welch and brought charges against McCarthy. The dramatic hearings, which ran for thirty-four days, starting April 22, were covered on TV and watching them became the country's chief preoccupation. In December, the Senate voted 67 to 22 to rebuke McCarthy for his tactics and behavior during the hearings, and his influence promptly began to fade. McCarthyism was substantially ended. ☐ One victim of the national witch-hunt was nuclear physicist J. Robert Oppenheimer, who had directed the wartime atomic bomb laboratory at Los Alamos, New Mexico, and headed the general advisory committee of the U.S. Atomic Energy Commission. In 1954 he was stripped of his AEC security clearance because of alleged past political associations. ☐ Thoreau's *Walden* was barred from U.S. Information Service libraries overseas as being Socialist. ☐ Public concern about the dangers of radioactive fallout and the disposal of radioactive waste grew as additional thermonuclear tests in the Pacific resulted in some injuries from radioactive particles. ☐ Lurid comic books came under attack from parents' groups as juvenile crime and delinquency rose. Twenty million copies of such comics were sold monthly; some states passed laws regulating the sale of *Uncanny*

Tales, Web of Mystery, and the like, to minors. ☐ A study revealed that the United States had 6 percent of the world's population and 60 percent of its automobiles, 57 percent of its telephones, 45 percent of its radio sets, and 34 percent of its railroads. Sixty percent of males and 30 percent of females smoked. ☐ Five congressmen were injured when Puerto Rican nationalists opened fire from the Ladies' Gallery in the House of Representatives.

SPORTS Roger Bannister of Great Britain broke the 4-minute mile, running the distance in 3 minutes, 59.4 seconds. ☐ Babe Didrikson Zaharias won the Women's National Open golf tournament following cancer surgery.

ARTS AND ENTERTAINMENT Arturo Toscanini retired, at 87, as conductor of the NBC Symphony Orchestra. ☐ The year 1954 is generally accepted as the birth year of rock 'n' roll, with top honors going to Bill Haley and his group, The Comets, with their "Shake, Rattle and Roll" and "Rock Around the Clock." A step away was hip-swivelling rhythm-and-blues singer Elvis Presley. ☐ Three out of five households now had television sets. ☐ Ernest Hemingway and his wife were injured in a plane crash in East Africa. Maxwell Bodenheim, twenties poet, novelist, and longtime familiar figure in Greenwich Village bars, was murdered, with his wife, Ruth, in their furnished Village room. ☐ *McCall's* magazine gave the world a new word—"togetherness."

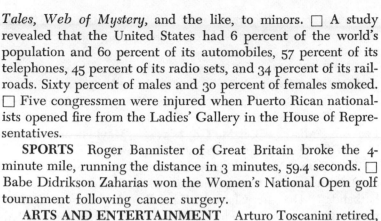

☐ 1955 "I thank God for high cheekbones every time I look in the mirror in the morning." —*Fashion model* SUZY PARKER, *who appeared on sixty magazine covers during the year*

INTRODUCED The Ford Thunderbird; McDonald's, with the opening of a restaurant in Des Plaines, Illinois; ultra-high-frequency waves, discovered at Massachusetts Institute of Technology; roll-on deodorants; filter cigarettes; big-money TV quiz shows

RETIRED   Dumont Television, which ceased operations

SONGS   "The Ballad of Davy Crockett" "Love and Marriage" "Love Is a Many Splendored Thing" "Sixteen Tons" "The Yellow Rose of Texas" "The Breeze and I" "Autumn Leaves" "Misty" "Let Me Go, Lover" "Maybellene"

FADS   Davy Crockett; painting by numbers

FASHION   Men's clothing began to lose its uniformity. A crucial break was the appearance of pink shirts and flashy hatbands. ☐ Designer Claire McCardell made the cover of *Time* magazine when she introduced tweed dirndl skirts and hooded sweaters for evening. Sheath dresses eased a bit at the waistline.

THE WORLD   Winston Churchill resigned as British prime minister and was succeeded by Anthony Eden. ☐ Nikolai Bulganin, Khrushchev's man, replaced Malenkov as Soviet premier. ☐ The sultan of Morocco abdicated, following riots. ☐ Border raids increased between Israel and Jordan. ☐ The heads of state of the United States, Great Britain, the USSR, and France held a summit meeting at Geneva. ☐ Germany became a member of the North Atlantic Treaty Organization.

THE UNITED STATES   President Eisenhower suffered a massive heart attack while vacationing in Denver, was hospitalized from September 24 to November 11, then recuperated at his Gettysburg farm. Talk was of Richard Nixon's being "a heartbeat away" from the presidency. The illness caused great concern and a sharp drop in the stock market. ☐ A polio vaccine developed by Dr. Jonas Salk was proved effective after tests in forty-four states; it was made generally available the following year. ☐ The United States extended $216 million in financial aid to Laos, South Vietnam, and Cambodia. President Eisenhower announced that nuclear bombs would be used in the event of war. The United States had four thousand stockpiled; the USSR one thousand. An increase in the United States Military Reserve was ordered; the force was to be raised gradually from 800,000 to 2,900,000. ☐ The AFL and CIO merged into a single labor federation, after a twenty-year schism. George Meany headed the AFL, and Walter Reuther the CIO at the time. ☐ Blacks in Montgomery, Alabama, began a bus boycott, under the leadership of the Rev. Martin Luther King, Jr., to protest segregation. The boycott, which followed Dr. King's principles of nonviolent direct action, started when Mrs. Rosa Parks, a black woman, was arrested for refusing to give up her bus seat to a white man. In Mississippi, a 14-year-old black youth, Emmett Till, who was accused of whistling at a white woman, was kidnapped and murdered by two white men; a white jury acquitted the men. ☐ The National Geographic Society announced that a study indicated there was no vegetation on the planet Mars. ☐ Salaries of Congress and federal judges were increased by 50 percent. Federal workers won a 7.5 percent pay boost and U.S. postal workers an 8 percent increase. ☐ Educators reported there was a shortage of 250,000 classrooms and 141,000 teachers in the nation, which now was faced with educating the postwar baby crop. ☐ The Presbyterian Church approved the ordination of women as ministers. ☐ It was a bad year for raccoons and a good one for novelty manufacturers as the country's kids went Davy Crockett-mad. The Disney film *King of the Wild Frontier* set off a fad for coonskin hats, fringed jackets, and toy flintlocks in holsters. More than three hundred products were spawned by Crockett, and some 4 million records of "The Ballad of Davy Crockett" were sold. ☐ Business mergers were on the rise; three times as many took place during 1955 as in 1949.

SPORTS Rocky Marciano knocked out Archie Moore in the ninth round. ☐ There were five thousand golf courses in the country and 3,800,000 players.

ARTS AND ENTERTAINMENT Contralto Marian Anderson made a belated debut, at the age of 53, at New York's Metropolitan Opera, singing in *Un Ballo in Maschera* and becoming the first black engaged as a permanent member of the opera company. ☐ Actor James Dean, 24, was killed when he crashed in his sports car. ☐ RCA put Elvis Presley under contract and within a year had sold 10 million of the charismatic performer's singles; he was without question the king of rock 'n' roll. Featured on the Ed Sullivan TV show, "Elvis the Pelvis" was shown only from the waist up; his sexy gyrations were considered unsuitable for Sullivan's Sunday evening family audience. □ The first of the big-money quiz shows, "The $64,000 Question," went on the air, starting a trend for extravagant cash and merchandise giveaways that was to continue until scandal exploded the bubble in 1959. □ NBC put color television to its first major use with a two-hour version of *Peter Pan*, starring Mary Martin and Cyril Ritchard. Children donned their Mouseketeer hats for the first time when "The Mickey Mouse Club" became a favorite. □ The Abstract Expressionist movement in painting received full recognition when New York's Museum of Modern Art mounted an exhibit called "The New Decade," with works by Jackson Pollack, Willem de Kooning, Robert Motherwell, and others. □ Less-talented Americans took to Sunday painting, a hobby developed through a combination of paint-by-the-numbers learning and the publicizing of the Eisenhower and Churchill dabblings. □ *The Reader's Digest*, which had scorned advertising throughout its history, announced that it would accept advertising for the first time but would carry no ads for liquor, tobacco, or remedies. Within two weeks the *Digest* was swamped with orders for three times as many ads as it could accommodate during the first year.

 **1956**

"The ability to get to the verge without getting into the war is the necessary art."
—SEC. OF STATE JOHN FOSTER DULLES, *summing up the Cold War in what became known as his "brink of war" statement*

ESTABLISHED The first private atomic energy plants, by Consolidated Edison at Indian Point, New York, and Commonwealth Edison at Grundy, Illinois

INTRODUCED Salk vaccine, the first to be proved effective against paralytic polio, available for the first time through normal channels of distribution; general use of the transistor, developed by Bell Labs in 1948; stereophonic sound on phonograph records

GONE FOREVER The Grand Army of the Republic, with the death of the last Union Army veteran, former drummer boy Albert Woolson, at 109

SONGS "Around the World in 80 Days" "I Could Have Danced All Night" "Love Me Tender" "On the Street Where You Live" "Blue Suede Shoes" "Hound Dog" "Standing on the Corner" "The Party's Over" "Que Sera, Sera" "True Love"

FADS Propeller beanies: the tiny propeller on the little hat whirled as children ran.

FASHION The fit of women's clothing continued to ease as Dior introduced the tunic dress. Turbans were back. Men sported jaunty Tyrolean hats.

THE WORLD Anti-Communist demonstrations in Hungary led to an invasion by Soviet tanks and troops, purges, and deportations. Some Hungarians were able to flee to the West. ☐ Nikita Khrushchev surprised the world by initiating a program of "de-Stalinization," denouncing the dead leader as "brutal, capricious, despotic." In short order, the Soviet Union invited more foreign trade, tourism, and foreign journalists. ☐ Egypt seized control of the Suez Canal Company. Britain and France, protecting their property, invaded Egypt at Port Said. Israel attacked Egypt's Sinai Peninsula. The UN intervened, a cease-fire was called, and a buffer peace-keeping force was established. ☐ Japan was admitted to the United Nations. ☐ Fidel Castro led an uprising in Oriente province in Cuba; it was suppressed by dictator Batista's forces, and Castro and his forces retreated to the southern tip of the island to begin two years of guerilla warfare.

THE UNITED STATES During the Montgomery, Alabama, bus boycott, the home of Dr. Martin Luther King, Jr. was bombed. Arthurine Lucy, the first black student to enroll at the University of Alabama, was suspended after three days of near riots, then permanently expelled for her accusations in a lawsuit against the school. ☐ The tents of the Ringling Brothers and Barnum and Bailey Circus were folded forever following

149

the July performances in Pittsburgh. John Ringling North called The Greatest Show on Earth "a thing of the past." The circus was reorganized the following year to play indoor arenas. □ President Eisenhower was renominated by the Republicans and, again with Richard Nixon as his running mate, once more defeated Adlai E. Stevenson. It was the first time a Republican president had won reelection since 1900. □ The wedding of the year took place in Monaco, when 26-year-old actress Grace Kelly became Her Serene Highness, as wife of Prince Rainier III. Commenting on the match, the bride's father said, "She went to the Riviera to make a film, *To Catch a Thief,* and look what she came back with." □ Yields from farm crops were the highest in U.S. history. It was a banner year for auto production, too, with 7 million cars and trucks coming off assembly lines. One out of every eight cars was a station wagon. □ The first American test rocket for sending a man-made satellite into orbit was fired from Patrick Air Force Base, Florida; it travelled at 4,000 mph, reached a height of 125 miles. □ A crew of five flew a helicopter from California to Washington, D.C. in thirty-seven hours, the first such transcontinental flight and, except for transporting helicopters, perhaps the last.

SPORTS Rocky Marciano retired undefeated as heavyweight boxing champ. Floyd Patterson defeated Archie Moore, who admitted to being 39 years old, in a fifth-round knockout victory, to become, at 21, the youngest heavyweight-title holder in history. □ The New York Yankees' Don Larsen pitched the first perfect game in World Series history against the Brooklyn Dodgers. □ Babe Didrikson Zaharias died.

ARTS AND ENTERTAINMENT As East-West relations eased, the Soviet Union sent its Bolshoi Ballet to London. □ Maria Callas, playing to a sold-out house, made her triumphant debut at the New York Metropolitan Opera, opening the season with *Norma.* □ Action painter Jackson Pollack died in an auto accident. □ The novel *Peyton Place,* recording scandalous carryings-on in a proper little town, was the most talked-about and juicy book of the year. □ Eugene O'Neill's *Long Day's Journey into Night,* written in 1940, received its first Broadway production. □ Following in the footsteps of Elvis Presley were Bobby

Darin, Fabian, and Frankie Avalon. Elvis made his first film and hit the top of the song charts with the title tune, "Love Me Tender." □ Ingrid Bergman, who six years earlier had been persona non grata in Hollywood because of her love affair with Roberto Rossellini, was warmly welcomed when she attended the Academy Awards and received the award as best actress for her role in *Anastasia*.

□ **1957** "That's not writing; that's typewriting."
—AUTHOR TRUMAN CAPOTE, *commenting on the meandering, undisciplined style of beat writer Jack Kerouac*

FOUNDED The European Common Market; Parents Without Partners, an organization of single parents; major league teams in San Francisco and Los Angeles, with the defection of the New York Giants and Brooklyn Dodgers; Gamblers Anonymous; SANE, a citizen's organization focussed on combatting the nuclear arms race

INTRODUCED Videotape, revolutionizing the television industry; senior citizens' apartment buildings, with the first in St. Petersburg, Florida; the portable electric typewriter; competitive Frisbee throwing; vinyl-coated raincoats; Ford's ill-fated Edsel automobile

RETIRED The U.S. Navy's last battleship, the *Wisconsin*; the Nash, Hudson, and Packard automobiles; New York City's last trolley car, which had plied the Queensboro Bridge since 1888; *Collier's* magazine, after years of carrying some of the country's liveliest writing

SONGS "Tammy" "Witchcraft" "Seventy-Six Trombones" "Banana Boat Song" "I'm Walkin'" "Jailhouse Rock" "Tonight" "That'll Be the Day" "Young Love" "Kisses Sweeter than Wine" "Yellow Bird"

DANCE HIT Calypso

FASHION Paris dictated the chemise, a waistless dress which contrasted sharply with the popular bouffant styles with fitted waists. Men thought it looked like a flour sack. American manufacturers insisted on copying one particular version, which featured a large, flat bow on the buttocks. The chemise flopped but rose again a few years later as a more sophisticated fashion.

THE WORLD   During the International Geophysical Year, sixty-seven cooperating nations started work on Antarctic exploration, the launching of space satellites, meteorological research. Soviet scientists launched *Sputnik I* and *Sputnik II,* the first man-made satellites to orbit the earth. *Sputnik II* carried a small dog, Laika. ☐ At the Central Committee meeting of the Party, Nikita Khrushchev won a majority, eliminating Kagonovich, Malenkov, and Molotov. Chinese Premier Chou En-lai visited Moscow. ☐ Regular plane service began between Moscow and London. ☐ Spain's Generalissimo Franco announced that the Spanish monarchy would be restored after his death. ☐ The Suez Canal was reopened to navigation; Israeli forces withdrew from the Sinai Peninsula. ☐ Great Britain exploded a thermonuclear bomb in the Pacific.

THE UNITED STATES   President Eisenhower formulated the Eisenhower Doctrine for the protection of Middle Eastern nations from Communist aggression. ☐ The Supreme Court ruled that state obscenity statutes were unconstitutional and that reading matter of adults could not be limited to protect children. Justice Felix Frankfurter wrote that such censorship was "burning the house to roast the pig." ☐ Desegregation of public schools in Little Rock, Arkansas, was violently opposed by segregationists; Gov. Orval Faubus called out the National Guard, later replaced, on presidential order, by federal troops. One little girl summed up the attitude: "I'd rather grow up an idiot than go to school with a nigger." ☐ The Teamsters Union was expelled from the AFL-CIO when its president, Jimmy Hoffa, refused to expel criminals within the union and the union refused to expel Hoffa. ☐ Wages for factory workers averaged $2.08 an hour, $82.99 a week. ☐ Members of the U.S. delegation to the World Youth Festival in Moscow were invited to tour Communist China by the All-China Youth Federation. The State Department, which had disapproved of the trip, confiscated the delegates' passports. ☐ Confessed Soviet spy Jack Sobel was sentenced to seven years in prison. Rudolph Abel, a Soviet counterintelligence officer, was sentenced to thirty years in prison; in 1962 he was exchanged for U-2 pilot Francis Gary Powers, imprisoned in the Soviet Union. □ *Confidential* magazine, which had spent much of its existence being sued for libel or defamation by celebrities whose lives it purported to cover, was charged by the state of California with conspiracy to commit criminal libel. Abandoning its coverage of Hollywood personalities, the magazine quickly lost its readers. □ The Rev. Billy Graham drew capacity audiences nightly to New York's Madison Square Garden, and 92,000 to Yankee Stadium, the largest crowd ever to jam "the House that Ruth Built." □ Bobby Fischer, 14 years old, won the American Rosenwald Memorial chess tournament.

ARTS AND ENTERTAINMENT The charms of the Caribbean islands hit the mainland; Americans whistled Calypso tunes, danced to the Calypso beat, and tried to imitate the elusive inflections of Calypso speech and songs. □ The beat movement, which started as a new form of artistic expression, with writer Jack Kerouac as its leader, became a new, anti-Establishment way of life with open use of drugs and more casual sex as a route to the beatific. It also developed its own vocabulary; beatniks "crashed" in "pads," earned "bread," "dug" good jazz. Beat poet Allen Ginsberg's long and serious poem, *Howl*, was seized by police as obscene. "Second generation" beatniks, those who affected the lifestyle but not the artistic output, adopted black leotards, no lipstick, lots of dark eye makeup if they were women, beards if they were men. Even soap operas wrote beat characters into the cast. To the dismay of the beats, black leotards became fashionable. □ Igor Stravinsky's 75th birthday was celebrated in Los Angeles with an all-Stravinsky program that included the world premiere of his ballet score, *Agon*. To mark Pablo Picasso's 75th birthday, New York's Museum of Modern Art mounted a comprehensive Picasso retrospective exhibit. □ The New York Philharmonic appointed Leonard Bernstein as one of its two principal conductors, then changed its mind and named him the sole conductor. □ The year's hit record was Debbie Reynolds singing "Tammy."

Buddy Holly and the Crickets hit it with "That'll Be the Day." Dick Clark made the transition from pop to rock.

Some high school and college boys affected crazy apache haircuts but the well-greased D.A., politely called ducktail, was more popular. A Massachusetts high school banned boys with ducktail cuts.

1958

"I wouldn't attach too much importance to those student riots. I remember when I was a student at the Sorbonne in Paris, I used to go out and riot occasionally."
—JOHN FOSTER DULLES *on student riots at the U.S. Embassy in Indonesia*

FOUNDED NASA, the National Aeronautics and Space Agency, to administer scientific exploration of space; American Association of Retired Persons; United Press International, through the merger of two news wire services, United Press and International News Service

INTRODUCED Large-scale use of commercial jet planes, with the introduction by Pan American of Boeing's 707 for North Atlantic service; trading stamps in supermarkets; Bank of America and Chase Manhattan Bank credit cards

SONGS "The Chipmunk Song" "I Enjoy Being a Girl" "Thank Heaven for Little Girls" "The Purple People Eater" "Volare" "Chanson d'Amour" "Tom Dooley" "Bird Dog"

DANCE The Cha-Cha

FASHION Young Yves St. Laurent, with his first collection for the House of Dior, introduced the trapeze silhouette—a tentlike shape that flowed out from the shoulders. The collection, really the ill-fated chemise in new—and attractively shorter—guise, was a success, and the more relaxed, less-fitted look for fashion slowly began to catch on. Mohair sweaters, roomy and brilliantly colored, were the big look in sportswear.

THE WORLD Pope Pius XII died and was succeeded by Pope John XXIII, whose coronation was seen on television. □

Egypt and Syria joined forces to become the United Arab Republic. ☐ Khrushchev replaced Bulganin as premier, becoming head of both the government and the Communist Party.

THE UNITED STATES   A poll revealed that Mrs. Eleanor Roosevelt was the most admired woman in America. ☐ In what was termed a recession, 7.7 percent of the work force was jobless. ☐ In January, three months after the Soviet launching of its *Sputnik*, U.S. scientists released the first American satellite, *Explorer I*, at Cape Canaveral, Florida. The Navy launched its *Vanguard I* in March and the Air Force, not to be outdone, launched an Atlas missile in December; it was equipped with a radio carrying a Christmas message from President Eisenhower. Four tries at reaching the moon with a missile failed. ☐ Nuclear-powered submarines were setting records. The *Skate* crossed the Atlantic underwater to England in eight days, eleven hours. The *Nautilus* crossed under the North Pole ice cap from the Pacific to the Atlantic, a distance of 1,830 miles. ☐ Cuba lost some of its popularity as an American vacation resort when Fidel Castro's forces in the Sierra Maestra hills began kidnapping American civilians and military personnel to gain recognition for their cause. The victims were freed, but tourism fell off. ☐ To avoid having to integrate, the public schools of Little Rock, Arkansas, closed, then reopened as private institutions. ☐ After thirty-four years in prison, Nathan Leopold of the 1924 Leopold-Loeb thrill-murder duo was paroled. He went to Puerto Rico where he became a social worker and married. ☐ Growing juvenile delinquency was causing alarm. An article in the *Ladies Home Journal* noted that crowded neighborhoods were breeding teenage junkies, turned criminal to support their habit. ☐ Automobile tail fins were in their full glory, ready to slice an unwary pedestrian in half. ☐ First class postage increased from 3¢ to 4¢ an ounce, airmail from 6¢ to 7¢. ☐ Four pacifists and their ship, *The Golden Rule*, were seized by the Coast Guard when they sought to reach an atomic testing area in the Pacific to protest nuclear tests. ☐ Sherman Adams, special assistant to President Eisenhower, resigned in the face of a scandal involving his acceptance of gifts, including a good Republican vicuna coat. ☐ Vice President Nixon made a trip to

South America in an effort to counteract anti-American sentiment there, but was met with hostile demonstrations.

SPORTS Althea Gibson, who had broken the color line in tennis and had won both the Wimbledon and U.S. women's singles for the second consecutive year, announced she would quit tennis to launch a career as a popular singer. □ Jockey Eddie Arcaro celebrated his 4,000th win during the year.

ARTS AND ENTERTAINMENT Texas-reared Van Cliburn, a 23-year-old pianist, became famous overnight when he took first place in the International Piano and Violin Competition in Moscow. □ Russia's Moiseyev dance company visited the United States and was widely acclaimed. □ The Nobel Prize for Literature was awarded Russian Boris Pasternak. He declined to accept it, under governmental pressure. Sales of his novel, *Doctor Zhivago*, skyrocketed in twelve languages, if not his own.

□ **1959** "We have beaten you to the moon, but you have beaten us in sausage-making."
—SOVIET PREMIER NIKITA KHRUSHCHEV, *after inspecting a meat-processing plant during his visit to the United States*

FOUNDED The U.S. manned space program; the American Professional Football League; a committee to study the possibility of New York City's becoming the fifty-first state

INTRODUCED The Douglas DC-8 jet plane; a food-stamp program for the poor; thin plastic garment covers for use by dry cleaners; a synthetic diamond, manufactured by De Beers; U.S. compact cars, introduced to compete with small foreign cars

WITHDRAWN Ford's Edsel, the biggest boner in the company's history (manufacture of the 1960 model was suspended November 19, 1959)

SONGS "Mack the Knife" "Stagger Lee" "High Hopes" "The Battle of New Orleans" "Everything's Coming Up Roses"

"Personality" "He's Got the Whole World in His Hands" "Climb Ev'ry Mountain"

FAD Hula hoops

FASHION The Chanel look was almost a uniform for women—easy-to-wear cardigan suits and loads of costume jewelry. Women's hair was long, often faked with falls or wiglets.

THE WORLD Cuba's dictator, Batista, fled the country on January 1 and Fidel Castro led his forces into Santiago de Cuba. In February, Castro was sworn in as premier. Later in the year, the new government expropriated sugar mills owned by U.S. companies. ☐ Charles de Gaulle was inaugurated as president of France. ☐ At an American exhibition in Moscow, Vice Pres. Richard Nixon debated Premier Khrushchev in a model kitchen in what became known, logically enough, as "the Kitchen Debate." ☐ The U.S.–Soviet race to conquer outer space quickened, with the USSR taking the lead; it launched a series of missiles carrying small animals and successfully hit the moon with *Lunik II*. The first U.S. satellite was put into orbit by the army; the navy sent two heroic monkeys named Able and Baker on a rocket trip to the Caribbean. ☐ The St. Lawrence Seaway, joining the Great Lakes with the Atlantic, was dedicated by Britain's Queen Elizabeth II and President Eisenhower.

THE UNITED STATES Alaska was admitted to the Union as the forty-ninth state on January 3 and Hawaii as the fiftieth on August 21. ☐ Seven astronauts were selected from the ranks of military test pilots to undergo training for the first manned space-capsule ride, scheduled to take place in two years. ☐ Oklahoma, which had been dry since it entered the Union fifty-one years earlier, legalized the sale of liquor, leaving Mississippi as the only remaining dry state. ☐ The Whammo Company introduced the hula hoop and it caught on like the flu. Long-vacant factories reopened as hula hoop plants. Thirty million hoops sold at $1.98. Although children were the primary market, M.D.s, chiropractors, and osteopaths were kept busy trying to straighten out adult hips and backs thrown out of kilter while wiggling the hoops. ☐ The Supreme Court declared unconstitutional a Louisiana law banning boxing matches between blacks and whites.

Public schools in Norfolk and Alexandria, Virginia, desegregated without incident. The Supreme Court declared unconstitutional the law under which Arkansas had converted its public schools to private institutions; they reconverted to public schools, with segregationists demonstrating. ☐ Soviet Premier Khrushchev visited the United States, accompanied by his wife, who charmed everyone. He saw a large part of the country but almost went home when a planned visit to Disneyland was cancelled for security reasons; he was shocked and embarrassed by a special can-can performance on a movie set. He also conferred with President Eisenhower. ☐ Just before Thanksgiving, the U.S. Health Department warned that a weed killer that caused cancer in rats had been used on cranberries grown in Washington and Oregon. People didn't listen too carefully, refused to buy cranberries from anyplace at all, and almost destroyed the growers.

ARTS AND ENTERTAINMENT Photography's elder statesman Edward Steichen organized an exhibit of 502 photographs from all over the world, "The Family of Man," which was seen by 4 million people in twenty-five countries. ☐ As part of the cultural exchange program between the U.S. and the Soviet Union, Dmitri Shostakovich, Dmitri Kabalevsky, and four other Soviet musicians made a month-long American tour. ☐ The magazine *TV Guide*, with fifty-three regional editions, had 6,500,000 readers each week. The average American family TV set was on six hours daily. ☐ Television quiz shows, whose prizes had grown increasingly enticing and whose audiences were enthralled as contestants vied for pots as high as $264,000, came to a sudden end in scandal when it was discovered that some contestants had been briefed on questions in advance. ☐ Swedish soprano Birgit Nilsson made her American debut as Isolde at the Metropolitan Opera House. *Wozzek*, Alban Berg's operatic masterpiece of thirty-four years earlier, finally was produced by the Met. ☐ Paperback books were now firmly established. There were six thousand titles in print. ☐ Radio was far from dead; 156 million sets were in operation in the U.S., 26 percent of them in automobiles. Radio had its own scandal when the Federal Communications Commission uncovered widespread use of "payola," payments made to disc jockeys to push records. □ One of Frank Lloyd Wright's last designs, the Guggenheim Museum, opened in New York. □ D. H. Lawrence's novel *Lady Chatterley's Lover* had the distinction of being banned from the mails, thirty-one years after it was written, by Postmaster General Arthur Summerfield, who said, "Any literary merit the book may have is far outweighed by the pornographic and smutty passages and words." Federal Judge Frederick van Pelt Bryan ruled the ban unconstitutional and Americans were finally able to read the unexpurgated version of the book.

□ **1960**   "I don't like life there. There is no greenery. It would make a stone sick."
—NIKITA KHRUSHCHEV *on New York City, following his second, shoe-banging visit to the UN.*

FOUNDED   The Richard III Society, to vindicate the fifteenth-century king vilified in Shakespeare's drama

INTRODUCED   Contraceptive pills for public sale; the heart pacemaker; laser beams; the first automated post office, in Providence, Rhode Island; Sun City, the first town for senior citizens, near Phoenix, Arizona; blue jeans shaped to the female figure; civil rights sit-ins

SONGS   "Never on Sunday" "The Second Time Around" "Teen Angel" "The Twist" "My Home Town" "Stairway to Heaven" A modern version of the gospel hymn "We Shall Overcome," with royalties assigned to the Freedom Movement

DANCE STEP   The Twist (in New York City, the chic jammed the Twist capital, a hitherto notably unchic night spot, the Peppermint Lounge)

FASHION   Women's heads doubled in size with bouffant hairdos. For those who weren't afraid to mess their hair, there were knitted white-wool watchcaps. Turtleneck sweaters, leather suits and coats were popular. In England, designer Mary Quant started the "Chelsea Look" of extraordinarily brief skirts but it

159

was a while before her influence was felt. Stretch pants, often held under the foot by a strap, were adapted from ski wear for women's fashion.

THE WORLD Queen Elizabeth's third child, Prince Andrew, became the first baby born to a reigning English monarch since 1857. The Queen's sister, Princess Margaret Rose, married a commoner, photographer Anthony Armstrong-Jones. ☐ President Eisenhower's goodwill tour of Latin America was marred by an anti-American demonstration and tear-gas bombing in Montevideo. Eisenhower's planned visit to Japan was cancelled, following violent demonstrations there protesting a new mutual cooperation treaty calling for U.S. bases in Japan. ☐ Israeli agents captured former Nazi SS General Adolph Eichmann in Argentina. ☐ A rocket shot down a U.S. U-2 reconnaissance plane, piloted by Francis Gary Powers, over Soviet territory. The incident wrecked plans for a Paris summit meeting of the United States, Britain, France, and the USSR. The Soviets sentenced Powers to ten years in prison for espionage; he was exchanged for Soviet spy Colonel Abel in 1962. ☐ The United States placed an embargo on shipments of any kind to Cuba. Following uprisings in Guatemala and Nicaragua, believed to have been instigated by Cuban Premier Fidel Castro, the United States was invited to patrol Central American waters.

THE UNITED STATES Despite the 1954 Supreme Court decision, only 6 percent of Southern schools were integrated. Black students in Greensboro, North Carolina, staged a sit-in demonstration at a segregated variety-store lunch counter. The movement quickly spread to other Southern cities. Woolworth and Kress stores throughout the country were picketed by sympathizers; by September 1961, more than seventy thousand whites and blacks had joined the sit-ins, which eventually forced the variety chains to integrate lunch-counter seating. ☐ The nuclear-powered submarine *Triton* circumnavigated the globe on an eighty-four-day underwater voyage. ☐ In the presidential elections, Democratic Sen. John F. Kennedy won by a hair over his Republican rival, Vice Pres. Richard M. Nixon. It was generally felt that Kennedy's more appealing appearance on the four nationwide television debates between the two candidates had provided the slim winning edge. ☐ Foreign heads of state descended on New York for the fifteenth meeting of the United Nations General Assembly. Soviet Premier Khrushchev caused a ruckus at one meeting by removing his shoe and pounding his desk with the heel to indicate disapproval of a speech. Equally gauche were the manners of the Cuban delegation; opting to prepare meals in their hotel rooms, they offended the fastidious by plucking chickens and tossing the feathers out windows. ☐ The U.S. population was 179,300,000, of which 33,500,000 was made up of children aged 5 to 14. The migration to suburbia was reflected in lawn and porch furniture sales, double those of 1950, and the child-orientation of the populace in children's book sales, which were triple those of 1950. Potato chip sales soared. ☐ The American Heart Association announced that coronary deaths among middle-aged men were far higher among heavy smokers than among nonsmokers.

SPORTS   Rafer Johnson won the Olympic decathlon gold medal. ☐ Carol Heiss won both the Olympic and U.S. national figure-skating competitions. ☐ Basketball star Wilt Chamberlain retired, then changed his mind and signed a new contract. ☐ Floyd Patterson regained the heavyweight boxing title with a fifth-round knockout of Ingemar Johansson. ☐ Bowling had become a favorite pastime; the number of lanes had doubled since 1950.

ARTS AND ENTERTAINMENT   There now were 85 million television sets in American homes. When NBC censored a joke on the successful "Tonight" show, star Jack Paar walked off the stage in protest, returning three weeks later. ☐ Opera star Leonard Warren died during a performance on the stage of the Metropolitan Opera House. ☐ D. H. Lawrence's *Lady Chatterley's Lover*, now sold and mailed legally, became, belatedly, an American bestseller. ☐ Showman Billy Rose donated his collection of modern sculpture, including works by Rodin and Maillol, to the National Museum in Jerusalem. ☐ An Actor's Equity strike closed New York's theaters for eleven days, the first such strike since 1919.

 **1961** "All my life, I've known better than to depend on the experts. How could I have been so stupid as to let them go ahead?" —PRES. JOHN F. KENNEDY, *after the Bay of Pigs fiasco in Cuba*

FOUNDED The Peace Corps, by executive order of President Kennedy; CORE, the Congress of Racial Equality, which led Freedom Rides in the South; the Green Berets, special forces for action in Vietnam

INTRODUCED Airline shuttle flights requiring no advance reservations, between Washington, D.C. and New York; the theatrical Antoinette Perry (Tony) Awards; the pop-top beverage can opening, invented by U.S. Shoe Machinery Co.; stereo FM radio

FAREWELL APPEARANCE The glamorous, mysterious Orient Express made its last run between Paris and Bucharest, after seventy-eight years.

SONGS "Moon River" "Roses Are Red, My Love" "Where the Boys Are" "Travelin' Man" "Please, Mr. Postman" "The Exodus Song" "Love Makes the World Go Round" "Calcutta"

DANCE STEPS La Pachanga joined the Twist. From Paris came Le Madison for a brief fling.

FASHION Kimono sleeves, three-quarter length, were the rule for women. Coats and suits left the lower arms bare, to be warmed by fashionable long gloves. Sleeveless dresses with fitted, double-breasted jackets replaced suits. Men's neckties were at their narrowest; fedoras were still standard headwear.

THE WORLD Tension over military occupation of Berlin increased when restrictions were imposed on travel from East to West Berlin; to halt defections of East Germans, the Berlin Wall —actually a twenty-five-mile structure—was built. □ Cuba requested the United States to reduce its embassy staff, claiming that most on the staff were FBI or CIA spies; the United States severed relations. In April, the new Kennedy administration became involved in a previously planned invasion of Cuba by CIA-trained Cuban exiles. The expedition, which became known as the Bay of Pigs fiasco, collapsed in three days. ☐ The Soviet Union successfully orbitted cosmonaut Yuri Gagarin around the earth in a spacecraft, then followed with a second trip with Gherman S. Titov. A month later, in May, the first U.S.-manned missile sent astronaut Alan B. Shepard, Jr. on a fifteen-minute suborbital flight from Cape Canaveral, Florida. ☐ The United States dispatched four thousand men and thirty-two helicopters to South Vietnam to "help Vietnam preserve its independence, protect its people against Communist assassins, and help them build a better life," according to President Kennedy. ☐ Dag Hammarskjöld, secretary general of the United Nations, was killed in a plane crash in Northern Rhodesia. ☐ The UN General Assembly rejected a USSR proposal to admit the People's Republic of China.

THE UNITED STATES   Following his inauguration, John F. Kennedy created a mood of action and "viguh." His Peace Corps attracted eighteen thousand volunteers in its first year. He called for broad participation in exercise, saying that five out of seven men called were rejected by the army. President Kennedy visited Paris, Vienna, and London during his first year in office; the elegant Jacqueline Kennedy set a new level of style for First Ladies. The French adored JFK when he said, "I'm the fellow who accompanied Jackie to Paris." Kennedy appointed Mrs. Eleanor Roosevelt a U.S. delegate to the UN General Assembly. ☐ Hijacking of American airliners and diverting them to Havana—three attempts were successful during the year—led to a law making hijacking a federal crime, punishable by death or prison. ☐ The National Council of Churches endorsed artificial birth control as a means of family limitation. ☐ The rightwing John Birch Society suggested that former presidents Roosevelt, Truman, and Eisenhower and former Secretary of State John Foster Dulles had advanced the cause of Communism. ☐ The *Journal* of the American Medical Association reported statistical evidence indicating a connection between smoking and heart disease. ☐ Nelson Rockefeller's son Michael was reported missing on an anthropological trip off the coast of New Guinea. No trace of him was ever found. ☐ The antisegregation movement gained strength with the formation of a biracial passive resistance group, CORE, which became instrumental in organizing Freedom Rides—trips by mixed white and black demonstrators into the South on interstate busses. Alabama turned out to be an unhealthy state for Freedom Riders, who were attacked in three cities and arrested by the hundreds in Montgomery. The groups succeeded in desegregating numerous public facilities. ☐ In his farewell speech, Pres. Dwight D. Eisenhower warned against "the acquisition of unwarranted influence, whether sought or unsought, by the military-industrial complex," adding that "the potential for the disastrous rise of misplaced power exists and will persist." ☐ Announcing his candidacy for governor of California, former Vice Pres. Richard M. Nixon said, "I shall not be a candidate for president in 1964," but made no commitment beyond that.

ARTS AND ENTERTAINMENT Ernest Hemingway committed suicide. Grandma Moses died at the age of 101. ☐ Joan Sutherland made a sensational Metropolitan Opera debut. Artur Rubinstein, at the age of 71, played ten Carnegie Hall recitals. ☐ During the Soviet Kirov Ballet's first visit to Paris, principle male dancer Rudolph Nureyev defected and sought permission to remain in France. ☐ New York's Metropolitan Museum of Art paid a record $2,300,000 for Rembrandt's *Aristotle Contemplating the Bust of Homer.* ☐ On the second show of "You're in the Picture," TV series host Jackie Gleason spent most of the time apologizing for how dreadful the first show had been. ☐ Cellist Pablo Casals, who had vowed not to play in public until Spain was free, relented when President Kennedy made a special request for him to play at the White House.

☐ **1962** "I found nothing but progress and hope for the future."
—SEC. OF DEFENSE ROBERT S. MC NAMARA, *on his return from a forty-eight-hour trip to Vietnam*

FOUNDED The Ragtime Society, to unearth and preserve musical classics

INTRODUCED *Telstar I*, launched by NASA to make possible transatlantic transmission of television pictures; two new National League baseball teams, the New York Mets and Houston Astros; singles weekends, by Grossinger's, New York State mountain resort; full integration in U.S. military reserve units

SONGS "Sherry" "The Sweetest Sounds" "Ramblin' Rose" "Return to Sender" "Breaking Up Is Hard to Do" "Days of Wine and Roses" "Go Away, Little Girl" "You Are My Sunshine" "A Taste of Honey"

DANCES Bossa Nova

FASHION Wigs arrived as fashion accessories, a boon to women who couldn't do a thing with their hair, had no time for hairdressers, or wanted to change their personalities. Jacqueline Kennedy quickly became the American fashion leader, wearing A-line dresses, suits and coats that skimmed the figure, skirts almost to knee level, and pillbox hats.

THE WORLD The United States established a Military Assistance Command in Vietnam, sending troops to provide technical training and assistance to the Vietnamese. The Pentagon admitted that American pilots were flying combat missions. □ Cuba released 1,113 prisoners taken during the Bay of Pigs invasion and 922 of the prisoners' relatives, in exchange for $53 million in medical supplies and baby food. □ After a trial in Israel covered by the world press, former Gestapo officer Adolph Eichmann was condemned to death; he was hanged in 1963. □ Algerians voted by plebiscite in favor of independence from France. European businesspeople fled the country, taking their capital with them. □ Vatican Council II convened in October, to meet in four annual sessions until December 8, 1965.

THE UNITED STATES John H. Glenn became the first American to orbit the earth, going three times around while millions watched on television; he became an instant hero. An unmanned interplanetary probe found Venus too hot to support life. □ Dr. Frances Kelsey, a minor civil service employee, was presented a medal by President Kennedy for doing nothing. She had deliberately dragged her feet in approving a pharmaceutical company's application to market a new drug for pregnant women that she considered unproved, saving thousands of American families from tragedy. The drug, thalidomide, was responsible for the birth of armless and legless babies in Europe. ☐ In October, President Kennedy revealed in a television speech to the nation a Soviet military buildup in Cuba, where it was establishing missile bases capable of firing nuclear rockets for distances of a thousand miles. He demanded immediate dismantling of the bases and ordered a blockade of military shipments to Cuba. The world held its breath for twelve days while American and Soviet leaders negotiated and the USSR finally agreed to withdraw the bases. ☐ The Pennsylvania and New York Central railroads, two of the nation's largest, merged into the single Penn-Central. ☐ In a continuing trend, major daily newspapers disappeared. The *Los Angeles Examiner* merged into the *Herald,* and in New York, a 114-day newspaper strike marked the end for several of the city's papers; by 1964, the metropolitan area's nine papers had dwindled to four. ☐ In what was the largest cash robbery in history, a gang held up a U.S. mail truck in Plymouth, Massachusetts, and made off with $1,551,000. ☐ Film star Marilyn Monroe was found dead in Hollywood of a barbiturate overdose. During the filming of a supercolossal *Cleopatra,* the romance of Richard Burton and Elizabeth Taylor surged in and out of headlines for most of the year. ☐ By Federal Court order, James Meredith became the first black to enter the University of Mississippi. Meredith tried four times to register, being blocked twice by Governor Barnett, then by the lieutenant governor and state troopers, then by a crowd of 2,500 whites. U.S. marshals finally escorted him in; in the riot that followed, 2 were killed and 375 injured. President Kennedy dispatched federal troops and National Guardsmen to insure Meredith's admission to classes. ☐ Mrs. Eleanor Roosevelt died.

SPORTS Fans who paid $100 for ringside seats for the Sonny Liston–Floyd Patterson heavyweight fight got little for their money when Liston knocked out Patterson in two minutes, six seconds, of the first round. ☐ The New York Mets, under Casey Stengel, finished their first season, having lost three out of every four games played; their stumblebum tactics drew a hoard of devoted fans.

ARTS AND ENTERTAINMENT Soviet defector Rudolph Nureyev debuted with Britain's Royal Ballet at Covent Garden in February, beginning a historic partnership with Margot Fonteyn. ☐ The first Beatles disc, "Love Me Do," was released; by the end of 1963, 7 million Beatles singles had sold in Britain alone. Two of the fastest-selling albums in U.S. recording history were Vaughn Meader's "The First Family," mimicking members of the Kennedy clan, and Allan Sherman's "My Son the Folksinger." A new sound in popular music came with the combination of Latin and Dixieland by the Tijuana Brass. ☐ Philharmonic Hall, the first building in New York's Lincoln Center cultural complex, opened with a flourish but enthusiasm died when it became apparent that someone had bungled the acoustics. ☐ The musical *My Fair Lady* closed after 2,717 performances. ☐ Johnny Carson became host of the "Tonight" show on TV. ☐ *The Silent Spring*, a book by eminent marine biologist Rachel Carson, was instrumental in focussing world attention on ecology; it described the effects on the balance of nature caused by irresponsible use of insecticides and herbicides. ☐ The woman of the year was Jacqueline Kennedy, who took the country on a TV tour of the White House, then became an international celebrity as she made goodwill missions to India, Pakistan, and Italy—visits that were considered political as well as personal successes. ☐ Andy Warhol had a one-man show at the Stable Gallery in New York, showing giant Campbell Soup cans, among the seminal works in the Pop Art movement.

"You certainly can't say that the people of Dallas haven't given you a nice welcome."
—MRS. JOHN B. CONNALLY, JR., *to Pres. John F. Kennedy, in the motorcade in Dallas, Texas, November 22*

ESTABLISHED A twenty-four-hour hot line between Washington and Moscow, to prevent accidental nuclear war

INTRODUCED The cassette recorder, by Phillips Co. of Holland (it arrived in the United States in 1964 as the Norelco Carry-Corder); an "artificial heart," used by Dr. M. De Bakey to take over circulation of patients' blood during heart surgery; a domestic Peace Corps; color Polaroid cameras; a safe, effective measles vaccine; postal zone zip codes in the United States

SONGS "Blowin' in the Wind" "Dominique" "Puff, the Magic Dragon" "Call Me Irresponsible" "Danke Shoen" "Those Lazy Hazy Crazy Days of Summer" "Louie, Louie" "If I Had a Hammer" "My Coloring Book"

FADS Swifties, adverbial puns named after boys' novel hero Tom Swift. ("It's a foggy day," Tom said hazily. "Which way to the Place de la Concorde?" Tom asked ruefully.)

THE WORLD Pres. John F. Kennedy was assassinated in Dallas, Texas, on November 22. Lee Harvey Oswald, arrested for the crime, was murdered two days later in front of television cameras by Jack Ruby, a Dallas nightclub owner. Vice Pres. Lyndon B. Johnson was sworn in as president within an hour after the announcement of Kennedy's death. For four days, the nation watched the incredible series of events from assassination to funeral on television, which suspended all commercial announcements. □ Earlier in the year, Great Britain's Secretary of State for War, John Profumo, admitted to a liaison with Christine Keeler, a call girl who had also been involved with a Soviet naval attaché. The scandal, one of a number of security leaks, shook the Macmillan government. The London *News of the World* offered Miss Keeler $23,000 for her life story. □ Pope John XXIII died; he was succeeded by Giovanni Battista Cardinal Montini, elected as Pope Paul VI. □ In a spectacular robbery, armed bandits took more than $7 million in cash from a mail train near Cheddington, England. Careless about fingerprints, all of the robbers were caught, but only one million dollars of the loot was recovered. ☐ In South Vietnam, Pres. Ngo Dinh Diem was killed in a military coup. The Cambodian government requested that U.S. troops stationed there withdraw.

THE UNITED STATES Immediately after President Kennedy's assassination, Pres. Lyndon B. Johnson set up a special commission, headed by Supreme Court Justice Earl Warren, to investigate whether Lee Harvey Oswald had acted alone. The Warren Commission studied the matter for nearly a year. ☐ George Wallace, sworn in as governor of Alabama, spoke for "segregation now, segregation tomorrow and segregation forever." ☐ Military aid to South Vietnam was increased. ☐ The U.S. nuclear submarine *Thresher* was lost in the Atlantic with all 129 hands. ☐ J. Robert Oppenheimer, who had been denied classified status in 1954, received the Enrico Fermi Award for his work in atomic science. Dr. Timothy Leary of Harvard University's psychology department was discharged for using undergraduates in experiments with LSD and other drugs. ☐ Some 250,000 Freedom Riders converged on Washington in August to support black demands for equal rights. The key event was Dr. Martin Luther King, Jr.'s speech in which he said, "I have a dream that this nation will rise up and live out the true meaning of its creed: 'We hold these truths to be self-evident: that all men are created equal.'"

SPORTS Jack Nicklaus became the youngest golfer ever to win the Masters Tournament at Augusta, Georgia; he also won the PGA. ☐ Surfing soared as a participation sport; it also spawned a subculture of full-time surfers, beachboys, and sun freaks.

ARTS AND ENTERTAINMENT Publication of Betty Friedan's *The Feminine Mystique*, raising sharp questions about woman's traditional role as wife, mother, and homemaker, marked the start of the feminist movement. On the other side of the issue, Helen Gurley Brown converted stodgy *Cosmopolitan* magazine into a how-to-nab-a-man-by-being-sexy educational vehicle. ☐ Another publication furor was created by Jessica

Mitford, who had America's morticians turning on their grave-sites with her attack on the country's funeral and burial customs in *The American Way of Death.* ☐ Efforts to save New York's neo-classic wonder, McKim, Mead and White's colonnaded Pennsylvania Station, failed; it came down to make room for a new Madison Square Garden. ☐ Folk-singing was undergoing a revival, with Bob Dylan and Joan Baez as cult figures: their songs, expressing the protest against injustice and war that was a growing sentiment with young people, were sharply different from the folk music of such forties figures as Burl Ives. In popu-lar music, Barbra Streisand hit it big, as did Stevie Wonder, then known as Little Stevie Wonder. ☐ The historic Armory art show of 1913 was re-created in its original setting, the Sixty-Ninth Armory in New York. History repeated itself as Marcel Duchamp's *Nude Descending a Staircase* became a main attrac-tion among the 350 of the original 1,300 works that were assem-bled. ☐ In television, "The Beverly Hillbillies," criticized as being insipid, promptly jumped to the top of the ratings.

☐   **1964**   "Unfortunately, many Americans live on the outskirts of hope—some because of their poverty, some because of their color, and all too many because of both. Our task is to help replace their despair with opportunity."
—PRES. LYNDON B. JOHNSON, *opening "the war on poverty" in his State of the Union message*

FOUNDED   A national wilderness system, 9,200,000 acres set aside by Act of Congress

INTRODUCED   Feature films on airplanes; touch-tone telephone dialing; the first legalized sweepstakes in U.S. his-tory, in New Hampshire; go-go dancers; presidential voting in the District of Columbia

ENDED   The poll tax for voters, with the Twenty-Fourth Amendment to the Constitution

SONGS "Hello, Dolly" "Amen" "As Tears Go By" "A Hard Day's Night" "Goin' Out of My Head" "I Want to Hold Your Hand" "Downtown" "People" "What Kind of Fool Am I?"

IN Discotheques; depending on the music and your part of the country, the dances were the frug, the swim, the Watusi, the surf, the monkey

MADNESS The Beatles

FASHION French couturier Courrèges introduced short, little-girl dresses, short white boots; they quickly caught on. American designer Rudy Gernreich created a flurry with topless swimsuits supported by two thin straps; three thousand were sold but they were not evident on beaches.

THE WORLD Soviet Premier Nikita Khrushchev was retired from power, accused of personal rule. Leonid Brezhnev became first secretary, Alexei Kosygin chairman of the Council of Ministers. ☐ The United States escalated its commitment in Vietnam after two U.S. destroyers were reportedly attacked by North Vietnamese torpedo boats in the Gulf of Tonkin. ☐ The People's Republic of China tested its first atomic bomb. ☐ Pope Paul VI visited the Holy Land, the first pope to do so. ☐ Yasir Arafat became the leader of the anti-Israeli Arab guerilla force, Al Fatah.

THE UNITED STATES Following the reported Gulf of Tonkin attack, Congress passed a resolution giving the president power to "take all necessary measures to repel any armed attack against the forces of the United States and to prevent further aggression." It became a virtual declaration of war. ☐ The bodies of three civil rights workers who had been reported missing in Mississippi in June were discovered in August, buried near Philadelphia, Mississippi. Seven of the twenty-one white men arrested for the crime were found guilty of conspiracy in the slaying, by an all-white jury. ☐ Boycotts of schools, protesting *de facto* segregation, took place in a number of Northern cities. Three months after a New York City high school boycott by 464,000 students, the city presented a desegregation plan acceptable to black groups. Similar boycotts took place in Chicago, Cleveland, Cincinnati, and Boston. ☐ The Rev. Martin

Luther King, Jr. won the Nobel Peace Prize; he gave the money to the Civil Rights movement. ☐ The Warren Commission released its report in September, concluding that Lee Harvey Oswald had been solely responsible for the assassination of President Kennedy. ☐ Students at the University of California at Berkeley started what became a nationwide campus movement of sit-in demonstrations and boycott of classes, protesting administrative control over students' political activities. The Berkeley "free speech" movement gained faculty support, the chancellor resigned, and a "free speech area" was set aside on campus. ☐ President Johnson pushed through Congress a series of measures, including the Anti-Poverty Bill and the Economic Opportunity Act, authorizing $947,500,000 for youth programs, community action programs, rural antipoverty measures, small business loans, and job training for youth. ☐ The moon lost its green-cheese image when the U.S. *Ranger 7* rocket made a hard landing, first sending back TV pictures of the moon's surface. Later in the year, *Mariner 4* probed Mars, learning that the planet's atmospheric pressure is a fraction of Earth's. ☐ President Johnson romped through the presidential election. With Hubert H. Humphrey as his running mate, he won 486 electoral votes to Sen. Barry M. Goldwater's 52. LBJ, who had attacked Goldwater as "trigger happy" during the campaign, escalated the Vietnam involvement shortly after his reelection. ☐ The U.S. Surgeon General issued a report linking smoking and cancer. ☐ Teamsters Union chief, James Hoffa, was found guilty of trying to bribe a juror in an earlier trial and sentenced to eight years in jail and a $10,000 fine. Later in the year, he and six colleagues were convicted of fraudulent use of union pension funds and sentenced to five years in jail. ☐ The State Department revealed it had found a network of forty microphones embedded in the walls of the U.S. Embassy in Moscow. ☐ A mammoth World's Fair in New York City was less than successful and widely criticized as a cultural desert. The most popular attractions were the General Motors Futurama, the Vatican Pavilion's display of Michelangelo's *Pietà*, and the Spanish Pavilion's restaurant. ☐ California overtook New York as the nation's most populous state.

SPORTS Cassius Clay turned out to be every bit as great as he said he was, gaining the heavyweight boxing title by knocking out Sonny Liston in the seventh round. ☐ The graceful Maria Bueno was women's champion at both Wimbledon and Forest Hills.

ARTS AND ENTERTAINMENT The Beatles took the United States by storm, making their first appearance on Ed Sullivan's television show before an estimated audience of 73 million, giving a triumphant concert in Carnegie Hall, creating teenage mob scenes wherever they went, and moving one after another of their songs to the top of the lists. They also succeeded in communicating some of the meaning of rock music to adults. The Beatles' dandified clothes and long haircuts, which seemed purely theatrical at first, were to have a revolutionary influence on men's fashions. ☐ Another kind of theatrical sensation was being created by ballet dancers Rudolph Nureyev and Dame Margot Fonteyn; following a performance of *Swan Lake* at the Vienna State Opera, they were forced to take eighty-nine curtain calls. ☐ Geometric Op Art was causing a furor. ☐ In the movies, there was a spate of beach-party films with such titles as *Muscle Beach Party*. ☐ Contralto Marian Anderson retired from the music world. ☐ Elizabeth Taylor and Richard Burton were married; his second, her fifth.

"The problem could be called a credibility gap. It represents a perceptibly growing . . . skepticism about the candor or validity of official declarations."
—MURRAY MARDER, *writing in the* Washington Post *about administration pronouncements on foreign policy*

INTRODUCED Fertility drugs; body stockings; the U.S. Surgeon General's warning that "cigarette smoking is dangerous to your health" on all cigarette packages; draft-card burnings
SONGS "Like a Rolling Stone" "What the World Needs

173

Now Is Love" "Help" "Sounds of Silence" "Mr. Tambourine Man" "Try to Remember" "Eve of Destruction" "Yesterday" "What Have They Done to the Rain?"

FASHION Miniskirts, inches above the knee, were the rule, starting as Mary Quant's young fashion, gradually worn by women of all ages, regardless of leg shape. London hairdresser Vidal Sassoon introduced an extreme, geometric cut for women. Trousers, snug at the top, belled at the bottom, were in for the young of both sexes. ☐ Some fairly conventional young men began to let their hair grow. The trend toward a breakdown of sharp sex differences in clothing, which was to lead to the "unisex" look, had started.

THE WORLD Rhodesia's white-majority regime proclaimed the country's independence from Britain. ☐ The United States bombed North Vietnam, setting off worldwide anti-American demonstrations. ☐ Soviet cosmonaut A. A. Leonov became the first man to float in space. In June, American astronaut Edward H. White stepped out of the *Gemini 4* capsule and walked in space before TV cameras for twenty-one minutes. He dismayed camera buffs by dropping his costly Hasselblad rig. ☐ In a bloodless coup, Algerian President Ben Bella was ousted by a group of military leaders. ☐ In the Soviet Union, Nikolai Podgorny was chosen head of state. ☐ Other U.S. and Soviet space achievements of the year included a rendezvous of Frank Borman and James A. Lovell, in *Gemini 7*, with Walter Shirra and Thomas Stafford in *Gemini 6*, and the voyage of the Soviet *Venera 3*, which became the first man-made object to strike another planet, Venus.

THE UNITED STATES A massive Civil Rights march, protesting voter registration rules and slow desegregation, was led by Dr. Martin Luther King, Jr. Starting in Selma, Alabama, site of recent demonstrations, it wended its way to the state capitol in Montgomery, Alabama, its ranks swelling from the thirty-two hundred who had started, to twenty-five thousand. President Johnson dispatched four thousand troops to guard the marchers on their route. Blacks in the Watts area of Los Angeles rioted for six days in August; thirty-five died, four thousand were arrested; property damage was estimated at more than

$200 million. ☐ Pope Paul VI visited New York, the first time a pope had been to America, and delivered an appeal for peace at the UN. ☐ Congress passed a Truth in Packaging bill, requiring that standard weights and measures be shown on all packages. ☐ Medical specialists confirmed what jet travellers had been saying all along, that jet travel through a number of time zones could disrupt psychological and physiological functions. ☐ Student demonstrations against the Vietnam war continued. Teach-ins were held on more than a hundred campuses. In New York and California, young men burned their draft cards in public rallies. As President Johnson announced that draft calls would be doubled, the demonstrations intensified. ☐ New York City was completely blacked out and most of the northeastern United States and Canada partially blacked out by a massive power failure on November 9. Hapless dental patients were caught with drills in their teeth; people spent the night in elevators, subways, on trains or, if they were fortunate, at the cocktail parties they were attending when the lights went out. ☐ A scandal swept the new Air Force Academy when it was discovered that some cadets had cheated on exams; 105 of them resigned. ☐ Consumer advocate Ralph Nader gained sudden celebrity with publication of his book, *Unsafe at Any Speed,* which accused automobile manufacturers of ignoring safety factors in rushing cars to market. The book set off the safety movement and the recall of cars to correct unsafe features.

ARTS AND ENTERTAINMENT President Johnson was host to a Festival of the Arts and Humanities at the White House; poet Robert Lowell declined an invitation, in protest against American foreign policy. ☐ For the first time in years, George Balanchine appeared as an active participant in a ballet, his new *Don Quixote* for his New York City Ballet. ☐ The Ford Foundation announced grants of $85 million to fifty symphony orchestras to enable them to lengthen their seasons and raise salaries. ☐ An exhibit at the New York Museum of Modern Art, "The Responsive Eye," acknowledged the important Op Art movement, based on principles of optics and illusion. ☐ Folk singer Bob Dylan startled his devotees and started a new movement in music when he merged elements of rock into his folk

175

protest songs. Others were quick to pick up the folk-rock blend. Top pop performers included The Lovin' Spoonful, The Jefferson Airplane. ☐ There were now 588 TV stations in the United States. Such superspy shows as "The Man from U.N.C.L.E." were popular. ☐ Among the Beautiful People, status was an invitation to author Truman Capote's masked black-and-white ball at New York's Plaza Hotel. Those who were not invited left town. The guest of honor was *Washington Post* publisher Katharine Graham, who found the chic and crowded gathering of better than five hundred elegants "cozy and glamorous."

☐ 1966   "[The United States] is succumbing to the arrogance of power."
—SEN. J. W. FULBRIGHT, *Chairman of the Senate Foreign Relations Committee (Sen. Barry Goldwater asked him to resign his chairmanship for "giving aid and comfort to the enemy")*

FOUNDED   Amnesty International of the U.S.A., working for release of "prisoners of conscience"; the League for Spiritual Discovery, by Timothy Leary, for the purpose of legalizing LSD and marijuana as religious sacraments

INTRODUCED   Medicare, a federal program to pay medical expenses of citizens over 65; the terms "hawks" and "doves" to define prowar and antiwar forces; the first black U.S. senator since Reconstruction, Edward W. Brooke of Massachusetts; the first black cabinet member, Robert C. Weaver, Secretary of the newly created Department of Housing and Urban Development; eight-track stereo cassette recorders as options in Ford cars; search-and-destroy warfare

FINALE   The crack Chicago–Los Angeles train, *Superchief*, an acknowledged pacesetter since 1936, made its final run (in its heyday, no movie star would be caught dead riding anything but the *Superchief*); the U.S. Catholic Church ended its dictum against the eating of meat on Fridays, except during Lent.

SONGS "It Was a Very Good Year" "These Boots Are Made for Walking" "You're Gonna Hear from Me" "Yellow Submarine" "Paint It Black" "Strangers in the Night" "The Revolver" "Georgy Girl" "A Day in the Life of a Fool" "Somewhere My Love" "A Man and a Woman"

THE WORLD Disastrous floods of the Po and Arno rivers struck Italy, doing terrible damage in Florence, where priceless art treasures and ancient landmarks were inundated. Art experts and restorationists from around the world converged on Florence to contribute to the effort to save masterpieces of painting, sculpture, and architecture. ☐ The Cultural Revolution started in the People's Republic of China, with a Red Guard of young people assigned to forcibly impressing the anti-Western movement on citizens. ☐ India's Prime Minister Lal Bahadur Shastri died, to be succeeded by Indira Gandhi, daughter of Jawaharlal Nehru. ☐ Two former Nazi ministers, Albert Speer and Baldur von Schirach, were released after twenty years in prison. ☐ Mammoth temples and statuary at Abu Simbel, Egypt, were moved to save them from the rising waters of the Aswan High Dam. ☐ Protests against the U.S. involvement in Vietnam became worldwide. ☐ The first photograph taken from the moon's surface was transmitted to earth, first via the Soviet *Luna 9*, then by the U.S. *Surveyor*, which made the first soft landing on the moon and sent back more than ten thousand photographs.

THE UNITED STATES Escalation of the Vietnam war continued and demonstrations increased in size and frequency. More than five thousand Americans had been killed and thirty thousand wounded. Rallying at the Washington monument, sixty-three thousand voters pledged to vote only for antiwar candidates; ten thousand people picketed the White House. When Defense Secretary McNamara was given an honorary degree by Amherst College, a group of graduating seniors walked out. President Johnson termed war critics "nervous Nellies." ☐ "Black Power" became the slogan of such new Civil Rights leaders as Stokely Carmichael and H. Rap Brown of the Student Nonviolent Coordinating Committee, who believed that blacks should control all institutions and businesses in black ghettoes. Another new phrase was "white backlash," describing reaction to the emerging black militancy. □ The word "psychedelic" gained currency and there was growing concern over the drug culture, particularly the use of LSD, which was simple to manufacture and whose effects were unpredictable. LSD was added to the Federal Drug Administration's list of dangerous drugs. Timothy Leary, fired from Harvard, assumed a kind of high-priest role among LSD trippers. □ Former Hollywood star and liberal Ronald Reagan, transformed into a politician and conservative, defeated incumbent Pat Brown for the governorship of California.

SPORTS   Billie Jean King won her first major tennis tournament—the women's singles at Wimbledon; Maria Bueno was again the winner at Forest Hills. □ Cassius Clay had an active year, outpointing George Chuvalo and knocking out Henry Cooper, Brian London, Karl Mildenberger, and Cleveland Williams.

ARTS AND ENTERTAINMENT   The famous gold curtain of the old Metropolitan Opera House in New York came down for the last time and was cut into small pieces that were sold as souvenirs. The new Metropolitan at Lincoln Center opened with a new opera, *Antony and Cleopatra* by Samuel Barber, commissioned for the occasion. □ Color television was well established and half of the 11 million sets bought by Americans during the year were equipped for color. The American passion for television was such that when two favorite programs, "Batman" and "The Virginian," were interrupted by ABC and NBC to announce that astronauts Neil Armstrong and David Scott had been forced to make an emergency landing of their *Gemini 8* spacecraft, stations were flooded with irate phone calls. All three major networks televised the wedding of President Johnson's daughter Luci and Patrick Nugent. □ Ralph Ginzburg, publisher of *Eros,* was sentenced to five years in prison for obscene advertising of his erotic magazine. □ A number of radio stations banned the playing of Beatles records after Beatle John Lennon remarked that the Beatles were more popular than Jesus. Discs that were being played in their place included those of such groups as The Hollies, The Mamas and the Papas, and Neil Diamond. □ The population of the United States stood at

178

195,287,000; there were 78 million cars and 16 million trucks on the roads.

□ 1967

"There never were any flower children. It was the biggest fraud ever perpetrated on the American public . . . The community is based on dope, not love."
—*Syndicated columnist* NICHOLAS VON HOFFMAN

INTRODUCED   The Twenty-Fifth Amendment to the Constitution, dealing with presidential disability; induction center sit-ins; flower children; the first popularly distributed film to portray explicit sex, the Swedish *I Am Curious, Yellow;* multimedia shows with flashing colored lights, later to become standard disco decor

FINALE   The *Twentieth Century Limited,* New York Central's New York–Chicago all-Pullman deluxe train, with its maids, valets, stenographers, barbers, and red-carpeted entrance —downgraded in 1957 when it added coaches—was retired (the Central's president noted that "the supremacy of the jet airplane for long-distance travel lies beyond argument"); the Frisco, with forty-six hundred miles of track, became a freight-only line; the Pennsylvania R.R. added coaches to its crack *Broadway Limited.*

SONGS   "Feelin' Groovy"   "Michelle"   "By the Time I Get to Phoenix"   "San Francisco (Be Sure to Wear Some Flowers in Your Hair)"   "Light My Fire"   "Happy Jack"   "Cabaret" "Sunrise, Sunset"   "Ode to Billy Joe"

SHOCKING THE ESTABLISHMENT   Hippies

FASHION   Maxis, ankle-length coats worn over miniskirts (now as much as seven inches above the knee) were adopted by some young women but it was a half-hearted fashion that didn't take; it hid the new erogenous zone, the thigh. Paper dresses were a flash in the pan.

THE WORLD   By December 474,000 American men were

in Vietnam. U.S. bombers attacked Hanoi. ☐ In June, Israel, attacked by Arab forces, smashed back against Egypt, Syria, and Jordon, capturing and occupying the Sinai Peninsula, the Golan Heights, Gaza Strip, and the east bank of the Suez Canal in the Six-Day War. ☐ Communist China announced that it had exploded a hydrogen bomb. ☐ Great Britain legalized homosexual behavior in private between consenting adults. ☐ Dr. Christiaan Barnard performed the first successful human heart transplant on Louis Washkansky, who died of pneumonia eighteen days later.

THE UNITED STATES Joseph Stalin's daughter, Svetlana Alliluyeva, who had left the USSR for Switzerland, arrived in the United States to become a resident. ☐ The House of Representatives, charging New York Representative Adam Clayton Powell with misuse of government funds and nepotism, denied him his seat. ☐ Several blacks moved into positions of influence: Thurgood Marshall became the first black U.S. Supreme Court Justice; Carl B. Stokes was elected mayor of Cleveland, Ohio, and Richard G. Hatcher mayor of Gary, Indiana. ☐ There was racial violence. In Newark, New Jersey, twenty-six died during July riots; later that month, racial violence flared in Detroit and seven thousand National Guardsmen came to the aid of police officers after forty-three had died during five nights of rioting. There were other less lethal riots in New York, Rochester, Birmingham, and New Britain, Connecticut. ☐ Antiwar demonstrations strengthened. At the Lincoln Memorial in Washington, 50,000 demonstrators assembled; in New York, 200,000 protesters marched from Central Park to the UN headquarters; 50,000 peace marchers demonstrated in San Francisco. ☐ It was announced that draft deferments would be cancelled for college students who interfered with recruiting or violated draft laws. ☐ The Pentagon announced that the United States had lost its 500th plane since air raids were started against North Vietnam in 1964. ☐ The National Student Association admitted that it had received more than $3 million secretly from the CIA between 1952 and 1966 for overseas programs. ☐ Young people converged on the Haight-Ashbury district of San Francisco and the East Village of New York City—hippies, flower children, whatever they chose to call themselves—into communal living, perhaps the drug culture, heavily amplified music, sometimes spiritualism. ☐ Three astronauts in NASA's Apollo program, Virgil Grissom, Edward White II, and Robert Chaffee, were killed in a spacecraft fire during a simulated launch. ☐ The "Boston Strangler," Albert de Salvo, who had confessed to thirteen murders, was sentenced to life imprisonment. ☐ Lynda Bird Johnson married Marine Captain Charles Robb. Former child star Shirley Temple Black failed in her run for a congressional seat on the Republican ticket. ☐ The 100-millionth telephone was installed in the United States, which had half of all the phones in the world.

SPORTS   Cassius Clay was stripped of his heavyweight title for refusing military service; the title was vacant until 1970. ☐ In tennis, Billie Jean King took every title in sight, while John Newcombe did the same in the men's division. ☐ Mickey Mantle hit his 500th homer. ☐ For the third consecutive year, the Green Bay Packers, under coach Vince Lombardi, won the NFL Conference and then the championship.

ARTS AND ENTERTAINMENT   The effort to save the art of Florence, Italy, continued. Mrs. John F. Kennedy was honorary president of the Committee to Rescue Italian Art, which raised several million dollars. The Red Cross, Boy Scouts, and Lions Clubs all raised money for restoration. ☐ Barbra Streisand drew 135,000 to Central Park in New York City for a concert. ☐ English singer Gerry Dorsey assumed the name of the composer of the opera *Hansel and Gretel* and, as Engelbert Humperdinck, made the grade. ☐ Jacqueline Susann's novel *Valley of the Dolls* set a record by selling 6,800,000 copies of the paperback edition in six months. ☐ Indian sitarist Ravi Shankar, who had been playing the subtle ragas of his country for many years, became a celebrity, and his elegant art was adopted by performers as diverse as the Beatles and Yehudi Menuhin. ☐ Folk singer Joan Baez was arrested during an induction center sit-in in Oakland, California.

 **1968**

FOUNDED The Jogging Association, to promote fitness

INTRODUCED Legalized abortion in Great Britain; Hong Kong flu, reaching epidemic proportions; vaginal deodorants; the alphabetical rating system for movies in the United States; fruit-flavored yoghurt

SONGS "Hey, Jude" "Mrs. Robinson" "Those Were the Days" "Little Green Apples" "Hold Me Tight" "Scarborough Fair" "Eleanor Rigby" "Abraham, Martin and John" "Mac-Arthur Park" "California Dreamin' "

ARRIVED Adult recognition that rock music was not going away

FASHION A revolution for men: Nehru jackets and turtlenecks acceptable in place of shirt and tie; pendants and other nonfunctional jewelry acceptable for he-men; the suit no longer the only choice for business and social occasions. □ For women: pants suits introduced and gratefully accepted; boots, no longer a cute fashion, became high and warm for winter; fashion-industry leaders tried to introduce midcalf "midi" fashions but mini devotees fought back and the manufacturers and retailers lost a bundle.

THE WORLD The U.S. intelligence ship *Pueblo* was seized by North Korea in the Sea of Japan. Nine months later, eighty-two men were released. □ A protest of New Left students in Nanterre, France, grew quickly into widespread civil strife; within a month, 10 million strikers had paralyzed the country; Paris was in a state of siege; President de Gaulle nevertheless gained a majority in the June general election, campaigning against a Communist conspiracy. □ Spain officially rescinded the 1492 edict that banned Jews from that country. □ Pope Paul VI issued an encyclical reaffirming the Church's opposition to birth control except by the rhythm method; a survey two

182

months later indicated that half of American priests disagreed with the stand. □ The Soviet Union invaded Czechoslovakia in August, putting an end to the liberalized regime of Alexander Dubcek.

THE UNITED STATES The Vietnam involvement became the longest war in U.S. history. Draft resistance and evasion gained many more adherents; antiwar sentiment ran high. Dr. Benjamin Spock and the Rev. William Sloane Coffin were convicted of counselling and aiding draft evaders. Fr. Daniel J. Berrigan and others were convicted of destroying Selective Service System draft files by pouring blood on them. □ Sen. Eugene J. McCarthy, a critic of U.S. policies in Vietnam, scored an unexpected triumph in the March presidential primary in New Hampshire, campaigning on an antiwar platform and prompting Sen. Robert F. Kennedy, another critic of the war, to enter the race. On March 31, President Johnson announced he would not seek reelection and ordered a limitation on the bombing of North Vietnam. □ The Rev. Martin Luther King, Jr. was assassinated April 4 in Memphis, Tennessee. Within the next ten days, rioting erupted in 125 cities; federal and National Guard troops were required in several of them. An escaped convict, James Earl Ray, pleaded guilty to the crime. □ On June 5, Sen. Robert F. Kennedy, following a huge win in the California primary, was assassinated in the Hotel Ambassador, Los Angeles. Sirhan B. Sirhan, a Jordanian, was convicted of the murder. □ Campus unrest was widespread; Columbia University students seized five buildings to protest building of a new gym in a ghetto area and the university's connection with a Pentagon project; they finally were evicted in a violent fracas with police. A strike at San Francisco State University lasted five months. □ In the Haight-Ashbury district of San Francisco, it was the Summer of Love. □ NASA's Apollo program came closer to a manned lunar landing. Astronauts in *Apollo 7* orbited the earth 163 times, and *Apollo 8* orbited the moon. □ The Kerner Commission report on civil disorders cited white racism as the chief cause of black violence. □ Richard M. Nixon won the Republican nomination for president. His choice of Spiro Agnew as his running mate was termed by the *Washington Post* as "perhaps the most eccentric political appointment since the Roman emperor Caligula named his horse a consul." ☐ Hubert H. Humphrey was nominated at the tumultuous Democratic convention in Chicago. Thousands of antiwar protesters converged on the city. Police drove the demonstrators back from convention headquarters in full view of TV cameras. ☐ Nixon won the election by a narrow margin. ☐ Jacqueline Kennedy married Greek shipping magnate Aristotle Onassis; president-elect Nixon's younger daughter Julie married David Eisenhower, Ike's grandson. ☐ A Gallup poll for the first time showed the public as considering crimes of violence the issue that disturbed them most. Drug abuse at all levels of society was becoming more severe. ☐ The liquor industry's gross sales for the year were $12 billion, more than the nation spent on education, medical care, and religion combined.

SPORTS   The United States took forty-five gold medals at the Summer Olympics in Mexico City. At the Winter Olympics, Peggy Fleming won the women's figure-skating events and Jean Claude Killy took gold medals for the ski downhill, giant slalom, and men's slalom. ☐ U.S. tennis went open, with professionals permitted to compete for the first time; amateur Arthur Ashe took the men's title, Virginia Wade the women's.

ARTS AND ENTERTAINMENT   C. Day Lewis was appointed poet laureate of England. ☐ Explicit sex was now common in films and a new rating system was introduced to accommodate new mores; a film rated "G" was general entertainment; "PG," parental guidance suggested; "M," for adults and mature young persons; "R," for films barred to those under 16, unless accompanied by an adult; "X," forbidden to those under 16. Filmmakers quickly learned that an X-rated film had a lot going for it. ☐ Plane hijackings were on the increase, with Cuba the most common destination. The Seaboard Railroad ran an ad, "If you want to go to Miami without a stopover in Havana, call us."

184

☐ **1969** "That's one small step for man, one giant leap for mankind."
—U.S. ASTRONAUT NEIL A. ARMSTRONG, *commander of the* Apollo 11 *mission, on becoming the first man to set foot on the moon*

FOUNDED Friends of the Earth, to restore and preserve the earth's resources

INTRODUCED Disposable diapers; two new American League baseball franchises—the Seattle Pilots and Kansas City Royals—and two National League teams—the Montreal Expos and San Diego Padres; the Boeing 747, capable of carrying up to five hundred passengers; *MS.* magazine; demonstration models of videotape recorders; the *Metroliner,* high-speed train between Washington, D.C. and New York, and the *Turbotrain,* between New York and Boston

SONGS "Aquarius" "Hurry on Down" "Raindrops Keep Falling on My Head" "Let the Sunshine In" "Everybody's Talkin'" "I'll Never Fall in Love Again" "Yesterday, When I Was Young" "My Cup Runneth Over" "Didn't We" "A Time for Us"

NEW INTEREST The occult for the masses: ordinary people bought ouija boards, studied up on reading of tarot cards, had their horoscopes cast; it was the start of the big occult movement of the 1970s.

FASHION There was lots of talk about unisex matching outfits for couples but nothing much came of it. For men, velvet suits and ruffled shirts were appropriate evening wear, no longer foppish. ☐ Pants suits for women meant that a change of costume was no longer required to go from job to evening party; pants were acceptable everywhere.

RETIRED Cyclamates, artificial sweeteners, were removed from the market.

THE WORLD Man walked—bounced, really—on the moon while an estimated 600 million people in forty-nine countries watched the live telecast. ☐ The United States Air Force began secret bombing of Cambodia, having bypassed the chain

185

of command at President Nixon's request. ☐ Violent fighting between Protestants and Roman Catholics broke out in Northern Ireland. ☐ Golda Meir became the fourth prime minister of Israel. Yasir Arafat, leader of Al Fatah, was elected chairman of the executive committee of the Palestinian Liberation Organization. ☐ Charles de Gaulle was narrowly defeated in a referendum; Georges Pompidou became president of France. The British-French *Concorde* supersonic plane made its first test flight. Prince Charles became England's Prince of Wales. ☐ Sixty-five planes were hijacked during the year.

THE UNITED STATES   War resistance heightened; a growing number of young men applied for conscientious-objector status; others fled the country, with Canada and Scandinavia being favored destinations. Canadian officials announced they would admit U.S. draft evaders and army deserters who qualified as immigrants. Moratorium Day was marked throughout the country. In Washington, ten thousand gathered before the Justice Department to protest government prosecution of dissenters; they were dispersed with tear gas. ☐ Following a noisy trial, the "Chicago Eight," indicted in connection with demonstrations during the 1968 Democratic Convention, were found not guilty. ☐ Army Staff Sgt. David Mitchell and Lt. William L. Calley, Jr. were ordered to stand trial before a court-martial for the premeditated murder of twenty-two South Vietnamese civilians at My Lai in 1968. ☐ Supreme Court Justice Abe Fortas resigned after disclosure of his questionable financial dealings. President Nixon appointed Warren Burger as chief justice of the Supreme Court. ☐ In one of his early explorations of rhetoric, Vice Pres. Spiro Agnew announced that Moratorium Day was "encouraged by an effete corps of snobs who characterized themselves as intellectuals." ☐ Sharon Tate and three others were found slaughtered in her Los Angeles home. A few months later, Charles Manson and members of his nomad cult were indicted for the brutal slayings. ☐ Actor Richard Burton bought his wife, Elizabeth Taylor, a sixty-nine-carat diamond from Cartier; the price was in excess of a million dollars. ☐ Writer Norman Mailer and journalist Jimmy Breslin ran for mayor and city council president of New York City. Both

186

lost, but the campaigns were lively, with Mailer running on a platform of "no more bullshit." ☐ A car driven by Sen. Edward M. Kennedy plunged off a bridge into the water at Chappaquiddick Island, Martha's Vineyard, Massachusetts. A young secretary with him, Mary Jo Kopechne, drowned. Senator Kennedy pleaded guilty to leaving the scene of a fatal accident and received a suspended two-month sentence.

SPORTS   The comically inept New York Mets took the National League pennant, then went on to defeat Baltimore 4 games to 1 in the World Series. ☐ Football's Joe Namath said he would rather retire from the game than give up his interest in a restaurant alleged to be a hangout for underworld characters; he later reversed his decision and went out of the restaurant business. ☐ Rod Laver took the men's tennis titles at Wimbledon and Forest Hills.

ARTS AND ENTERTAINMENT   Leonard Bernstein conducted his final concert as permanent conductor of the New York Philharmonic. Pierre Boulez was appointed to conduct a series of sixteen concerts. ☐ The New York Museum of Modern Art purchased the late Gertrude Stein's art collection; it included thirty-eight early Picassos. ☐ *Oh, Calcutta,* New York's first play with nudity, opened off-Broadway. ☐ TV's popular Smothers Brothers Show was cancelled by CBS because the brothers failed to submit a show for prescreening. The network considered their material controversial. ☐ Tiny Tim, the ukelele-playing falsetto singer who had brought new life to "Tip Toe Through the Tulips," married a young woman known as Miss Vicki, live and in color, on Johnny Carson's "Tonight" show.

CHECKLISTS

Books

Here are the books lots of people were reading in any given year. Quality and lasting value have nothing to do with the choices, although here and there you'll find books that were significant as well as popular. Following this list is another, Publishing Landmarks, that includes children's books.

BESTSELLERS

1910   *The Rosary*, Florence Barclay; *When a Man Marries*, Mary Roberts Rinehart

1911   *The Winning of Barbara Worth*, Harold Bell Wright; *The Harvester*, Gene Stratton Porter

1912   *How to Live on 24 Hours a Day*, Arnold Bennett; *Mark Twain*, Albert Bigelow Paine

1913   *Pollyanna*, Eleanor H. Porter; *Laddie*, Gene Stratton Porter; *The New Freedom*, Woodrow Wilson; *Auction Bridge Today*, Milton C. Work

1914   *Penrod*, Booth Tarkington; *The Prince of Graustark*, George Barr McCutcheon

1915   *K*, Mary Roberts Rinehart; *The Lone Star Ranger*, Zane Grey

1916   *Seventeen*, Booth Tarkington; *Mr. Britling Sees It Through*, H. G. Wells; *Dear Enemy*, Jean Webster

1917   *Over the Top*, Arthur Guy Empey; *Rhymes of a Red Cross Man*, Robert W. Service; *The Hundredth Chance*, Ethel M. Dell

1918   *Dere Mable*, Edward Streeter; *The U.P. Trail*, Zane Grey; *My Four Years in Germany*, James W. Gerard

1919   *The Four Horsemen of the Apocalypse*, V. Blasco Ibañez; *The Tin Soldier*, Temple Bailey; *The Education of Henry Adams*, Henry Adams

1920   *The Economic Consequences of the Peace*, John M.

Keynes; *Now It Can Be Told*, Philip Gibbs; *The Great Impersonation*, E. Phillips Oppenheim

1921 *Main Street*, Sinclair Lewis; *The Outline of History*, H. G. Wells; *The Sheik*, Edith M. Hull

1922 *If Winter Comes*, A. S. M. Hutchinson; *Simon Called Peter*, Robert Keable; *The Story of Mankind*, Hendrik Willem Van Loon

1923 *Black Oxen*, Gertrude Atherton; *The Life of Christ*, Giovanni Papini; *Babbitt*, Sinclair Lewis; *Etiquette*, Emily Post; *The Sea-Hawk*, Rafael Sabatini

1924 *So Big*, Edna Ferber; *The Plastic Age*, Percy Marks; *Ariel*, André Maurois; *The Cross Word Puzzle Book*, Prosper Buranelli and others

1925 *Arrowsmith*, Sinclair Lewis; *When We Were Very Young*, A. A. Milne; *The Man Nobody Knows*, Bruce Barton; *The Perennial Bachelor*, Anne Parrish

1926 *Gentlemen Prefer Blondes*, Anita Loos; *The Private Life of Helen of Troy*, John Erskine; *Why We Behave Like Human Beings*, George A. Dorsey; *Sorrell and Son*, Warwick Deeping

1927 *Elmer Gantry*, Sinclair Lewis; *Jalna*, Mazo de la Roche; *Napoleon*, Emil Ludwig; *Ask Me Another*, Julian Spafford and Lucien Esty; *We*, Charles A. Lindbergh

1928 *The Bridge of San Luis Rey*, Thornton Wilder; *Strange Interlude*, Eugene O'Neill; *Bad Girl*, Viña Delmar; *Mother India*, Katherine Mayo

1929 *All Quiet on the Western Front*, Erich Maria Remarque; *Dodsworth*, Sinclair Lewis; *The Art of Thinking*, Ernest Dimnet; *The Bishop Murder Case*, S. S. Van Dine

1930 *Cimarron*, Edna Ferber; *The Story of San Michele*, Axel Munthe; *The Strange Death of President Harding*, Gaston B. Means and May Dixon Thacker; *Young Man of Manhattan*, Katharine Brush

1931 *The Good Earth*, Pearl Buck; *Grand Hotel*, Vicki Baum; *Education of a Princess*, Grand Duchess Marie; *Washington Merry-Go-Round*, Anonymous (the authors were Drew Pearson and Robert S. Allen); *Boners* (a collection); *Back Street*, Fannie Hurst; *Culbertson's Summary* and *Culbertson's Bridge Blue Book*, Ely Culbertson

1932 *The Fountain*, Charles Morgan; *Only Yesterday*, Frederick Lewis Allen; *Van Loon's Geography*, Hendrik Willem Van Loon; *Magnificent Obsession*, Lloyd C. Douglas

1933 *Anthony Adverse*, Hervey Allen; *The Master of Jalna*, Mazo de la Roche; *Life Begins at Forty*, Walter Pitkin; *100,000,000 Guinea Pigs*, Arthur Kallet and F. J. Schlink

1934 *While Rome Burns*, Alexander Woollcott; *Nijinsky*, Romola Nijinsky; *Private Worlds*, Phyllis Bottome; *So Red the Rose*, Stark Young

1935 *Green Light*, Lloyd C. Douglas; *North to the Orient*, Anne Morrow Lindbergh; *Skin Deep*, M. C. Phillips; *Life with Father*, Clarence Day; *Lost Horizon*, James Hilton; *Personal History*, Vincent Sheean

1936 *Gone With the Wind*, Margaret Mitchell; *Wake Up and Live!*, Dorothea Brande; *Man the Unknown*, Alexis Carrel; *Inside Europe*, John Gunther; *Live Alone and Like It*, Marjorie Hillis

1937 *The Citadel*, A. J. Cronin; *Northwest Passage*, Kenneth Roberts; *Of Mice and Men*, John Steinbeck; *How to Win Friends and Influence People*, Dale Carnegie; *The Return to Religion*, Henry C. Link; *The Rains Came*, Louis Bromfield

1938 *The Yearling*, Marjorie Kinnan Rawlings; *My Son, My Son!*, Howard Spring; *Rebecca*, Daphne du Maurier; *The Importance of Living*, Lin Yutang

1939 *The Grapes of Wrath*, John Steinbeck; *All This, and Heaven Too*, Rachel Field; *Days of Our Years*, Pierre Van Paassen; *Inside Asia*, John Gunther

1940 *Kitty Foyle*, Christopher Morley; *For Whom the Bell Tolls*, Ernest Hemingway; *Bet It's a Boy*, Betty B. Blunt; *Mrs. Miniver*, Jan Struther

1941 *The Keys of the Kingdom*, A. J. Cronin; *Berlin Diary*, William L. Shirer; *The White Cliffs of Dover*, Alice Duer Miller; *Out of the Night*, Jan Valtin; *Blood, Sweat and Tears*, Winston Churchill; *This Above All*, Eric Knight

1942 *The Song of Bernadette*, Franz Werfel; *The Moon Is Down*, John Steinbeck; *The Robe*, Lloyd C. Douglas; *Kings Row*, Henry Bellamann; *See Here, Private Hargrove*, Marion Hargrove; *The Last Time I Saw Paris*, Elliot Paul; *They Were Expendable*, William L. White

1943   *The Valley of Decision*, Marcia Davenport; *Under Cover*,
       John Roy Carlson; *One World*, Wendell Willkie; *Here Is
       Your War*, Ernie Pyle
1944   *Strange Fruit*, Lillian Smith; *A Tree Grows in Brooklyn*,
       Betty Smith; *I Never Left Home*, Bob Hope; *Brave Men*,
       Ernie Pyle; *Forever Amber*, Kathleen Winsor; *Leave Her
       to Heaven*, Ben Ames Williams
1945   *The Black Rose*, Thomas B. Costain; *Dear Sir*, Juliet
       Lowell; *Up Front*, Bill Mauldin; *Anything Can Happen*,
       George and Helen Papashvily; *The Egg and I*, Betty
       MacDonald; *Earth and High Heaven*, Gwethalyn Graham
1946   *This Side of Innocence*, Taylor Caldwell; *The Hucksters*,
       Frederic Wakeman; *Peace of Mind*, Joshua L. Liebman;
       The River Road, Frances Parkinson Keyes
1947   *The Miracle of the Bells*, Russell Janney; *Information
       Please Almanac, 1947*; *Gentleman's Agreement*, Laura Z.
       Hobson; *The Moneyman*, Thomas B. Costain
1948   *The Big Fisherman*, Lloyd C. Douglas; *The Naked and
       the Dead*, Norman Mailer; *Dinner at Antoine's*, Frances
       Parkinson Keyes; *Crusade in Europe*, Dwight D. Eisen-
       hower; *How to Stop Worrying and Start Living*, Dale
       Carnegie
1949   *The Egyptian*, Mika Waltari; *Mary*, Sholem Asch; *A Rage
       to Live*, John O'Hara; *White Collar Zoo*, Clare Barnes,
       Jr.; *How to Win at Canasta*, Oswald Jacoby; *The Greatest
       Story Ever Told*, Fulton Oursler; *Cheaper by the Dozen*,
       Frank B. Gilbreth, Jr. and Ernestine Gilbreth Carey
1950   *The Cardinal*, Henry Morton Robinson; *Joy Street*,
       Frances Parkinson Keyes; *The Baby*, a picture book;
       Look Younger, Live Longer, Gayelord Hauser; *Kon-Tiki*,
       Thor Heyerdahl
1951   *From Here to Eternity*, James Jones; *The Caine Mutiny*,
       Herman Wouk; *Washington Confidential*, Jack Lait and
       Lee Mortimer; *The Sea Around Us*, Rachel Carson
1952   *The Silver Chalice*, Thomas B. Costain; *East of Eden*,
       John Steinbeck; *Giant*, Edna Ferber; *The Old Man and
       the Sea*, Ernest Hemingway; *A Man Called Peter*,
       Catherine Marshall
1953   *The Robe*, Lloyd C. Douglas; *Battle Cry*, Leon Uris;
       The Power of Positive Thinking, Norman Vincent Peale;
       Désirée, Annemarie Selinko

1954 *Not as a Stranger,* Morton Thompson; *No Time for Sergeants,* Mac Hyman; *I'll Cry Tomorrow,* Lillian Roth; *The Tumult and the Shouting,* Grantland Rice

1955 *Marjorie Morningstar,* Herman Wouk; *Auntie Mame,* Patrick Dennis; *Gift from the Sea,* Anne Morrow Lindbergh; *The Family of Man,* Edward Steichen; *The Man in the Gray Flannel Suit,* Sloan Wilson

1956 *Peyton Place,* Grace Metalious; *The Last Hurrah,* Edwin O'Connor; *Arthritis and Common Sense,* Dan Dale Alexander; *The Search for Bridey Murphy,* Morey Bernstein; *Andersonville,* MacKinlay Kantor; *The Mandarins,* Simone de Beauvoir

1957 *By Love Possessed,* James Gould Cozzens; *Compulsion,* Meyer Levin; *Kids Say the Darndest Things!,* Art Linkletter; *Atlas Shrugged,* Ayn Rand

1958 *Dr. Zhivago,* Boris Pasternak; *Anatomy of a Murder,* Robert Traver; *Lolita,* Vladimir Nabokov; *Only in America,* Harry Golden

1959 *Exodus,* Leon Uris; *Hawaii,* James Michener; *Advise and Consent,* Allen Drury; *Lady Chatterley's Lover,* D. H. Lawrence; *Folk Medicine,* D. C. Jarvis; *Act One,* Moss Hart; *The Elements of Style,* William Strunk, Jr. and E. B. White

1960 *The Chapman Report,* Irving Wallace; *The Leopard,* Giuseppe di Lampedusa; *Ourselves to Know,* John O'Hara

1961 *The Agony and the Ecstasy,* Irving Stone; *Franny and Zooey,* J. D. Salinger; *To Kill a Mockingbird,* Harper Lee; *The Carpetbaggers,* Harold Robbins

1962 *Ship of Fools,* Katherine Anne Porter; *Seven Days in May,* Fletcher Knebel and Charles W. Bailey II; *The Prize,* Irving Wallace; *Calories Don't Count,* Dr. Herman Taller; *O Ye Jigs & Juleps,* Virginia Cary Hudson; *Happiness Is a Warm Puppy,* Charles M. Schulz

1963 *The Shoes of the Fisherman,* Morris L. West; *The Group,* Mary McCarthy; *Caravans,* James A. Michener; *Profiles in Courage,* John F. Kennedy; *City of Night,* John Rechy

1964 *The Spy Who Came in from the Cold,* John Le Carré; *Herzog,* Saul Bellow; *Four Days,* United Press and American Heritage; *The Kennedy Wit,* compiled by Bill Adler; *Convention,* Fletcher Knebel and Charles W. Bailey

1965 *The Source*, James A. Michener; *Up the Down Stair-case*, Bel Kaufman; *How to Be a Jewish Mother*, Dan Greenburg; *A Gift of Prophecy*, Ruth Montgomery; *Games People Play*, Eric Berne; *A Thousand Days*, Arthur M. Schlesinger, Jr.; *The Making of the President, 1964*, Theodore H. White

1966 *Valley of the Dolls*, Jacqueline Susann; *The Adventurers*, Harold Robbins; *How to Avoid Probate*, Norman Dacey; *In Cold Blood*, Truman Capote; *Human Sexual Response*, William H. Masters and Virginia E. Johnson; *Rush to Judgement*, Mark Lane

1967 *The Arrangement*, Elia Kazan; *Confessions of Nat Turner*, William Styron; *The Chosen*, Chaim Potok; *The Plot*, Irving Wallace; *Death of a President*, William Manchester; *Our Crowd*, Stephen Birmingham

1968 *Airport*, Arthur Hailey; *Couples*, John Updike; *Listen to the Warm*, Rod McKuen; *The Doctor's Quick Weight Loss Diet*, Irwin M. Stillman and Samm Sinclair Baker; *The Money Game*, Adam Smith

1969 *Portnoy's Complaint*, Philip Roth; *The Godfather*, Mario Puzo; *The Love Machine*, Jacqueline Susann; *The Peter Principle*, Lawrence J. Peter and Raymond Hull; *Between Parent and Teenager*, Dr. Haim G. Ginott

PUBLISHING LANDMARKS

Most of the books listed here never made the bestseller lists. But they have shaped minds and lives, shocked entire generations into new ways of thinking, or revolutionized the way that writers write and readers read. Many of them are taught in schools and colleges. All of them are still in print. Not every year produced one.

At the end of this list, you'll find another brief one of Children's Landmarks for the same period.

1910 *Howard's End*, E. M. Forster; *Principia Mathematica*, Bertrand Russell

1911 *Ethan Frome*, Edith Wharton; *Poems*, Rupert Brooke; *Zuleika Dobson*, Max Beerbohm; *The White Peacock*, D. H. Lawrence

1912 *Trent's Last Case,* E. C. Bentley; the first English translation of Dostoyevsky's *The Brothers Karamazov*

1913 *Totem and Taboo,* Sigmund Freud; *Sons and Lovers,* D. H. Lawrence; *Death in Venice,* Thomas Mann; *Swann's Way,* Marcel Proust; *O Pioneers,* Willa Cather

1914 *Dubliners,* James Joyce; *The Golden Bowl,* Henry James; *North of Boston,* Robert Frost; *Chance,* Joseph Conrad; *Caves of the Vatican,* André Gide

1915 *Victory,* Joseph Conrad; *Of Human Bondage,* W. Somerset Maugham; *Spoon River Anthology,* Edgar Lee Masters; *The Thirty-Nine Steps,* John Buchan

1916 *Portrait of the Artist as a Young Man,* James Joyce; *Democracy and Education,* John Dewey; *Chicago Poems,* Carl Sandburg

1917 *Introduction to Psychoanalysis,* Sigmund Freud; *The Love Song of J. Alfred Prufrock and Other Poems,* T. S. Eliot; *South Wind,* Norman Douglas; *The Unconscious,* Carl Jung

1918 *Eminent Victorians,* Lytton Strachey; *My Antonia,* Willa Cather; *Exiles,* James Joyce; *New Poems,* D. H. Lawrence; *Decline of the West,* Oswald Spengler

1919 *Winesburg, Ohio,* Sherwood Anderson; *Jurgen,* James Branch Cabell; *Collected Poems,* Thomas Hardy; *The Moon and Sixpence,* W. Somerset Maugham; *The American Language,* H. L. Mencken; *Corn Huskers,* Carl Sandburg

1920 *The Age of Innocence,* Edith Wharton; *Ten Days That Shook the World,* John Reed; *Kristin Lavransdatter,* Sigrid Undset; *Smoke and Steel,* Carl Sandburg; *Cheri,* Colette; *This Side of Paradise,* F. Scott Fitzgerald; *A Country Doctor,* Franz Kafka; *Bliss,* Katharine Mansfield

1921 *Three Soldiers,* John Dos Passos; *Chrome Yellow,* Aldous Huxley; *Women in Love,* D. H. Lawrence; *Poems 1918–1921,* Ezra Pound; *Queen Victoria,* Lytton Strachey; *Monday or Tuesday,* Virginia Woolf

1922 *The Wasteland,* T. S. Eliot; *Tales of the Jazz Age* and *The Beautiful and the Damned,* F. Scott Fitzgerald; *Forsyte Saga,* John Galsworthy; *The Thibaults,* Roger Martin du Gard; *Siddhartha,* Herman Hesse; *Ulysses,* James Joyce (published in Paris); *The Garden Party,*

Katherine Mansfield; *Jacob's Room*, Virginia Woolf; *Last Poems*, A. E. Housman

1923   *A Lost Lady*, Willa Cather; *The Rover*, Joseph Conrad; *The Ballad of the Harp-Weaver*, Edna St. Vincent Millay; *The Enormous Room*, E. E. Cummings; *The Ego and the Id*, Sigmund Freud

1924   *A Passage to India*, E. M. Forster; *The Magic Mountain*, Thomas Mann; *Autobiography*, Mark Twain; *In Our Time*, Ernest Hemingway; *My Life in Art*, Konstantin Stanislavsky

1925   *The Great Gatsby*, F. Scott Fitzgerald; *The Counterfeiters*, André Gide; *The Trial*, Franz Kafka; *Manhattan Transfer*, John Dos Passos; *Mrs. Dalloway*, Virginia Woolf; *An American Tragedy*, Theodore Dreiser

1926   *The Castle*, Franz Kafka; *The Plumed Serpent*, D. H. Lawrence; *Soldier's Pay*, William Faulkner; *The Sun Also Rises*, Ernest Hemingway

1927   *Men Without Women*, Ernest Hemingway; *To the Lighthouse*, Virginia Woolf; *Remembrance of Things Past*, Marcel Proust; *Steppenwolf*, Hermann Hesse; *Amerika*, Franz Kafka

1928   *John Brown's Body*, Stephen Vincent Benét; *Point Counter Point*, Aldous Huxley; *Lady Chatterley's Lover* (Europe only), D. H. Lawrence; *The Buck in the Snow*, Edna St. Vincent Millay; *Good Morning, America*, Carl Sandburg; *Death Comes for the Archbishop*, Willa Cather; *Decline and Fall*, Evelyn Waugh

1929   *Sartoris* and *The Sound and the Fury*, William Faulkner; *A Farewell to Arms*, Ernest Hemingway; *Look Homeward, Angel*, Thomas Wolfe; *A Room of One's Own*, Virginia Woolf; *The Universe Around Us*, James Jeans

1930   *Poems*, W. H. Auden; *The Bridge*, Hart Crane; *Ash Wednesday*, T. S. Eliot; *As I Lay Dying*, William Faulkner; *The 42nd Parallel*, John Dos Passos; *Vile Bodies*, Evelyn Waugh; *The Revolt of the Masses*, Ortega y Gasset; *Civilization and Its Discontents*, Sigmund Freud

1931   *Sanctuary*, William Faulkner; *Collected Poems*, Robert Frost; *The World of Physics*, Arthur E. Eddington

1932   *Voyage to the End of the Night*, Louis F. Céline; *Light in August*, William Faulkner; *Brave New World*, Aldous

Huxley; *1919*, John Dos Passos; *Young Lonigan*, James
T. Farrell

1933 *Blood Wedding*, Federico García Lorca; *Man's Fate*,
André Malraux; *Joseph and His Brethren* (Vol. 1),
Thomas Mann; *Down and Out in Paris and London*,
George Orwell; *The Shape of Things to Come*, H. G.
Wells

1934 *Tender Is the Night*, F. Scott Fitzgerald; *I, Claudius* and
Claudius the God, Robert Graves; *Patterns of Culture*,
Ruth Benedict; *A Study of History*, Arnold Toynbee;
And Quiet Flows the Don, Mikhail Sholokhov

1935 *Murder in the Cathedral*, T. S. Eliot; *The Dog Beneath
the Skin*, W. H. Auden and Christopher Isherwood; *Mr.
Norris Changes Trains*, Christopher Isherwood; *Growing
Up in New Guinea*, Margaret Mead; *The Young Manhood
of Studs Lonigan*, James T. Farrell

1936 *The Crack-Up*, F. Scott Fitzgerald; *Twenty-five Poems*,
Dylan Thomas; *General Theory of Employment, Interest
and Money*, John M. Keynes

1937 *The Neurotic Personality of Our Time*, Karen Horney;
Nausea, Jean-Paul Sartre; *Man's Hope*, André Malraux;
USA (trilogy of *42nd Parallel*, *1919*, *The Big Money*),
John Don Passos

1938 *The Evolution of Physics*, Albert Einstein, Leopold In-
field; *The Culture of Cities*, Lewis Mumford; *The Un-
vanquished*, William Faulkner; *Goodbye to Berlin*,
Christopher Isherwood

1939 *Finnegan's Wake*, James Joyce; *Lotte in Weimar*,
Thomas Mann; *Journal 1885–1939*, André Gide; *Family
Reunion*, T. S. Eliot

1940 *Portrait of the Artist as a Young Dog*, Dylan Thomas;
Native Son, Richard Wright; *The Interpretation of Personality*, Carl Jung

1941 *The Last Tycoon*, F. Scott Fitzgerald (posthumously);
To the Finland Station, Edmund Wilson

1942 *The Stranger*, Albert Camus; *Four Quartets*, T. S. Eliot;
Go Down, Moses, William Faulkner; *The Flies*, Jean-Paul
Sartre

1943 *The Witness Tree*, Robert Frost; *Being and Nothingness*,
Jean-Paul Sartre

1944 *Psychology and Religion*, Carl Jung; *The Condition of Man*, Lewis Mumford; *Full Employment in a Free Society*, William Beveridge; *No Exit*, Jean-Paul Sartre; *Caligula*, Albert Camus

1945 *Animal Farm*, George Orwell

1946 *All Men Are Mortal*, Simone de Beauvoir; *Deaths and Entrances*, Dylan Thomas

1947 *The Plague*, Albert Camus; *Lord Weary's Castle*, Robert Lowell; *Dr. Faustus*, Thomas Mann

1948 *The Age of Anxiety*, W. H. Auden; *Ape and Essence*, Aldous Huxley; *Notes Toward a Definition of Culture*, T. S. Eliot

1949 *1984*, George Orwell; *The Second Sex*, Simone de Beauvoir

1950 *70 Cantos*, Ezra Pound; *The God That Failed*, Arthur Koestler

1951 *The Lonely Crowd*, David Riesman; *The Rebel*, Albert Camus; *The Sea Around Us*, Rachel Carson; *Catcher in the Rye*, J. D. Salinger

1952 *Collected Poems*, Marianne Moore; *Collected Poems*, Dylan Thomas; *The Invisible Man*, Ralph Ellison; *Waiting for Godot*, Samuel Beckett

1953 *The Confidential Clerk*, T. S. Eliot

1954 *Felix Krull*, Thomas Mann; *Lord of the Flies*, William Golding; *Under Milkwood*, Dylan Thomas (posthumously); *Lord of the Rings*, J. R. R. Tolkien; *Tragedy Is Not Enough*, Karl Jaspers; *The Doors of Perception*, Aldous Huxley

1955 *Why Johnny Can't Read*, R. Flesch; *The Diary of Anne Frank*, Anne Frank; *Catch 22*, Joseph Heller

1956 *The Organization Man*, W. H. Whyte; *History of the English-Speaking People*, Winston S. Churchill

1957 *The Town*, William Faulkner; *On the Road*, Jack Kerouac

1958 *Brave New World Revisited*, Aldous Huxley; *The Affluent Society*, John K. Galbraith; *Letters 1902–1924*, Franz Kafka

1959 *Two Cultures and the Sciences*, C. P. Snow; *Dogmatics in Outline*, Karl Barth; *The Phenomenon of Man*, Pierre Teilhard de Chardin

1960 *The Rise and Fall of the Third Reich*, William L. Shirer

1961 *Letters 1889–1936*, Thomas Mann; *The Self and the*

Drama of Society, Reinhold Niebuhr; *Sinclair Lewis: An American Life*, M. Schorer

1962 *Notebooks 1935-1942*, Albert Camus; *In the Interlude*, Boris Pasternak; *One Day in the Life of Ivan Denisovich*, Aleksandr Solzhenitsyn; *The Guns of August*, Barbara Tuchman

1963 *The Silent Spring*, Rachel Carson; *The Tin Drum*, Gunter Grass; *In the Clearing*, Robert Frost; *Pictures from Brueghel*, William Carlos Williams; *The Fire Next Time*, James Baldwin; *Eichmann in Jerusalem: A Report on the Banality of Evil*, Hannah Arendt

1964 *The Words*, Jean-Paul Sartre; *Anti-Intellectualism in American Life*, Richard Hofstadter

1965 *The Union Dead*, Robert Lowell

1966 *Collected Stories*, Katherine Anne Porter; *Quotations of Chairman Mao*, Mao Tse-tung

1967 *Collected Shorter Poems: 1927-1957*, W. H. Auden

1968 *The Double Helix*, James Watson; *Psychoanalysis and Politics*, Herbert Marcuse

CHILDREN'S LANDMARKS

1912 *Just So Stories*, Rudyard Kipling
1916 *Otto of the Silver Hand*, Howard Pyle
1922 *The Voyages of Dr. Doolittle*, Hugh Lofting
1923 *Bambi*, Felix Salten
1924 *The Complete Peterkin Papers*, Lucretia Hale
1926 *Smoky*, Will James; *Winnie the Pooh*, A. A. Milne
1928 *The House at Pooh Corner*, A. A. Milne
1929 *Hitty, Her First Hundred Years*, Rachel Field
1933 *The Story of Babar*, Jean de Brunhoff
1934 *Mary Poppins*, P. L. Travers
1935 *Caddie Woodlawn*, Carol Brink
1936 *The Story of Ferdinand*, Monro Leaf
1937 *Ballet Shoes*, Noel Streatfield
1938 *The Hobbit*, J. R. R. Tolkien
1939 *Madeleine*, Ludwig Bemelmans
1940 *Lassie Come Home*, Eric Knight
1941 *My Friend Flicka*, Mary O'Hara; *Black Stallion*, Walter Farley
1942 *The Little House*, Virginia Burton

Periodicals

A heartening number of magazines and other periodicals that were already well established in 1910 are still around today—*Good Housekeeping, Harper's, Harper's Bazaar, Ladies' Home Journal, McCall's, National Geographic, Popular Science,* and *Vogue* among them. Here are some of the periodicals that have been born, lived, or died during your Real or Assumed Lifetime:

The American   Started 1906. Ceased publication 1956. Celebrated middle-class American life.

The American Home   Started 1928.

American Mercury   Started 1924 by George Jean Nathan and H. L. Mencken. Its heyday ended with Mencken's retirement in 1933.

American Spectator   Started 1932; ceased 1937. Also had George Jean Nathan as co-editor.

Argosy   Started 1882, has been through many incarnations. Discontinued as a pulp magazine in 1941; revived in 1949 as a different magazine.

Ballyhoo   Started 1931; ceased 1939. Burlesqued advertising, politicians, the American way of life. A great tease which had a short, spectacular success.

Better Homes and Gardens   Started 1922.

Bride's magazine   Started 1934.

Bridge World   Started 1929, when the game was new and a craze.

Business Week   Started 1929.

Century Magazine   Started 1881; ended 1930.

College Humor   Started 1923, soon had 800,000 readers. A digest of jokes and cartoons from various college publications. A Depression victim.

Collier's   Started 1888, became one of America's great weeklies, publishing major writers of its day including, in the 1930s, Winston Churchill. Discontinued 1957.

The Delineator   Once edited by Theodore Dreiser. Discontinued 1937.

Esquire   Started 1933.

Family Circle   Started 1932, distributed through large grocery chains.

Flair   Started and discontinued 1950 but was a beauty while it lasted; died of high production costs related to its die cuts, accordian folds, etc.

Fortune   Started 1930 by Time, Inc.; large format, expensive look.

Glamour   Started 1939; directed to young workingwomen.

Gourmet   Started 1941; devoted to fine food, good eating.

Harper's Weekly   Started 1857; discontinued 1916. Briefly revived in the 1970s.

Holiday   Started 1946 by Curtis Publishing; large format, new idea. Later reduced in size. Survived into the 1970s.

Judge   Started 1881, hit its peak as a humor magazine in the 1920s. Bankrupt 1932.

Leslie's Weekly   Started as *Frank Leslie's Illustrated Newspaper*, 1855. Expired 1922.

Life (No. 1)   Referred to in the text for the year 1910 as "the old *Life*"; started 1883 as magazine of gentle social satire and humor, became a synonym for smartness, with such writers as Robert Benchley and Dorothy Parker. Ceased 1936, when Henry Luce bought the name for his new picture magazine.

Life (No. 2)   Started 1936 with name of older publication. Became the first primarily picture magazine, the unofficial recorder of changes in social mores, and one of the country's most popular publications. Discontinued in the 1970s, then revived.

The Literary Digest Started 1890; discontinued 1938, after learning, with its guarantee that Alfred Landon would beat FDR in the 1936 election, that it was out of touch with the times.

Look Started 1937; like *Life*, emphasized photo-journalism.

Mademoiselle Started 1935; one of the first fashion magazines directed to women younger than those who read the established *Vogue* and *Harper's Bazaar*.

MS. Feminist-oriented magazine, started 1969.

National Review Conservative publication started 1955 by William F. Buckley, Jr.

New Republic Started as a weekly, 1914.

New York Started 1968, rising from the ashes of the defunct *New York Herald Tribune's* Sunday magazine section.

The New Yorker Started 1925 by Harold Ross. Became and remains a leading showcase for important writers, the best cartoonists, and serious critics of the arts and entertainment.

Newsweek News weekly, started 1933.

Parade Sunday newspaper supplement, started 1941.

Penthouse American version started 1969.

Playboy Started 1953; invented the centerfold, with Marilyn Monroe as the first subject.

Psychology Today Started 1967; quickly successful.

Ellery Queen's Mystery Magazine Started 1941.

Quick Started 1949. A pocket-sized digest of the news. Quick disappearance came in 1953.

Rolling Stone Started 1967 as a contemporary popular music publication, grew into one covering contemporary culture, politics, arts, and music.

The Saturday Evening Post Founded 1728 by Benjamin Franklin; went through many hands; purchased 1897 by Curtis Publishing Company, which developed it into one of the most widely read periodicals in publishing history. The name survives, in the hands of another publisher; the weekly *SEP* suspended publication 1969.

The Saturday Review Founded 1924 as *The Saturday Review of Literature*.

Scribner's Started 1887. A serious publication. Ceased 1939.

Seventeen Started 1944. The first fashion publication directed to teenagers and the most successful.

Sports Illustrated Started by Time-Life, Inc., 1954.

St. Nicholas Started 1873. A fine children's magazine which published *Tom Sawyer Abroad* and Kipling's *Jungle Book* serially; also printed the writing of its young readers, including, at one time, Edna St. Vincent Millay.

Stereo Review Started 1958.

Sunset Started 1917.

Time Started by Henry Luce in 1923 as the first news magazine. Originally noted for its peculiar backward sentence structure, it gradually rejoined the English language.

True Confessions Started 1922.

TV Guide Started as a national magazine in 1953, pulling together a group of regional TV publications just as the medium was taking off.

Weight Watchers Magazine Started 1968.

Woman's Day Started 1937 by the A & P for exclusive distribution in its stores.

Woman's Home Companion Started 1870. Under editor Gertrude Lane for thirty years, it published such writers as Willa Cather, John Galsworthy, Arnold Bennett, and Sinclair Lewis. Discontinued 1957.

Youth's Companion Started 1827; discontinued 1929.

Vanity Fair Founded 1914; discontinued 1936. Under editor Frank Crowninshield, this was the stylish and elegant magazine of the 1920s and 1930s, with such writers as Robert Benchley, Dorothy Parker, Aldous Huxley.

Comic Strips

Even if they were dead serious adventures, they've always been called funnies or comic strips. An amazing number of them have endured over many decades. Some went through many hands; the name given in parentheses is that of the original artist or creator.

1910 Already firmly entrenched were the following funnies: *Katzenjammer Kids* (Rudolph Dirks), first strip with talk

balloons, featuring brats Hans and Fritz and Der Captain. Also known as *The Captain and the Kids*. Lasted into the 1970s.
Happy Hooligan (Fred Opper). Last appeared in 1932.
Buster Brown (R. F. Outcault). Last appeared in 1920; the haircut lingered on.
Little Jimmy (James Swinnerton). Last appeared in 1958.
Little Nemo (Winsor McCay). Became *The Land of Wonderful Dreams*. Last appeared in 1927.
Hairbreadth Harry (C. W. Kahles). Last appeared in 1939.
Mutt and Jeff (Bud Fisher). Began in 1907 as A. *Mutt*; Jeff appeared shortly. It's still going.

Started after 1910 were:

1912 *Polly and Her Pals* (Cliff Sterrett). Last ran in 1958.
1913 *Krazy Kat* (George Herriman). Last appeared in 1944.
 Hawkshaw the Detective (Gus Mager). Last appeared in the late 1940s.
 Bringing Up Father (George McManus), featuring Maggie and Jiggs.
1914 *Abie the Agent* (Harry Hershfield).
1915 *Boob McNutt* (Rube Goldberg); the cast included Ike and Mike, they look alike. Last appeared in 1934.
 Toonerville Folks (Fontaine Fox, Jr.); daily panel featuring the Toonerville Trolley and its Skipper, the Terrible Tempered Mr. Bang, and others. Last appeared in 1955.
1917 *Schools Days* (Clare Victor Dwiggins). Last appeared in 1932.
 The Gumps (Sidney Smith), with the memorably chinless Andy Gump.
1918 *The Bungle Family* (Harry Tuthill); originally *Home Sweet Home*. Last appeared in 1945.
 Gasoline Alley (Frank King), the first strip in which characters grew up along with the readers.
 Minute Movies (Edgar Wheeler). Last appeared in the mid-1930s.
1919 *Barney Google and Spark Plug* (Billy De Beck), later called *Barney Google and Snuffy Smith* but always with his knock-kneed horse, Spark Plug.
 S'Matter Pop? (Charles M. Payne). Last ran in 1949.

1921 *Out Our Way* (J. R. Williams). These were reissued in the 1950s.

1923 *Felix the Cat* (Pat Sullivan). Began as an animated cartoon before hitting the funny papers.
Our Boarding House (Gene Ahern), single panel featuring the braggart Major Hoople.
Moon Mullins (Frank Willard).

1924 *Captain Easy* (Roy Crane), the first comic adventure strip, began as *Washington Tubbs II* and *Wash Tubbs*.
Little Orphan Annie (Harold Gray). The strip discontinued a few years ago but Annie and Daddy Warbucks live on.
Wash Tubbs (Roy Crane), became Captain Easy.

1927 *Bobby Thatcher* (George Storm), boys' adventure strip. Last appeared in 1937.
Nize Baby (Milt Gross), dialect script. Last appeared in 1929.

1928 *Tarzan* (Hal Foster).
Skippy (Percy Crosby). Last appeared in 1943.

1929 *Buck Rogers* (Dick Calkins); the first science fiction strip, set in the 25th Century. Last appeared in 1967.
Count Screwloose (Milt Gross). Last appeared in 1934, when Screwloose from Tooloose moved to *Dave's Delicatessen*.
Popeye the Sailor (E. C. Segar) made his first appearance in the *Thimble Theatre* strip, already inhabited by Olive Oyl. Wimpy came later.

1930 *Blondie* (Chic Young) debuted as a gold digger but quickly became a model wife when she married Dagwood Bumstead.
Mickey Mouse (Floyd Gottfredson from the Walt Disney character).

1931 *Dick Tracy* (Chester Gould).
Dave's Delicatessen (Milt Gross).

1932 *Secret Agent X-9* (Alex Raymond); became *Secret Agent Corrigan*.

1933 *Alley Oop* (V. T. Hamlin).
White Boy (Garrett Price); later called *Skull Valley*. Last appeared in 1936.

1934 *Li'l Abner* (Al Capp).
Terry and the Pirates (Milton Caniff).

1937   *Prince Valiant* (Hal Foster).
       Abbie an' Slats (Al Capp, Raeburn Van Buren). Last appeared in 1971.
1938   *Superman* (Jerry Siegel and Joe Shuster).
1939   *Batman.*
1940   *Captain Marvel.*
1941   *Gordo* (Gus Arriola).
1942   *Barnaby* (Crockett Johnson); the small boy with the cigar-chomping fairy godfather, Mr. O'Malley. Discontinued in 1952; briefly revived 1962.
1947   *Steve Canyon* (Milt Caniff).
1948   *Pogo* (Walt Kelly), the politically hip possum. Discontinued in 1974.
1950   *Peanuts* (Charles Schulz). The comic strip that became an industry.
       King Aroo (Jack Kent). Last appeared in 1965.
       Beatle Bailey (Mort Walker).
1954   *Hi and Lois* (Mort Walker).
1957   *Miss Peach* (Mell Lazarus).
1958   *B.C.* (Johnny Hart).
1964   *The Wizard of Id* (Brant Parker).
1965   *Tumbleweeds* (Tom K. Ryan).
1968   *Doonesbury* (Garry Trudeau) debuted in the *Yale Record*, moved to the *Yale Daily News*, was nationally syndicated in 1970.

Movies

Almost everyone goes away mad from lists of movies year by year. Individual favorites are bound to be left out. What follows is not a list of the best or even the most meaningful; it's a picture of what was going on.

1910   D. W. Griffith made cans and cans of short films for Biograph.
1911   Griffiith, *Enoch Arden;* the first of Tom Mix's film; Mack

Sennett, one of Griffith's actors, struck out on his own, to become the king of slapstick, originator of the pie-in-the-face routine, and inventor of the Keystone Kops and the bathing beauty.

1912   Among the many shorts was *The New York Hat,* with Mary Pickford and Lionel Barrymore; Sarah Bernhardt made the French movie *Queen Elizabeth*; the important Italian film was *Quo Vadis.*

1913   Sennett's short films kept the crowds laughing; Cecil B. De Mille directed his first film, *The Squaw Man.*

1914   Charlie Chaplin made fourteen films, among them *Tillie's Punctured Romance,* his first full-length comedy, and *Kid Auto Races in Venice,* in which he wore his tramp costume for the first time; the first of the Pearl White serials, *Perils of Pauline; The Spoilers,* with William Farnum.

1915   D. W. Griffith's *Birth of a Nation,* the first full-length serious drama (Lillian Gish, Mae Marsh, Henry B. Walthall); *The Lamb* (Douglas Fairbanks); *The Tramp* (Chaplin, Edna Purviance, Mack Swain); *A Fool There Was* (Theda Bara); Cecil B. De Mille's *Carmen*

1916   D. W. Griffith's *Intolerance* (Lillian Gish, Mae Marsh, Constance Talmadge, Erich von Stroheim); Chaplin's *The Pawnshop* and *The Rink*; Geraldine Farrar in *Joan the Woman*

1917   *The Little Princess* (Mary Pickford); *Wild and Woolly* (Douglas Fairbanks); Chaplin's *The Immigrant and Easy Street*

1918   The first Tarzan film, with Elmo Lincoln as the Ape Man; Chaplin's *A Dog's Life* and *Shoulder Arms*; Ernst Lubitsch's *Carmen*

1919   *Broken Blossoms* (Lillian Gish, Richard Barthelmess); *Daddy Long Legs* (Mary Pickford); *Male and Female* (Gloria Swanson)

1920   *The Cabinet of Dr. Caligari* and *The Golem,* German classics; *The Mark of Zorro* (Douglas Fairbanks); *Way Down East* (Lillian Gish, Richard Barthelmess); *Polly-anna* (Mary Pickford)

1921   *The Kid* (Charlie Chaplin, Jackie Coogan); *Orphans of the Storm* (Lillian and Dorothy Gish, Joseph Schildkraut, Monte Blue); *The Sheik* (Rudolph Valentino); *The*

Three Musketeers (Douglas Fairbanks); Fritz Lang's *The Weary Death*

1922   *Grandma's Boy* (Harold Lloyd); Robert Flaherty's classic documentary, *Nanook of the North*; Fritz Lang's *Dr. Mabuse*; *The Hunchback of Notre Dame* (Lon Chaney); *Robin Hood* (Douglas Fairbanks, Wallace Beery). Buster Keaton shorts included *The Electric House*

1923   *The Covered Wagon*; *Our Hospitality* (Buster Keaton, Natalie Talmadge)

1924   *Manhandled* (Gloria Swanson); *The Navigator* (Buster Keaton); *The Thief of Bagdad* (Douglas Fairbanks, Anna May Wong); Emil Jannings' *The Last Laugh*

1925   Sergei Eisenstein's *Potemkin*; *The Phantom of the Opera* (Lon Chaney); *The Pony Express* (Ricardo Cortez); *The Gold Rush* (Charlie Chaplin); *The Eagle* (Rudolph Valentino, Vilma Banky); Charlie Chan in the first of forty-six screen appearances; *The Big Parade* (John Gilbert, Renée Adorée)

1926   *The General* (Buster Keaton, Marian Mack); *Tramp, Tramp, Tramp* (Harry Langdon's first full-length film); *Dancing Mothers* (Clara Bow as a flapper); *The Black Pirate* (Douglas Fairbanks, Billie Dove); *Son of the Sheik* (Rudolph Valentino, Vilma Banky); *Ben Hur* (Ramon Navarro); *Beau Geste* (Ronald Colman, Noah Beery)

1927   De Mille's *The King of Kings*; *Seventh Heaven* (Janet Gaynor); *Flesh and the Devil* (Greta Garbo); *The Way of All Flesh* (Emil Jannings); Fritz Lang's *Metropolis*; *Steamboat Bill* (Buster Keaton); the first Laurel and Hardy film, *Putting Pants on Phillip*; the first film with synchronized sound, *The Jazz Singer* (Al Jolson)

1928   *Coquette* (Mary Pickford); *In Old Arizona* (Warner Baxter); *Our Dancing Daughters* (Joan Crawford); René Clair's *The Italian Straw Hat*; Sergei Eisenstein's *Ivan the Terrible*; *The Last Command* (Emil Jannings); Mickey Mouse in his film debut, *Steamboat Willie*

1929   Two of the first of the big musicals: *Broadway Melody* and *The Love Parade*; *Disraeli* (George Arliss, Joan Bennett); *The Divorcee* (Norma Shearer); Alfred Hitchcock's *Blackmail*; the dance team of Buck and Bubbles made a two-reeler for Pathé.

1930   *Anna Christie* (Greta Garbo); *The Blue Angel* (Marlene Dietrich); the first of the prison films: *The Big House* (Wallace Beery); Jean Cocteau's *The Blood of the Poet; With Byrd at the South Pole*

1931   The Marx Brothers' first: *Monkey Business; City Lights* (Charlie Chaplin); *Min and Bill* (Marie Dressler, Wallace Beery); *Frankenstein* (Boris Karloff); *A Connecticut Yankee* (Will Rogers); *Little Caesar* (Edward G. Robinson); René Clair's *Le Million; Skippy* (Jackie Cooper)

1932   The all-star *Grand Hotel; Dr. Jekyll and Mr. Hyde* (Fredric March); *The Sin of Madelon Claudet* (Helen Hayes); *A Farewell to Arms* (Gary Cooper); *Shanghai Express* (Marlene Dietrich); Fritz Lang's *M, the Kidnapper* (Peter Lorre); Johnny Weissmuller in his first Tarzan film; Katharine Hepburn's first film, *A Bill of Divorcement*, with John Barrymore

1933   *The Private Life of Henry VIII* (Charles Laughton); *Little Women* (Katharine Hepburn); *The Invisible Man* (Claude Rains); *She Done Him Wrong* (Mae West); *King Kong* (Fay Wray, Bruce Cabot); *42nd Street* (Ruby Keeler, Dick Powell); Noel Coward's *Cavalcade*; the smash hit, Disney's *Three Little Pigs; Flying Down to Rio* (Fred Astaire and his new partner, Ginger Rogers); *Rasputin and the Empress* (John, Ethel, and Lionel Barrymore); *I Am a Fugitive from a Chain Gang* (Paul Muni)

1934   *It Happened One Night* (Clark Gable, Claudette Colbert); *Of Human Bondage* (Leslie Howard, Bette Davis); *The Thin Man* (William Powell, Myrna Loy); *Catherine the Great* (Elizabeth Bergner); *Twentieth Century* (John Barrymore, Carole Lombard); Fred Astaire and Ginger Rogers danced in *The Gay Divorcee*, and the acrobatic tap dancers, the Nicholas Brothers, in Eddie Cantor's *Kid Millions.*

1935   *The Informer* (Victor McLaglen); *Mutiny on the Bounty* (Clark Gable, Charles Laughton, Franchot Tone); Hitchcock's *The 39 Steps* (Robert Donat, Madeleine Carroll); *Dangerous* (Bette Davis); *David Copperfield* (Freddie Bartholomew, W. C. Fields); Fred Astaire and Ginger Rogers in both *Roberta* and *Top Hat; A Night at the*

Opera (Marx Brothers); Shirley Temple and Bill Robinson doing their step dance in *The Little Colonel*; *Captain Blood*, making a star of Errol Flynn

1936 *Mr. Deeds Goes to Town* (Gary Cooper); *The Great Ziegfeld* (Luise Rainer, William Powell); *Dodsworth* (Walter Huston); *Louis Pasteur* (Paul Muni); *Rose Marie* (Nelson Eddy, Jeanette MacDonald); *The Garden of Allah* (Charles Boyer, Marlene Dietrich); *La Kermesse Héroique,* directed by Jacques Feyder; *The Ghost Goes West* (Robert Donat); *Winterset* (Burgess Meredith, Margo)

1937 *Stella Dallas* (Barbara Stanwyck); *The Good Earth* (Paul Muni, Luise Rainer); *Captains Courageous* (Spencer Tracy); *Camille* (Greta Garbo, Robert Taylor); *A Day at the Races* (Marx Brothers); *In Old Chicago* (Tyrone Power, Don Ameche, Alice Faye); *The Awful Truth* (Cary Grant, Irene Dunne); *A Star Is Born* (Janet Gaynor, Fredric March); *Lost Horizon* (Ronald Colman); Tyrone Power and former Olympic star Sonja Henie in *Thin Ice*

1938 *You Can't Take It With You* (James Stewart, Jean Arthur); Disney's *Snow White and the Seven Dwarfs;* *Pygmalion* (Leslie Howard, Wendy Hiller); Hitchcock's *The Lady Vanishes* (Michael Redgrave); *The Goldwyn Follies*, with George Gershwin's final score; *Four Daughters* (introducing John Garfield, starring Rosemary, Priscilla, and Lola Lane); *The Adventures of Robin Hood* (Errol Flynn); *Holiday* (Katharine Hepburn, Cary Grant); *Love Finds Andy Hardy* (Mickey Rooney, Judy Garland)

1939 John Ford's *Stagecoach* (John Wayne, Claire Trevor); *Wuthering Heights* (Laurence Olivier, Merle Oberon); *Gone With the Wind* (Clark Gable, Vivien Leigh); *Ninotchka* (Greta Garbo, Melvyn Douglas); *Mr. Smith Goes to Washington* (James Stewart, Jean Arthur); *The Wizard of Oz* (Judy Garland); *Goodbye Mr. Chips* (Robert Donat, Greer Garson); *Intermezzo* (Ingrid Bergman, Leslie Howard); the first of twenty-seven Blondie films, featuring Baby Dumpling

1940 *The Grapes of Wrath* (Henry Fonda, Jane Darwell); *Rebecca* (Laurence Olivier, Joan Fontaine); *The Great*

Dictator (Charlie Chaplin, Jack Oakie); *The Baker's Wife* (Raimu); *The Westerner* (Gary Cooper, Walter Brennan); *The Philadelphia Story* (Katharine Hepburn, Cary Grant, James Stewart); Bob Hope and Bing Crosby in the first *Road* picture—to Singapore; Disney's *Fantasia; Kitty Foyle* (Ginger Rogers); *His Girl Friday* (Cary Grant, Rosalind Russell, Ralph Bellamy)

1941 *Citizen Kane* (Orson Welles); *Never Give a Sucker an Even Break* (W. C. Fields); *Major Barbara* (Rex Harrison, Wendy Hiller); *Sergeant York* (Gary Cooper); *How Green Was My Valley* (Donald Crisp, Roddy McDowall); *Here Comes Mr. Jordan* (Robert Montgomery, Claude Rains); *The Maltese Falcon* (Humphrey Bogart, Mary Astor, Sidney Greenstreet); *Two-faced Woman*, Garbo's final film

1942 *Casablanca* (Humphrey Bogart, Ingrid Bergman); *Mrs. Miniver* (Greer Garson, Walter Pidgeon); *Yankee Doodle Dandy* (James Cagney); *Woman of the Year* (Katharine Hepburn, Spencer Tracy); *Sullivan's Travels* (Joel McCrea, Veronica Lake); *In Which We Serve* (Noel Coward); *Kings Row* (Ronald Reagan, Ann Sheridan); *Now, Voyager* (Bette Davis, Paul Henreid); Disney's *Bambi; For Me and My Gal* (Gene Kelly, Judy Garland); *Holiday Inn* (Fred Astaire, Bing Crosby)

1943 *The Ox-Bow Incident* (Henry Fonda, Dana Andrews); *For Whom the Bell Tolls* (Gary Cooper, Ingrid Bergman); *Sahara* (Humphrey Bogart); *Thank Your Lucky Stars* (all-star wartime musical); *The Song of Bernadette* (Jennifer Jones); *Air Force* (John Garfield, Faye Emerson)

1944 *Up in Arms* (Danny Kaye); *Going My Way* (Bing Crosby, Barry Fitzgerald); *Meet Me in St. Louis* (Judy Garland, Margaret O'Brien); *Gaslight* (Ingrid Bergman); *Lifeboat* (Tallulah Bankhead); *To Have and Have Not* (Humphrey Bogart, Lauren Bacall); *Les Enfants du Paradis* (Jean Louis Barrault); *Pin Up Girl* (Betty Grable); *Jane Eyre* (Joan Fontaine, Orson Welles)

1945 *The Lost Weekend* (Ray Milland, Jane Wyman); *Laura* (Gene Tierney, Dana Andrews); *Anchors Aweigh* (Frank Sinatra, Gene Kelly, Kathryn Grayson); *The Corn Is Green* (Bette Davis); *Spellbound* (Ingrid Bergman,

Gregory Peck); *Mildred Pierce* (Joan Crawford); *State Fair* (Jeanne Crain, Dick Haymes); *Brief Encounter* (Celia Johnson, Trevor Howard); *National Velvet* (Elizabeth Taylor)

1946   *Notorious* (Cary Grant, Ingrid Bergman); *To Each His Own* (Olivia de Havilland, John Lund); *The Yearling* (Gregory Peck, Jane Wyman); *Anna and the King of Siam* (Irene Dunne, Rex Harrison); *The Best Years of Our Lives* (Myrna Loy, Fredric March); Roberto Rossellini's *Paisan; Henry V* (Laurence Olivier); Jean Cocteau's *Beauty and the Beast*

1947   *Gentleman's Agreement* (Gregory Peck, John Garfield); *Great Expectations; Life with Father* (William Powell, Irene Dunne); *Miracle on 34th Street* (Maureen O'Hara); *Odd Man Out* (James Mason); *Nightmare Alley* (Tyrone Power); *Crossfire* (Robert Ryan); *The Red Shoes* (Moira Shearer); *The Bicycle Thief*

1948   *Monsieur Verdoux* (Charlie Chaplin); *Easter Parade* (Fred Astaire, Judy Garland); *Treasure of the Sierra Madre* (Humphrey Bogart, Walter Huston); *Johnny Belinda* (Jane Wyman, Lew Ayres); *Louisiana Story; Hamlet* (Laurence Olivier); *The Snake Pit* (Olivia de Havilland); *Key Largo* (Humphrey Bogart, Lauren Bacall, Claire Trevor); *Red River* (John Wayne, Montgomery Clift)

1949   *All the King's Men* (Broderick Crawford, Mercedes McCambridge); *The Barkleys of Broadway* (Fred Astaire, Ginger Rogers, Oscar Levant); *Champion* (Kirk Douglas); *The Heiress* (Olivia de Havilland); *Lost Boundaries; Command Decision* (Gregory Peck, Dean Jagger); *The Fallen Idol* (Ralph Richardson)

1950   *All About Eve* (Bette Davis, Anne Baxter); *Born Yesterday* (Judy Holliday, William Holden, Broderick Crawford); *Kind Hearts and Coronets* (Alec Guinness); *Sunset Boulevard* (Gloria Swanson, William Holden); *Stromboli* (Ingrid Bergman), Roberto Rossellini director; *The Third Man* (Orson Welles, Joseph Cotten)

1951   *The African Queen* (Humphrey Bogart, Katharine Hepburn); *A Streetcar Named Desire* (Marlon Brando, Vivien Leigh, Karl Malden); *An American in Paris* (Gene Kelly); *The Great Caruso* (Mario Lanza); *A Place in the*

Sun (Montgomery Clift, Elizabeth Taylor); *Death of a Salesman* (Fredric March)

1952 *Come Back, Little Sheba* (Shirley Booth, Burt Lancaster); *Cry, the Beloved Country* (Sidney Poitier); *High Noon* (Gary Cooper, Grace Kelly); *Singin' in the Rain* (Gene Kelly, Donald O'Connor, Debbie Reynolds)

1953 *Moulin Rouge* (Jose Ferrer); *From Here to Eternity* (Montgomery Clift, Burt Lancaster, Deborah Kerr, Frank Sinatra); *Gentlemen Prefer Blondes* (Marilyn Monroe, Jane Russell); *Shane* (Alan Ladd, Van Heflin); *Stalag 17* (William Holden)

1954 *La Strada* (Anthony Quinn); *On the Waterfront* (Marlon Brando); *The Country Girl* (Bing Crosby, Grace Kelly, William Holden); *Seven Brides for Seven Brothers* (Jane Powell, Howard Keel); *Beat the Devil* (Humphrey Bogart, Robert Morley, Gina Lollobrigida); *A Star Is Born* (Judy Garland, James Mason)

1955 *East of Eden* (Julie Harris, James Dean); *The Seven-Year Itch* (Marilyn Monroe); *Marty* (Ernest Borgnine); *Bad Day at Black Rock* (Spencer Tracy); *The Rose Tattoo* (Anna Magnani); *Rebel Without a Cause* (James Dean); *Strategic Air Command* (James Stewart); *It's Always Fair Weather* (Gene Kelly, Michael Kidd, Dan Dailey); *To Catch a Thief* (Cary Grant, Grace Kelly); *The Red Balloon*

1956 Mike Todd's *Around the World in 80 Days* (David Niven and all-star cast); *The King and I* (Yul Brynner, Deborah Kerr); *The Ten Commandments* (Charlton Heston, Anne Baxter); *Anastasia* (Ingrid Bergman, Yul Brynner); *High Society* (Bing Crosby, Grace Kelly); *I'll Cry Tomorrow* (Susan Hayward); *Bus Stop* (Marilyn Monroe); *The Rainmaker* (Burt Lancaster, Katharine Hepburn)

1957 *The Bridge on the River Kwai* (Alec Guinness, William Holden, Jack Hawkins); *Pal Joey* (Rita Hayworth, Frank Sinatra); *The Three Faces of Eve* (Joanne Woodward); *The Prince and the Showgirl* (Sir Laurence Olivier, Marilyn Monroe); *12 Angry Men* (Henry Fonda, Lee J. Cobb); Ingmar Bergman's *Wild Strawberries*

1958 *Gigi* (Leslie Caron, Maurice Chevalier); *Peyton Place* (Lana Turner, Hope Lange); *Auntie Mame* (Rosalind

Russell); *The Horse's Mouth* (Alec Guinness); *Cat on a Hot Tin Roof* (Elizabeth Taylor, Paul Newman); Ingmar Bergman's *The Seventh Seal*; *Mon Oncle* (Jacques Tati)

1959   *Ben Hur* (Charlton Heston, Martha Scott); *Anatomy of a Murder* (James Stewart, Lee Remick, Ben Gazzara); *North by Northwest* (Cary Grant, Eva Marie Saint); *The Nun's Story* (Audrey Hepburn, Peter Finch); *Pillow Talk* (Doris Day, Rock Hudson, Thelma Ritter); François Truffaut's *The 400 Blows; Some Like It Hot* (Marilyn Monroe, Jack Lemmon, Tony Curtis); *On the Beach* (Fred Astaire, no dancing)

1960   *Exodus* (Paul Newman, Eva Marie Saint); *G.I. Blues* (Elvis Presley); *Psycho* (Anthony Perkins, Janet Leigh); *Suddenly Last Summer* (Katharine Hepburn, Elizabeth Taylor); *Tunes of Glory* (Alec Guinness, John Mills); *Never on Sunday* (Melina Mercouri); *The Apartment* (Jack Lemmon, Shirley MacLaine); *Elmer Gantry* (Burt Lancaster, Jean Simmons)

1961   *West Side Story* (Natalie Wood); *Judgment at Nuremberg* (Maximilian Schell, Spencer Tracy, Marlene Dietrich); *Two Women* (Sophia Loren); *La Dolce Vita* (Anita Ekberg, Marcello Mastroianni); *Splendor in the Grass* (Warren Beatty, Natalie Wood); *The World of Suzie Wong* (Nancy Kwan, William Holden)

1962   *Lawrence of Arabia* (Peter O'Toole); *The Miracle Worker* (Patty Duke, Anne Bancroft); *Sweet Bird of Youth* (Paul Newman, Ed Begley); *Sundays and Cybele; Last Year at Marienbad; To Kill a Mockingbird* (Gregory Peck)

1963   *Hud* (Paul Newman, Patricia Neal, Melvyn Douglas); *Tom Jones* (Albert Finney); Federico Fellini's *8½; The L-Shaped Room* (Leslie Caron)

1964   *Mary Poppins* (Julie Andrews); *My Fair Lady* (Rex Harrison, Audrey Hepburn); *Topkapi* (Melina Mercouri, Peter Ustinov); *Zorba the Greek* (Anthony Quinn); *Dr. Strangelove* (Peter Sellers, George C. Scott, Sterling Hayden); *A Hard Day's Night* (the Beatles)

1965   *Ship of Fools* (Simone Signoret, Oskar Werner, Vivien Leigh); *Darling* (Julie Christie); Fellini's *Juliet of the Spirit; The Sound of Music* (Julie Andrews); *Cat Ballou* (Jane Fonda, Lee Marvin)

1966 *A Man for All Seasons* (Paul Scofield); *Who's Afraid of Virginia Woolf?* (Elizabeth Taylor, Richard Burton); Claude Lelouch's *A Man and a Woman*; *Georgy Girl* (Lynn Redgrave, James Mason); *The Shop on Main Street*; *Blow Up* (David Hemmings, Vanessa Redgrave); *The Russians Are Coming, The Russians Are Coming* (Carl Reiner, Alan Arkin)

1967 *In the Heat of the Night* (Rod Steiger, Sidney Poitier); *Cool Hand Luke* (Paul Newman); *The Graduate* (Dustin Hoffman); *La Guerre Est Finie* (Yves Montand); *Elvira Madigan*; *Guess Who's Coming to Dinner?* (the final Katharine Hepburn–Spencer Tracy film); *Bonnie and Clyde* (Faye Dunaway, Warren Beatty)

1968 *The Lion in Winter* (Katharine Hepburn, Peter O'Toole); *The Heart Is a Lonely Hunter* (Alan Arkin); *Rachel, Rachel* (Joanne Woodward); *Rosemary's Baby* (Mia Farrow); *Funny Girl* (Barbra Streisand)

1969 *Z* (Yves Montand); *Midnight Cowboy* (Jon Voight, Dustin Hoffman); *They Shoot Horses, Don't They?* (Jane Fonda); *The Prime of Miss Jean Brodie* (Maggie Smith); *Alice's Restaurant* (Arlo Guthrie); *The Wild Bunch* (William Holden, Ernest Borgnine, Robert Ryan)

Theater

The list below records Broadway opening dates, unless otherwise noted. You may have seen (or claim to have seen) shows of your lifetime at an earlier date—at an out-of-town tryout or in Europe—or, later, on tour or in revival.

1910 *Alias Jimmy Valentine*; Maurice Maeterlinck's *The Blue Bird*. MUSICALS: *Madame Sherry*; Victor Herbert's *Naughty Marietta*; *The Ziegfeld Follies*, introducing Fannie Brice and Bert Williams

1911 *The Garden of Allah*; *Disraeli* (George Arliss); *Kismet*

(Otis Skinner); Dublin's Abbey Theatre with J. M. Synge's *The Playboy of the Western World*. MUSICAL: *Jumping Jupiter* (Edna Wallace Hopper, Ina Claire)

1912 *Peg o' My Heart* (Laurette Taylor); Max Reinhardt's Deutsches Theater tableaux production, *Sumurun*. MUSICALS: Rudolf Friml's *The Firefly*; the first *Passing Show* revue. In burlesque, the Minsky brothers staged the first of their bawdy productions at the National Winter Garden.

1913 George M. Cohan's comedy-thriller, *Seven Keys to Baldpate*. MUSICALS: Victor Herbert's *Sweethearts*; Rudolf Friml's *High Jinks*; Vernon and Irene Castle's first show, *The Sunshine Girl*. Vaudeville's top "musical and flash act" was the Coccias. Mary Garden and John McCormack toured with Victor Herbert's grand opera, *Natoma*.

1914 Elmer Rice's *On Trial*; *It Pays to Advertise*; *Too Many Cooks*; *Twin Beds*. MUSICALS: *Chin-Chin*; George M. Cohan's *Hello, Broadway*; Irving Berlin's *Watch Your Step*; Victor Herbert's *The Only Girl*

1915 *The Great Lover*; *The House of Glass*; *The Unchastened Woman*. MUSICALS: *Very Good, Eddie*; *The Princess Pat*; *Katinka*. At New York's Hippodrome, the spectacle *Hip-Hip Hooray* featured a galaxy of stars plus John Philip Sousa's band.

1916 John Galsworthy's *Justice* (John Barrymore); *A Kiss for Cinderella* (Maude Adams). MUSICALS: *The Ziegfeld Follies*; *The Big Show* at the Hippodrome, with Anna Pavlova dancing two shows daily, earning $8,500 a week.

1917 Jesse Lynch Williams' *Why Marry?* (the first play to win a Pulitzer Prize); *Tiger Rose*; *Polly with a Past*. MUSICALS: *Maytime* (Peggy Wood); *Hitchy-Koo* (Irene Bordoni). Will Rogers, the "cowboy philosopher," joined *The Ziegfeld Follies*.

1918 *Lightnin'* (the first play to pass the 1,000-performance mark); *Dear Brutus* (Helen Hayes); *East Is West* (Fay Bainter); Henrik Ibsen's *A Doll's House*, *Hedda Gabler*, and other plays, with Alla Nazimova. MUSICALS: Irving Berlin's army show *Yip Yip Yaphank*; *Sometime* (Mae West)

1919 *Up in Mabel's Room*; Booth Tarkington's *Clarence* (Alfred Lunt); *The Jest* (John and Lionel Barrymore); *The Gold Diggers* (Ina Claire). MUSICALS: Victor Herbert's *The Velvet Lady*; *Irene*; *Apple Blossoms*

1920 Eugene O'Neill's *Beyond the Horizon* as well as his *The Emperor Jones*. The musical hit was Jerome Kern's *Sally*.

1921 *Dulcy* (Lynn Fontanne); *The Green Goddess* (George Arliss); Eugene O'Neill's *Anna Christie*; *Kiki* (Lenore Ulric). MUSICALS: Noble Sissle and Eubie Blake's *Shuffle Along* (Broadway's first all-black show); Sigmund Romberg's *Blossom Time*; *The Perfect Fool* (Ed Wynn)

1922 *Abie's Irish Rose* opened for a record run. *The Cat and the Canary*; *Seventh Heaven*; *Rain* (Jeanne Eagles); Karel Capek's robot melodrama *R.U.R.*; George Bernard Shaw's *Back to Methuselah*; Luigi Pirandello's *Six Characters in Search of an Author*; *Merton of the Movies*. MUSICALS: Irving Berlin's *Music Box Revue*. A Russian dance, burlesque, and folk song company, Chauve Souris, was a long-run favorite.

1923 *Cyrano de Bergerac* (Walter Hampden); *Icebound*; John Barrymore as *Hamlet*. MUSICALS: *Kid Boots* (Eddie Cantor); the annual *Music Box Revue* and *Ziegfeld Follies*

1924 Maxwell Anderson and Lawrence Stallings' *What Price Glory?*; Sidney Howard's *They Knew What They Wanted*; Eugene O'Neill's *Desire Under the Elms*; *The Guardsman* (Alfred Lunt and Lynn Fontanne); George Kelly's *The Show-Off*. MUSICALS: George and Ira Gershwin's *Lady Be Good*; Sigmund Romberg's *The Student Prince*; Rudolf Friml's *Rose Marie*

1925 *Craig's Wife*; George S. Kaufman's *The Butter and Egg Man*; *The Last of Mrs. Cheyney*. MUSICALS: *No! No! Nanette*; *The Vagabond King* (Dennis King); *Sunny* (Marilyn Miller); *The Coconuts* (Marx Brothers); George White's *Scandals*; Earl Carroll's *Vanities*

1926 Eugene O'Neill's *The Great God Brown*; *Gentlemen Prefer Blondes*; Ferenc Molnár's *The Play's the Thing*; Somerset Maugham's *The Constant Wife*. MUSICALS: George Gershwin's *Oh, Kay*; Sigmund Romberg's *The Desert Song*; Richard Rodgers and Lorenz Hart's *The Girl Friend*

1927 The George S. Kaufman–Edna Ferber *The Royal Family*;

Du Bose Hayward's *Porgy*. MUSICALS: *Hit the Deck*; *Good News*; Richard Rodgers and Lorenz Hart's *A Connecticut Yankee*; George and Ira Gershwin's *Funny Face*; Jerome Kern's *Show Boat*

1928 Eugene O'Neill's *Strange Interlude*; Ben Hecht and Charles MacArthur's *The Front Page*; Philip Barry's *Holiday*; Mae West in *Diamond Lil*. MUSICALS: *Blackbirds;* Sigmund Romberg's *The New Moon; Whoopee* (Eddie Cantor); *Animal Crackers* (Marx Brothers)

1929 Elmer Rice's *Street Scene*; *Journey's End*; *The Criminal Code*; *June Moon*; *Death Takes a Holiday*. MUSICALS: Noel Coward's *Bitter Sweet*; *The Little Show*

1930 Marc Connelly's *The Green Pastures*; George S. Kaufman and Moss Hart's *Once in a Lifetime*; *Grand Hotel*. MUSICALS: *Three's a Crowd*; two Gershwin shows: *Strike Up the Band* and *Girl Crazy*

1931 *Mourning Becomes Electra*; Noel Coward's *Private Lives*; *The Barretts of Wimpole Street*; *Counsellor at Law* (Paul Muni); *Reunion in Vienna* (Alfred Lunt and Lynn Fontanne). MUSICALS: George and Ira Gershwin's *Of Thee I Sing* (the first musical to win a Pulitzer Prize); *The Band Wagon*; Jerome Kern's *The Cat and the Fiddle*

1932 Philip Barry's *The Animal Kingdom*; the George S. Kaufman–Edna Ferber *Dinner at Eight*; S. N. Behrman's *The Late Christopher Bean*. MUSICALS: *Face the Music*; Jerome Kern's *Music in the Air*; Vincent Youman's *Take a Chance*; *The Gay Divorcee*

1933 *Tobacco Road* opened for a 3,182-performance run; Maxwell Anderson's *Both Your Houses*; Sidney Kingsley's *Men in White*; Eugene O'Neill's only comedy, *Ah, Wilderness!* MUSICALS: Irving Berlin's *As Thousands Cheer*; Ira and George Gershwin's *Let 'Em Eat Cake*; Jerome Kern's *Roberta*

1934 Lillian Hellman's *The Children's Hour*; *Dodsworth*. MUSICALS: Cole Porter's *Anything Goes*; Noel Coward's *Conversation Piece* (London)

1935 Zoë Akin's *The Old Maid*; Robert E. Sherwood's *The Petrified Forest*; Noel Coward and Gertrude Lawrence in his *Tonight at 8:30*; Clifford Odets' *Awake and Sing*; *Three Men on a Horse*; *Winterset*; *Dead End*; *Boy Meets Girl*; *Victoria Regina*. MUSICALS: Cole Porter's *Jubilee*;

Richard Rodgers and Lorenz Hart's *Jumbo* (presented by Billy Rose as a three-ring circus at the Hippodrome)

1936 Robert E. Sherwood's *Idiot's Delight*; *Stage Door*; *Tovarich*; *You Can't Take It with You*; *The Women*; John Gielgud appeared in *Hamlet*. MUSICALS: Richard Rodgers and Lorenz Hart's *On Your Toes*; Cole Porter's *Red, Hot and Blue*

1937 Maxwell Anderson's *High Tor*; *Having Wonderful Time*; *Room Service*; *Susan and God* (Gertrude Lawrence); Clifford Odets' *Golden Boy*; *Amphitryon 38* (Alfred Lunt and Lynn Fontanne); Orson Welles' "Mercury Theatre" staged a modern-dress version of *Julius Caesar*. MUSICALS: Richard Rodgers and Lorenz Hart's *Babes in Arms*; George M. Cohan in *I'd Rather Be Right*; the International Ladies' Garment Workers Union's *Pins and Needles*

1938 Thornton Wilder's *Our Town*; *What a Life*, introducing the character of Henry Aldrich (Ezra Stone). MUSICALS: two Richard Rodgers and Lorenz Hart shows, *I Married an Angel* and *The Boys from Syracuse*; Kurt Weill's *Knickerbocker Holiday*; *Hellzapoppin*

1939 Howard Lindsay and Russel Crouse's *Life with Father* (in for an eight-year run); Lillian Hellman's *The Little Foxes* (Tallulah Bankhead); *The Philadelphia Story* (Katharine Hepburn); George S. Kaufman and Moss Hart's *The Man Who Came to Dinner*; William Saroyan's *The Time of Your Life*. MUSICALS: *DuBarry Was a Lady* (Ethel Merman); *The Hot Mikado* (Bill Robinson)

1940 Robert E. Sherwood's *There Shall Be No Night*; James Thurber and Elliott Nugent's *The Male Animal*; *My Sister Eileen* (Shirley Booth); *The Corn Is Green* (Ethel Barrymore). MUSICALS: Irving Berlin's *Louisiana Purchase*; *Pal Joey* (the Richard Rodgers and Lorenz Hart show with the anti-hero); *Panama Hattie* (Ethel Merman); *Cabin in the Sky* (Ethel Waters)

1941 *Angel Street*; *Arsenic and Old Lace* (Boris Karloff, Josephine Hull); Noel Coward's *Blithe Spirit*; Lillian Hellman's *Watch on the Rhine*; Maurice Evans in *Macbeth*. MUSICALS: Kurt Weill's *Lady in the Dark* (Gertrude Lawrence); Danny Kaye in *Let's Face It*; *Best Foot Forward*

1942 Thornton Wilder's *The Skin of Our Teeth*; *The Pirate* (Alfred Lunt and Lynn Fontanne); *Guest in the House*. MUSICALS: *Star and Garter*; *By Jupiter*; Irving Berlin's *This Is the Army* (with an all-star cast of draftees)

1943 *Tomorrow the World* (Skippy Homeier as a pubescent Nazi); *The Voice of the Turtle* (Margaret Sullavan); Paul Robeson, Jose Ferrer, Uta Hagen in *Othello*. MUSICALS: *Oklahoma!* (the Richard Rodgers and Oscar Hammerstein show, in for a record run); Ogden Nash and Kurt Weill's *One Touch of Venus*

1944 *Jacobowsky and the Colonel*; *Anna Lucasta*, with an all-black cast; *I Remember Mama* (introducing Marlon Brando); *Harvey*; *A Bell for Adano*; *The Late George Apley*. MUSICAL: The Leonard Bernstein–Betty Comden–Adolph Green *On The Town*

1945 Howard Lindsay and Russel Crouse's *The State of the Union*; Tennessee Williams' *The Glass Menagerie*; *The Hasty Heart*; *Dream Girl*. MUSICALS: Richard Rodgers and Oscar Hammerstein's *Carousel*; *Up in Central Park*

1946 Eugene O'Neill's *The Iceman Cometh*; *O Mistress Mine* (Alfred Lunt and Lynn Fontanne); *Born Yesterday* (Judy Holliday, Paul Douglas); Laurence Olivier and London's Old Vic Repertory Company appeared on Broadway in *Henry V*, Parts I and II, and other Shakespearean works. MUSICAL: *Annie Get Your Gun*

1947 Tennessee Williams' *A Streetcar Named Desire* (Marlon Brando, Jessica Tandy); Arthur Miller's *All My Sons*; *The Heiress* (Basil Rathbone, Wendy Hiller); *Medea* (Judith Anderson). MUSICALS: E. Y. Harburg's *Finian's Rainbow*; Alan Jay Lerner and Frederick Loewe's *Brigadoon*

1948 *Mister Roberts* (Henry Fonda, David Wayne); Jean-Paul Sartre's *The Respectful Prostitute*; Jean Giradoux's *The Madwoman of Chaillot* (Martita Hunt); *Life with Mother*. MUSICALS: *Where's Charley?* (Ray Bolger); Cole Porter's *Kiss Me, Kate*; the revue *Lend an Ear*

1949 Arthur Miller's *Death of a Salesman* (Lee J. Cobb); *Detective Story*. MUSICALS: Richard Rodgers and Oscar Hammerstein's *South Pacific* (Mary Martin, Ezio Pinza); *Gentlemen Prefer Blondes* (Carol Channing); Kurt Weill's *Lost in the Stars*

1950   *Come Back, Little Sheba* (Shirley Booth); *The Member of the Wedding* (Julie Harris, Ethel Waters); T. S. Eliot's *The Cocktail Party* (Alec Guinness); *The Country Girl*; Katharine Hepburn appeared in *As You Like It.* MUSICALS: Frank Loesser's *Guys and Dolls*; Irving Berlin's *Call Me Madam* (Ethel Merman)

1951   Tennessee Williams' *The Rose Tattoo*; *The Four Poster* (Jessica Tandy, Hume Cronyn); *The Moon Is Blue*; *I Am a Camera*; *Stalag 17*; *Gigi* (Audrey Hepburn). MUSICALS: *The King and I* (Gertrude Lawrence, Yul Brynner); *Paint Your Wagon*; *A Tree Grows in Brooklyn*; *Top Banana* (Phil Silvers)

1952   Joseph Kramm's *The Shrike* (Jose Ferrer); *Dial "M" for Murder*; *The Time of the Cuckoo* (Shirley Booth); Laurence Olivier and Vivien Leigh appeared in Shakespeare's *Antony and Cleopatra* and George Bernard Shaw's *Caesar and Cleopatra*; Beatrice Lillie did a one-woman show. MUSICAL: *Wish You Were Here*

1953   William Inge's *Picnic*; Arthur Miller's *The Crucible*; *Camino Real*; *Tea and Sympathy* (Deborah Kerr); *The Teahouse of the August Moon*; *The Solid Gold Cadillac* (Josephine Hull). MUSICALS: Leonard Bernstein's *Wonderful Town* (Rosalind Russell); Cole Porter's *Can-Can* (Gwen Verdon); *Kismet*; Leontyne Price played in a notable revival of *Porgy and Bess.*

1954   *The Caine Mutiny Court Martial*; *The Bad Seed* (Patty Duke); *Anastasia*; *Witness for the Prosecution*. MUSICALS: *Peter Pan* (Mary Martin); *The Pajama Game*; *Fanny*; *The Boy Friend* (Julie Andrews); Bertolt Brecht and Kurt Weill's *The Threepenny Opera* was revived off-Broadway for a long run.

1955   Tennessee Williams' *Cat on a Hot Tin Roof*; *The Diary of Anne Frank* (Susan Strasberg); *Bus Stop*; *Tiger at the Gates*; *Inherit the Wind* (Paul Muni, Ed Begley); *No Time for Sergeants*; Samuel Beckett's *Waiting for Godot*. MUSICALS: *Damn Yankees*; Cole Porter's *Silk Stockings*

1956   Eugene O'Neill's *Long Day's Journey into Night*; *Separate Tables*; *Auntie Mame* (Rosalind Russell). MUSICALS: Alan Jay Lerner and Frederick Loewe's *My Fair Lady* (Julie Andrews, Rex Harrison); *Mr. Wonderful*

(Sammy Davis, Jr.); Judy Holliday in *Bells Are Ringing*; Frank Loesser's *The Most Happy Fella*

1957 *Look Homeward, Angel*; Gore Vidal's *A Visit to a Small Planet* (Cyril Ritchard); John Osborne's *Look Back in Anger*; *The Dark at the Top of the Stairs*; Tennessee Williams' *Orpheus Descending*. MUSICALS: Leonard Bernstein's *West Side Story*; Meredith Willson's *The Music Man*; *New Girl in Town* (Gwen Verdon)

1958 *Two for the Seesaw* (Henry Fonda, Anne Bancroft); *The Visit* (Alfred Lunt and Lynn Fontanne); Eugene O'Neill's *A Touch of the Poet*; Archibald MacLeish's *J.B.*; *Sunrise at Campobello*. MUSICALS: *La Plume de Ma Tante*; *Flower Drum Song*

1959 *Rashomon*; *Sweet Bird of Youth*; *A Raisin the Sun* (Sidney Poitier); *The Miracle Worker*; Edward Albee's one-act play, *The Zoo Story*, played off-Broadway; John Gielgud and Margaret Leighton played in *Much Ado About Nothing*. MUSICALS: Stephen Sondheim and Jule Styne's *Gypsy*; *The Sound of Music*; *Fiorello*. Off-Broadway, *Once Upon a Mattress* made a star of Carol Burnett.

1960 Tad Mosel's *All the Way Home*; Lillian Hellman's *Toys in the Attic* (Jason Robards, Jr.); *A Thurber Carnival*; Anthony Quinn, Laurence Olivier in *Becket*; Gore Vidal's *The Best Man*; a British import, *A Taste of Honey*. MUSICALS: *Bye Bye Birdie* (Chita Rivera, Dick Van Dyke); Alan Jay Lerner and Frederick Loewe's *Camelot* (Richard Burton); Michael Flanders and Donald Swann in *At the Drop of a Hat*; *An Evening with Mike Nichols and Elaine May*

1961 Eugene Ionesco's *Rhinoceros* (Zero Mostel, Eli Wallach); *A Man for All Seasons* (Paul Scofield); *The Caretaker* (Donald Pleasance); *Purlie Victorious* (Ossie Davis and Ruby Dee); Tennessee Williams' *The Night of the Iguana*. MUSICALS: *Carnival*; *How to Succeed in Business Without Really Trying*

1962 Edward Albee's *Who's Afraid of Virginia Woolf?*; *A Passage to India*; *Brecht on Brecht* off-Broadway; *A Thousand Clowns*. MUSICALS: *A Funny Thing Happened on the Way to the Forum* (Zero Mostel, Jack Gilford); *Stop the World—I Want to Get Off*; Richard Rodgers'

No Strings; I Can Get It for You Wholesale, with a star-making, show-stopping number for Barbra Streisand

1963   *The Typists* and *The Tiger,* one-act plays with Eli Wallach and Anne Jackson; *Luther* (Albert Finney); Bertolt Brecht's *Mother Courage* (Anne Bancroft); *Oh Dad, Poor Dad.* MUSICAL: *Oliver*

1964   *Luv* (Alan Arkin, Eli Wallach, Anne Jackson); Arthur Miller's *After the Fall; The Deputy;* James Baldwin's *Blues for Mister Charlie; Dylan* (Alec Guinness). MUSICALS: *Funny Girl* (Barbra Streisand); *Fiddler on the Roof* (Zero Mostel); *High Spirits* (Bea Lillie); *Hello, Dolly!* (Carol Channing). Richard Burton did *Hamlet* on Broadway.

1965   Frank D. Gilroy's *The Subject Was Roses; The Royal Hunt of the Sun; Marat-Sade;* Neil Simon's *The Odd Couple* (Walter Matthau, Art Carney). MUSICAL: *Man of La Mancha*

1966   Edward Albee's *A Delicate Balance; I Do! I Do!* (Mary Martin, Robert Preston). MUSICALS: *Mame* (Angela Lansbury); *Cabaret* (Jill Haworth, Joel Grey, Lotte Lenya)

1967   Tom Stoppard's *Rosencrantz and Guildenstern Are Dead;* Harold Pinter's *The Homecoming;* Neil Simon's *You Know I Can't Hear You When the Water's Running;* Eugene O'Neill's *More Stately Mansions* (Ingrid Bergman); *Black Comedy* (Lynn Redgrave)

1968   *Joe Egg* (Albert Finney); *The Great White Hope* (James Earl Jones); *The Man in the Glass Booth* (Donald Pleasance); *Plaza Suite* (George C. Scott); *The Prime of Miss Jean Brodie; The Boys in the Band.* MUSICALS: *Hair,* with a long-haired, vigorous young cast that upset a whole generation of adults, *Your Own Thing, Promises, Promises*

1969   *Butterflies Are Free; Hadrian VII* (Alec McCowen); *Last of the Red Hot Lovers; Oh! Calcutta* (renowned for introducing nudity to the conventional theater). MUSICALS: *1776; Coco* (Katharine Hepburn)

Radio

Regularly scheduled radio broadcasting generally is dated from November 2, 1920, when Westinghouse station KDKA, Pittsburgh, carried the returns of the Harding–Cox election. Within two years, radio-listening was a popular pastime. The transformation of radio from big-time entertainment to a primarily news and music medium coincided with the defection of shows and stars to television starting in the late 1940s. Here is a sampling of some of radio's memorable long-run shows and their stars.

1920   Vaughn de Leath, singing in a low-voiced style called crooning, became "The First Lady of Radio."

1921   Vincent Lopez ("Lopez speaking") and his band broadcast from the Hotel Pennsylvania Grill.

1922   Paul Whiteman, "The King of Jazz," who stayed with radio twenty-five years; American Tobacco's "Lucky Strike Radio Show"

1923   "The Happiness Boys," Billy Jones and Ernie Hare, the first regular comedy show; "Roxy and His Gang," S. L. Rothafel, with broadcasts from New York's Capitol Theater, a show that ran until the late 1930s; sports announcer Graham McNamee at the mike for the first football broadcast—the 1923 Army–Navy game

1924   The Republican National Convention, the first to be broadcast, was reported by McNamee and Maj. John Andrew White.

1925   Singers John McCormack and Lucrezia Bori, first of a long series of serious musicians to be heard on radio; "The A & P Gypsies"; "The Gold Dust Twins"; "The Goodrich Silvertown Orchestra," with the Silver Masked Tenor; the "Atwater Kent Program," featuring great musicians; "The Grand Ol' Opry," which went on to television fame

1926   Uncle Don and his bedtime stories. (He spent years denying that once, thinking the mike dead after his sign-off, he said, "There! I guess that'll hold the little bastards for another night.")

1927   Moran and Mack, the "Two Black Crows"; Ida Bailey Allen and her cooking school; Ted Husing was a popular announcer. Opera broadcasts from Chicago Civic Auditorium started a long run.

1928   "National Farm and Home Hour"; "Music Appreciation Hour," with Dr. Walter Damrosch, broadcast for schools and colleges; "The Voice of Firestone"; Father Coughlin went on the air, with what started as a series of children's Sunday broadcasts.

1929   Announcers began to be celebrities; besides Husing and McNamee, there were Milton Cross and Norman Brokenshire. H. V. Kaltenborn was a news commentator. "Amos 'n' Andy" went on. Kate Smith, the "Songbird of the South"; Rudy Vallee, the "Vagabond Lover," with radio's first variety show, "The Fleischmann Hour"; "The Rise of the Goldbergs," with Gertrude Berg; Singer Morton Downey. Red (Arthur) Godfrey, the "Warbling Banjoist," sang into a mike for the first time.

1930   The first national radio-rating service, Crossley, was organized. New shows: "The American School of the Air"; Walter Winchell, with his staccato coverage of news and gossip; Alexander Woollcott, with his "Town Crier" commentary; news broadcaster Lowell Thomas; the durable children's program, "Let's Pretend."

1931   "The March of Time"; "Lum and Abner"; Jessica Dragonette, with the Cities Service concert; Eddie Cantor with his violinist, Rubinoff; Russ Columbo. For children: "Little Orphan Annie"; Irene Wicker, "The Singing Lady." CBS took Father Coughlin off the air for the increasingly political, sometimes anti-Semitic, tone of his broadcasts; he formed his own network and became bigger than ever.

1932   New: Fred Allen and Portland Hoffa; Jack Benny and Mary Livingstone; "One Man's Family"; Ed Wynn, the Texaco Fire Chief, who demanded a live studio audience; "Vic and Sade," which became a classic soap opera; Jack Pearl as "Baron Munchausen," with the line, "Vass you dere, Sharlie?"; "Captain Henry's Maxwell House Show

Boat," with Charles Winninger, Lanny Ross; George Burns and Gracie Allen, with their own show. Already popular: Irene Bordoni as "The Coty Playgirl"; radio's first child star, Baby Rose Marie (she started at five); "The American Album of Familiar Music"; Ben Bernie's orchestra; Joe Cook; storyteller Irvin S. Cobb; torch singer Ruth Etting; Lawrence Tibbett; the Boswell Sisters. Daytime had soap opera: "Just Plain Bill" and "Red Davis," forerunner of "Pepper Young's Family."

1933　New: "The Lone Ranger"; "Helen Trent," who started soap opera tribulations that were to last until 1960; "Ma Perkins." Among the top ten shows and performers were "Show Boat," Ed Wynn, Al Jolson, "Myrt and Marge," Jack Benny, and "The Sinclair Wiener Minstrels." Walter O'Keefe was on for Lucky Strike and Erno Rapee conducted the orchestra on the "Linit Seven-Star Revue."

1934　"The Lux Radio Theatre," with radio versions of hit movies and Cecil B. De Mille as host; Ozzie Nelson's band, with singer Harriet Hilliard. "Hollywood Hotel" started, with Louella Parsons (she got her stars free until the union stopped her four years later). Other popular shows: Joe Penner, whose catchline, "Wanna buy a duck?" swept the country; Phil Spitalny and his All-Girl Orchestra. For the kids: "Buck Rogers in the 25th Century"; Bobby Benson at the H Bar O Ranch; "Jack Armstrong, the All-American Boy" (he ate Wheaties)

1935　New: Lucky Strike's "Your Hit Parade," playing the week's top fifteen tunes; Bing Crosby for Woodbury; "Cavalcade of America"; the scary "Lights Out"; Fibber McGee and Molly; "One Man's Family"; the "Metropolitan Auditions of the Air"; Major Bowes, with his gong and "Amateur Hour." Jack Benny hit the top.

1936　Radio was used lavishly for the first time in a presidential campaign, especially by the Republicans, who retained an ad agency. "Professor Quiz" introduced the quiz show to the world; "Columbia Workshop" bowed, to introduce the work of such writers as Norman Corwin, Arch Oboler, and Archibald MacLeish. Comedy was tops; a favorite was the screwball comedy of "Stoopnagle and Budd."

1937　Don Ameche, who had made his mark on "The First Nighter" dramas, became host of "The Chase and Sanborn Hour," whose regular star was Edgar Bergen with Charlie McCarthy; Bob Burns and his musical bazooka joined Bing Crosby.

1938 "Information Please," with moderator Clifton Fadiman, settled in for a long run; Bob Hope's "Pepsodent Show" became an instant hit; Kay Kyser debuted with his "Kollege of Musical Knowledge." Edward G. Robinson in "Big Town" was in the top ten. The radio event of the year was Orson Welles' "Mercury Theatre" dramatization of H. G. Wells' *The War of the Worlds,* which terrified half the country with its realism. The long-run soap opera "Life Can Be Beautiful" premiered.

1939 Established shows and stars continued as favorites. "The Chase and Sanborn Hour" and Jack Benny led the list. "The Aldrich Family" was number six, Bob Hope number seven of the top ten.

1940 Radio's importance as a news medium grew as World War II deepened. H. V. Kaltenborn, who had reported Hitler's rise and the Munich crisis, was a familiar voice. Prime Minister Winston Churchill was heard around the world and CBS correspondent Edward R. Murrow reported from London. Quiz shows came in batches this year: "Truth or Consequences," "The Quiz Kids," "Take It or Leave It." Jean Hersholt was popular as "Dr. Christian."

1941 Millions of Americans were listening to their radios, many to the New York Philharmonic Sunday afternoon broadcast, when news of the Japanese attack on Pearl Harbor came. On December 8, almost every radio in the country was on as President Roosevelt asked Congress to declare a state of war with Japan. Among regular programs at the top: "Mr. District Attorney"; Red Skelton; Arthur Godfrey, who had a morning variety show, "Arthur Godfrey Time."

1942 Disc jockeys were ordered by the War Department to stop playing listener requests which, it was decided, could be used as a means of code communication by enemy agents. From around the world, the voices of Ed Murrow, Eric Sevareid, William L. Shirer, Bill Henry, and Elmer Davis became familiar presenting news and commentary.

1943 "The $64 question" entered the language to represent a real poser; that sum was the top money on the popular "Take It or Leave It." Other popular shows: "The Great Gildersleeve," "Abie's Irish Rose," Abbott and Costello, Jimmy Durante with Garry Moore. Five nights a week for fifteen minutes, on "Here's Morgan," Henry Morgan played tricks with language and spoofed his sponsors.

1944 Commercial broadcasts were cancelled in June to make way for reports of the American landings on the Normandy beaches. Programs with such titles as "The Man Behind the Gun" and "The FBI in Peace and War" were popular; so were "Nick Carter," "The Life of Riley," and the mind-reader Dunninger.

1945 Martha Rountree and Lawrence Spivak introduced "Meet the Press." Favorite entertainment shows: "The Danny Kaye Show," "Beulah," the Pickens Sisters, the "Westinghouse Sunday Concert," the CBS Symphony "Gateway to Music," and, on daytime radio, "Queen for a Day."

1946 Benny, Allen, and the other favorites stayed on top. Arthur Godfrey had a new show, "Talent Scouts"; Marie Wilson was a dumb blonde on "My Friend Irma"; bandleader Harry James had his own show.

1947 Groucho Marx started with "You Bet Your Life"; "America's Town Meeting of the Air" was popular. A special favorite was Fannie Brice as Baby Snooks.

1948 Walter Winchell led the lists. A new quiz show, "Stop the Music," came on with prizes of as much as $165,000 and took the top spot. From Hollywood, the rapid-fire delivery of Jimmy Fidler and the flat, earnest voice of Louella Parsons provided the latest gossip. "Duffy's Tavern" was in the top ten.

1949 "Dragnet" started on radio but TV was making strong inroads. "The Voice of Firestone" concerts were discontinued. Many of the shows, including Bob Hope, continued. So did the morning husband-and-wife talk shows and the soaps.

1950 The big stars started moving to TV. Among notable holdouts were Tallulah Bankhead, whose ninety-minute "The Big Show" debuted; Gracie Fields; the "Steve Allen Show"; and even the dramatic "Grand Central Station." Radio gradually switched over, in the subsequent years, to a format emphasizing service programs, news, and music, including, with the advent of FM, a surge of classical-music stations.

By 1955 the disc jockeys had taken over most of radio. But there were exceptions: braving the trend, some new radio shows started up.

1952 "Gunsmoke" began and lasted in radio until 1961. 1952 was the year Robert Sarnoff said, "Radio is dead."

1955 "Monitor," a magazine-format weekend show of news, records, and sports, went on and lasted until 1974.

1961 "The Romance of Helen Trent," a soap opera started in 1933, ended after 7,222 episodes.

1968 Radio proved to be far from dead. There were 275 million radios in the U.S., 136.1 for every 100 people. A new show started, the "Walter Cronkite Report."

Television

It started with tiny screens in big wooden boxes, occasional wrestling matches, demonstration programs, and lots of test patterns to let people know their sets were working when nothing was programmed. But as early as 1938, NBC aired scenes from a Broadway show, *Susan and God*, with Gertrude Lawrence. The defection of radio shows to TV started in 1947, the same year that TV began its own unique programming.

1947 Radio's "Meet the Press," with Lawrence Spivak and Martha Rountree, moved to TV. "The Kraft Theater" went on and "Howdy Doody" debuted. Viewers loved the rough and tumble and frequent fights of the Roller Derby and the outrageously hoked-up wrestlers, particularly the marcelled and peroxided Gorgeous George. Douglas Edwards became the first regular news anchorman.

1948 Milton Berle became TV's first major star with "Texaco Star Theatre"; Bill Boyd's "Hopalong Cassidy" went on and caught on. "Ford Theater," "America's Town Hall Meeting," with host John Daly, and, for the kids, Buffalo Bob Smith. Arthur Godfrey moved to TV and Ed Sullivan's Sunday night "Toast of the Town" began a twenty-two-year run. Edward R. Murrow and Don Hollenbeck teamed up for one of the first commentary-and-interview programs. An early game show was "Break the Bank," with Bert Parks as host.

1949   Sid Caesar and Imogene Coca's fabled "Your Show of Shows" went on with ninety live minutes of totally original comedy each Saturday night. Easy-going Dave Garroway, with "Garroway at Large," was chief exponent of the Chicago School of TV, which also spawned "Kukla, Fran and Ollie." "The Aldrich Family" moved over from radio. Arthur Godfrey had his first show, Ted Mack had the "Original Amateur Hour"; TV's first science fiction show was "Captain Video."

1950   The pace of defections quickened. Jack Benny moved his team, including Mary Livingstone and Rochester, over from radio, avoided the overexposure of weekly programs but showed up on everyone else's show, as well. Other defectors from radio were Gertrude Berg with her "The Goldberg Show"; "The Lucky Strike Hit Parade"; "Superman"; Groucho Marx, whose "You Bet Your Life" was a smash. Dinah Shore went on for Chevrolet; Eddie Cantor, Abbott and Costello and Jerry Lewis all served at one time as hosts of "The Colgate Comedy Hour." "Broadway Open House," a forerunner of the "Tonight Show," starred Jerry Lester and Morey Amsterdam.

1951   TV's two longest-surviving soap operas, "Search for Tomorrow" and "Love of Life," started. Edward R. Murrow covered news events in depth with "See It Now." Art Linkletter's "People Are Funny" featured men and women in the street coping with impossible situations. "Kraft Theatre," "Philco Playhouse," "Studio One," "Playhouse 90," and others of the sixty- and ninety-minute television-theater shows presented four hundred live dramas during the year. Daytime TV held people enthralled during the Kefauver Committee hearings on crime, with a parade of pimps, gangsters, and ladies of the evening.

1952   New shows: The "Today" show, the first to start at 7:00
       A.M., with puckish, surprising Dave Garroway as its host;
       another long-run soap opera, "The Guiding Light"; Jackie
       Gleason's variety show, which ran until 1955; the "Ad-
       ventures of Ozzie and Harriet," with the husband-and-
       wife team and their real sons, Rick and David; Garry
       Moore with "I've Got a Secret," with Henry Morgan and
       Jayne Meadows; Ralph Edwards with "This Is Your Life";
       Art Linkletter's daytime show, "House Party." Jack Webb
       moved Sgt. Joe Friday from radio to TV in "Dragnet"
       ("Just the facts, Ma'am"). Mr. and Mrs. Arthur Murray
       had a "Dance Party."

1953   Millions followed Lucille Ball's real-life pregnancy on
       "I Love Lucy." "Goodyear Playhouse" presented one of
       TV's most celebrated dramas, Paddy Chayevsky's
       "Marty." Red Skelton moved from radio, applying his
       talent for pantomime in TV. Edward R. Murrow started
       "Person to Person," remote interviews with celebrities.
       Other new shows: "The Adventures of Superman," "The
       Life of Riley" with William Bendix, the "Danny Kaye
       Show." An early TV special was Ford's two-hour 50th
       anniversary, featuring many stars but best remembered
       for the duo of Mary Martin and Ethel Merman.

1954   The show of the year was ABC's presentation of the
       Army-McCarthy hearings. New shows: "Tonight" with
       Jack Paar as host; "Lassie," whose canine heroine tri-
       umphed for seventeen years; "Walt Disney's Wonderful
       World of Color," exploiting the newly introduced color
       TV; "Blondie and Dagwood," with Penny Singleton and
       lots of different Dagwoods over the years. Sid Caesar and
       Imogene Coca split after 102 memorable airings of "Your
       Show of Shows."

1955   Big-money quiz shows hit with "The $64,000 Question."
       Other entries of the season: Lawrence Welk with his
       champagne music; "Gunsmoke," the adult Western that
       had a twenty-year run; Phil Silvers in "You'll Never Get
       Rich." For children: "Captain Kangaroo" and "The
       Mickey Mouse Club" with its Mouseketeers. "Father
       Knows Best" went on, was cancelled, moved to another
       network, and settled in. Landmark shows: Judy Garland's

special and "Peter Pan," starring Mary Martin. Jackie Gleason and Art Carney starred in "The Honeymooners."

1956   Steve Allen was host of the "Steve Allen Variety Show," opposite Ed Sullivan on Sundays. Tennessee Ernie Ford was a Thursday regular. Another soap started, "As the World Turns," as did the long-run "Leave It to Beaver." Chet Huntley and David Brinkley's "goodnights" to one another became a running gag.

1957   Steve Allen became host of the "Tonight" show, continuing until 1959. Dick Clark's daytime "American Bandstand" for teenagers went on. Other new shows: James Garner in "Maverick"; "Have Gun, Will Travel"; Gisele MacKenzie had her own show. "Perry Mason," based on the Erle Stanley Gardner character, began a long series of trials, never lost a case.

1958   Americans were mesmerized by the big-money quiz shows, "The $64,000 Question" and "Twenty-One," as intellectual contestants with seemingly unlimited knowledge squirmed in anguish in their isolation booths. "77 Sunset Strip" started.

1959   The quiz-show bubble burst when a disgruntled contestant revealed that he and others were briefed on the tough questions they would have to answer on camera; the audiences stopped watching and the shows died. New shows included "The Untouchables," "Bonanza," and a new Steve Allen show.

1960   The year's highlights were the Nixon-Kennedy debates. Hollywood stars June Allyson, Barbara Stanwyck, Ann Sothern, and Dick Powell all had their own shows. Perry Como was the star of the "Kraft Music Hall." The prehistoric "Flintstones" went on; so did Andy Griffith, in a small-town comedy show.

1961   Vince Edwards became a star as Dr. "Ben Casey." Other hits: "The Dick Van Dyke Show," Jackie Gleason's "You're in the Picture," "Sing Along with Mitch," and "Car 54, Where Are You?"

1962   Johnny Carson took over the "Tonight" show. Dave Garroway left the "Today" show. New and instant hits were "The Virginian," "The Beverly Hillbillies," and the "Roy Rogers–Dale Evans Variety Hour." Jacqueline Kennedy took the country on a TV tour of the White House.

1963 David Janssen as "The Fugitive" started running. Bob Hope had not only his weekly Chrysler Theater comedy-variety show but a monthly special, a pace he kept up until 1967.

1964 "Peyton Place," based on Grace Metalious' bestselling book, became a kind of nighttime soap opera with plenty of sex. David Frost faced the nation for the first time on "That Was the Week That Was." "The Man from U.N.C.L.E." started.

1965 There was something for everyone in the family: "Flipper" for the kids, "The King Family" for the family, and Steve Lawrence, "Dr. Kildare," and "I Spy" for everyone.

1966 Daytime game shows, with prize or money giveaways, were big time; some spilled over into evening hours. "The Dating Game" was a popular one. A cult started with "Star Trek." Hollywood star Joan Bennett had a weird daytime soap opera, featuring spooks, vampires, and the occult, called "Dark Shadows."

1967 The top shows and stars in the United States were "The Lucy Show," Andy Griffith, "Bonanza," Red Skelton, and "Gunsmoke." Adults over fifty gave the top spot to Lawrence Welk, and young children favored "The Flying Nun." "The Smothers Brothers Comedy Hour" was going strong. Carol Burnett's show, with Harvey Korman and every guest you could want, started, ran until 1978. Barbara Walters of the "Today" show was named "Woman of the Year" by the Father's Day Committee of America.

1968 Rowan and Martin's "Laugh-In," with quick cuts, sight gags, one-liners, and Goldie Hawn was an instant hit; the show's line, "Sock it to me," moved into the language. "The Beautiful Phyllis Diller Show" was another leader.

1969 David Frost, now on his own, interviewed stars. "The Bold Ones" continued the interest in doctor series but added lawyers, as well. Leslie Uggams had her own show; so did Debbie Reynolds. "Hawaii Five-O" was a winner. In September, Mary Tyler Moore, who had played Dick Van Dyke's zingy wife on a previous show, signed an ownership deal for a show of her own for the following season.

Catastrophes

Fires and explosions; aviation and railroad accidents; losses at sea; storms, floods, earthquakes, and other natural catastrophes. Not all of them; just those you might need to date.

1911 Fire in the Triangle Shirtwaist Co., a New York sweatshop, killed 146, triggered new fire protection laws.

1912 The "unsinkable" British liner *Titanic* struck an iceberg on its maiden voyage, with the loss of 1,503 lives.

1913 Storms destroyed nineteen ships in the Great Lakes. A mine explosion in Dawson, New Mexico, killed 263.

1914 The liner *Empress of Ireland* sank after a collision in the St. Lawrence River, killing 1,024.

1915 A passenger train and troop train collided in Scotland, killing 227. The Great Lakes excursion steamer *Eastland* capsized in the Chicago River; 812 dead.

1917 In France, 543 killed in derailment of an overcrowded troop train near the mouth of the Mt. Cenis tunnel.

1918 The U.S.S. *Cyclops,* a naval auxiliary, disappeared on a voyage from Rio de Janeiro to Baltimore, with 324 aboard.

1919 A hurricane swept through Florida, Louisiana, and Texas, killing 284. Another 488 persons caught in storms at sea drowned.

1920 Bubonic plague in India; 2 million dead.

1921 British dirigible ZR-2, on trial run near Hull, England, broke in two, killing all sixty-two aboard.

1922 More than three-fifths of the city of Smyrna, Asia Minor, was destroyed in fire following the Turkish occupation. Many dead, 100,000 left homeless.

1923 In the great Japanese earthquake and fire, 50 percent of Tokyo and all of Yokohama were destroyed; 200,000 perished over the 45,000-square-mile area of the quake. Frank Lloyd Wright's newly opened H-shaped Imperial Hotel survived.

1924 Cholera in India; 300,000 dead.

1925 A series of tornadoes destroyed thirty-five towns in Missouri, Illinois, Indiana, Kentucky, Tennessee, and Alabama, killing 792, injuring 13,000.

1926   A hurricane struck the Florida east coast, killing 373, leaving 40,000 homeless, causing $165,000,000 in property damage and putting an end to the Florida real estate boom.

1927   Twenty thousand square miles of the Mississippi Valley flooded, leaving 700,000 homeless.

1928   An explosion in a Mather, Pennsylvania, coal mine killed 195; some survivors were found alive below after five days. The British steamer *Vestris,* badly overloaded, foundered and sank off the Virginia Capes with a loss of 110 passengers and crew.

1929   Spontaneous combustion of X-ray film produced poisonous fumes, killing 125 in Clinic Hospital, Cleveland, Ohio.

1930   The world's largest dirigible, *R-101,* crashed into a hillside in France on a flight to India, with loss of 47, including high British officials. An earthquake in Naples, Italy, killed 883. Fire swept through four blocks of the Ohio State Penitentiary, killing 317 convicts, injuring 231. A hurricane killed 4,000 in Santo Domingo.

1932   Earthquake in Kansu, China; 70,000 dead.

1933   The dirigible *Akron,* forced down at sea near Barnegat, New Jersey, during a storm, broke up; seventy-three died.

1934   The luxury liner *Morro Castle,* en route to New York from a Caribbean cruise, caught fire off the New Jersey coast and finally was beached at Asbury Park, New Jersey, where it burned to a hulk; 134 died.

1935   A disastrous earthquake in Quetta, Pakistan, killed 50,000. A hurricane swept the Florida Keys with 150 to 200 mph winds, killing 376.

1937   The giant German dirigible *Hindenburg* exploded in midair and crashed in flames just before tying up at her mooring at Lakehurst, New Jersey. Of ninety-seven aboard, thirty-seven perished in view of a crowd there to meet it. The disaster marked the end of dirigibles in commercial transportation.

1938   A hurricane hit Long Island and New England with winds up to 186 mph, killing 680, injuring 1,754, causing $400 million in property damage.

1939   More than 500 perished in a fire which destroyed the oil town of Lagunillas, Venezuela. A Chilean earthquake left

237   CATASTROPHES

30,000 dead. An earthquake destroyed Erzingan, Turkey; 100,000 casualties.

1942   The Cocoanut Grove nightclub in Boston, Massachusetts, jammed with about 1,000 people, caught fire; panic and inadequate exits resulted in 493 deaths. An explosion at Honkeiko Colliery in Manchuria killed 1,549 miners.

1944   A U.S. Air Force B-24 bomber crashed into a school at Freckleton, England, killing all 40 on board and 51 schoolchildren. The audience of 7,000 stampeded when the canvas "big top" of the Ringling Brothers and Barnum and Bailey circus caught fire and collapsed at Hartford, Connecticut; 163 died, 261 were injured. In a train stalled in a tunnel near Salerno, Italy, 426 suffocated.

1945   A U.S. Army bomber crashed into the Empire State Building, New York, killing thirteen.

1946   Tidal waves swept down on the Hawaiian Islands, the Aleutians, and the west coast of North America, killing 205, leaving 10,000 homeless. In Atlanta, Georgia, the supposedly fireproof Winecoff Hotel caught fire, killing 119.

1947   Most of Texas City, Texas, was destroyed, an estimated thousand were killed, and four thousand injured when a fire and explosion on the French ship *Grandcamp* set off a series of other explosions. All DC-6 planes were grounded and modified after a defective cabin heater caused a fire and crash near Bryce Canyon, Utah; fifty-two dead.

1948   A Pan American Constellation crashed in fog at Shannon Airport, killing fifty. Fire and explosion wrecked the I. G. Farben chemical works at Ludwigshafen, Germany, killing 200.

1949   Fire on the Chunking, China, waterfront killed 1,700. The Great Lakes passenger ship *Noronic* burned at a pier in Toronto, Canada. The only exit was blocked and 128 of the 695 aboard perished.

1950   An earthquake devastated a sparsely populated 30,000-square-mile area of Assam and Tibet, killing about 1,000. Two Long Island Railroad trains collided at Rockville Center, New York, killing 79, injuring 153. A chartered British Avon Tudor V, returning from an Irish soccer game, crashed off Cardiff, Wales, killing 80.

1951   Floods in Kansas and Missouri caused an estimated $1 billion in property damage but killed only 41. When a typhoon struck the Philippine Islands, 764 were killed and 60,000 left homeless. A Pennsylvania Railroad commuter train plunged through a temporary overpass at Woodbridge, New Jersey, killing 79.

1952   A three-train crash at Harrow-Wealdstone station, England, killed 112. A tornado in six Mississippi Valley states killed 239. A typhoon in the Philippines killed 431.

1953   A U.S. Air Force C-124 Globemaster crashed near Tokyo, killing all 129 aboard. In New Zealand, the Wellington-Auckland Express plunged into the swollen Whangaehu River, killing an estimated 155. Storms and floods ravaged eastern England and inundated a sixth of Holland, killing more than 2,000. Tornadoes in Texas killed 124, six tornadoes in Michigan and Ohio killed 139, and one in Massachusetts killed 92.

1954   A twelve-second earthquake in northern Algeria killed between 1,460 and 1,600 people. Hurricane "Carol" swept the eastern seaboard of the United States, killing 68, doing more than a half billion dollars' property damage. Hurricane "Hazel" followed, killing 410 in Haiti, then 184 on the U.S. Atlantic seaboard and in Canada.

1955   All 66 servicemen aboard died when two U.S. Air Force Flying Boxcars collided over Stuttgart, Germany. A bad hurricane year: "Diane" caused 191 deaths and devastating floods in New England; "Hilda" and "Janet" killed 788 in Mexico and the Caribbean. A racing car in the Grand Prix exploded, crashed into a crowd at Le Mans, France; 82 dead.

1956   A TWA Super-Constellation and a United Airlines DC-7 collided over the Grand Canyon, killing all 128. In Cali, Colombia, seven army trucks loaded with ammunition exploded, killing an estimated 1,200. The Italian liner *Andrea Doria* collided with the Swedish liner *Stockholm* in fog off the Massachusetts coast; the French liner *Ile de France* rushed to the rescue and, though the *Doria* sank, only 52 lives were lost; 1,600 were saved.

1957   An earthquake in Iran killed 1,564, injured 5,000. An excursion train in Jamaica, B.W.I., plunged into a ravine, killing 175, injuring 400. Hurricane "Audrey" devastated southwestern Texas and Louisiana, and a tidal wave all but wiped out the town of Cameron, Louisiana.

1958   A fire at Our Lady of the Angels Roman Catholic parochial school in Chicago killed 87 children and three nuns. A New Jersey Central Railroad commuter train plunged through an open lift bridge into Newark Bay, killing 48.

1959   Floods in Ohio and Pennsylvania and tornadoes in the southwest United States killed 110; typhoon "Vera" killed 4,464, left more than 1,500,000 homeless in Honshu, Japan; a hurricane and floods killed more than 1,000 in central Mexico; flood waters burst the Malpasset Dam near the Riviera, killing a reported 412.

1960   All 128 aboard and 6 people on the ground were killed when a United Airlines DC-8 jet and a TWA Super-Constellation collided over Staten Island, New York, one crashing there, one in Brooklyn. A U.S. Navy plane collided in midair with a Brazilian DC-3 over Rio de Janeiro Bay, killing 61, including navy musicians en route to perform at a dinner in Rio for President Eisenhower. An estimated 12,000 were killed in two earthquakes, a tidal wave, and fires that devastated Agadir, Morocco. Earthquakes, volcanic eruptions, and tidal waves battered southern and central Chile, killing an estimated 5,700. A fire aboard the aircraft carrier *Constellation,* at the Brooklyn Navy Yard, killed 50 civilian workers. Hurricane "Donna" caused the worst destruction in U.S. recorded history, hitting Puerto Rico, the Florida Keys, and roaring up the Atlantic Coast.

1961   In a Sabena Airlines 707 jet crash near Brussels, 18 members of the U.S. ice figure-skating team en route to a championship meet were killed. In a circus fire set by an ex-employee, more than 320 were killed near Rio de Janeiro. Hurricane "Carla" hit the Texas and Louisiana gulf coasts; typhoon "Nancy" struck central Japan; hurricane "Hattie" hit British Honduras.

1962   An avalanche on an extinct Andean volcano in Peru buried over 3,000. In a freak accident in Japan, a commuter train plowed into the wreckage and survivors of an earlier crash of a freight and commuter train; 162 died. Ten thousand died in a western Iran earthquake.

1963   A volcanic eruption on the island of Bali killed 1,584. Some 10,000 were killed when storms and a tidal wave struck East Pakistan. The 2,000-year-old city of Skopje, Yugoslavia, was devastated by an earthquake; 2,000 died.

1964   A powerful earthquake hit Alaska, killing 115. Nineteen crewmen on the Norwegian tanker *Stolt Dagali* died when it was sliced in two by the Israeli liner *Shalom* in fog off the New Jersey coast. Hurricane "Cleo" swept Guadeloupe, Haiti, and Cuba, then the Florida coast; typhoons "Iris" and "Joan" killed 7,000 in South Vietnam.

1965   An Eastern Airlines DC-7B crashed into the Atlantic shortly after takeoff from New York; eighty-four died.

1966   A British jet crashed on Mount Fuji, Japan, killing 124. In Florence, Italy, masterpieces of painting, sculpture, and architecture were lost or damaged when storms flooded the Po and Arno rivers, knocking out the economy of one-third of Italy.

1967   In one of the great oil spills, the U.S. tanker *Torrey Canyon* ran aground west of Cornwall, England; the oil contaminated 120 miles of French and English shoreline and killed marine life and sea birds.

1968   A series of major earthquakes in Iran killed 18,000 and left 100,000 homeless. The U.S. nuclear submarine *Scorpion* was lost in the Atlantic, with 99 men on board.

1969   In Maracaibo, Venezuela, a Viasa DC-9 plane crashed into a residential district, killing all eighty-four aboard and seventy-one on the ground. Torrential rains in California caused floods and mudslides that killed ninety-one, left 9,000 homeless.

Great Ocean Liners

Did you cross the Atlantic on one of the great luxury liners before jet planes did them in? Do you recall the luxury of morning bouillon served to you at your deck chair—or wish you did?

Do you recall dancing in the main salon, dining at the captain's table, travelling four in a cabin in third-class or playing shuffleboard on deck—and want to forget?

Here are the great liners that plied the Atlantic and the years you sailed—or could have sailed—on them. Flying the Atlantic as a passenger became possible in 1939, common in the 1950s. By 1960, when jets had taken over the North Atlantic route, 70 percent of transatlantic traffic was by plane; by 1969, only four out of a hundred travellers went by sea and most of the great ships had retired or were surviving with cruises. The *Queen Elizabeth 2* was the sole survivor in 1978, still making thirty Atlantic crossings a year.

SHIP	REGISTRY	MAIDEN VOYAGE	FATE
Aquitania	British	1914	Retired 1950
Berengaria	British	*	Retired 1938
Bismarck	German	1914	Became British *Majestic* after World War I
Bremen	German	1929	Sunk by RAF bombers in World War II
Coronia I	British	1904	Retired 1930
Coronia II	British	1949	Retired 1968
Constitution	American	1950	Mothballed, early 1970s
Andrea Doria	Italy	1952	Collided with *Stockholm,* sank, 1956
Europa	German	1933	Became the French *Liberté* after World War II
France I	French	1912	Retired, 1934
France II	French	1961	Withdrawn from service, 1974
Ile de France	French	1927	Sold to Japanese, 1958
Imperator	German	1913	Became British *Berengaria* after World War I

* German *Imperator,* acquired during World War I.

SHIP	REGISTRY	MAIDEN VOYAGE	FATE
Independence	American	1951	Retired, early 1970s
Leviathan	American	**	Retired, 1938
Liberté	French	†	Retired, 1962
Majestic	British	††	Retired, 1940
Mauretania	British	1907	Retired, 1935
Michelangelo	Italian	1965	Since 1975, a floating accommodation in the Persian Gulf
Nieuw Amsterdam	Dutch	1938	Retired from the Atlantic route in 1973
Normandie	French	1935	Burned at New York pier, 1942, while being refitted as a troop ship
Olympic	British	1911	Retired, 1935
Queen Elizabeth	British	1940	Scrapped in Hong Kong harbor, 1972
Queen Elizabeth 2	British	1969	Still afloat
Queen Mary	British	1936	Retired 1967; now on exhibit in Long Beach, California
Rex	Italian	1933	Sunk by German bombers, 1944
Titanic	British	1912	Sank on maiden voyage
United States	American	1952	Laid up in Norfolk, 1969
Vaterland	German	1914	Became American *Leviathan*, 1917; retired, 1938

** German *Vaterland,* acquired during World War I.
† German *Europa,* acquired during World War II.
†† German *Bismarck,* acquired during World War I.